D0302780

ORDINAL
TIME SERIES
ANALYSIS

WITHDRAWN
IOWA STATE UNIVERSITY
LIBRARY

ORDINAL TIME SERIES ANALYSIS

Methodology and Applications in Management Strategy and Policy

Edited by
TIMOTHY W. RUEFLI

THE IC² MANAGEMENT AND MANAGEMENT SCIENCE SERIES
W. Cooper and George Kozmetsky, Series Editors

QUORUM BOOKS
New York • Westport, Connecticut • London

Library of Congress Cataloging-in-Publication Data

Ordinal time series analysis : methodology and applications in
  management strategy and policy / edited by Timothy W. Ruefli.
      p.   cm.—(The IC² management and management science series)
   Includes bibliographical references.
   ISBN 0-89930-571-7 (lib. bdg. : alk. paper)
   1. Management—Statistical methods.   2. Strategic planning—
Statistical methods.   3. Time-series analysis.   I. Ruefli, Timothy
W.   II. Series.
HD30.215.074   1990
658.4'012'0151955—dc20   90-30011

British Library Cataloguing in Publication Data is available.

Copyright © 1990 by IC² Institute

All rights reserved. No portion of this book may be
reproduced, by any process or technique, without the
express written consent of the publisher.

Library of Congress Catalog Card Number: 90-30011
ISBN: 0-89930-571-7

First published in 1990

Quorum Books, 88 Post Road West, Westport, CT 06881
An imprint of Greenwood Publishing Group, Inc.

Printed in the United States of America

The paper used in this book complies with the
Permanent Paper Standard issued by the National
Information Standards Organization (Z39.48-1984).

10 9 8 7 6 5 4 3 2 1

Contents

Preface

The title of this book, while an accurate description of its contents, is likely to conjure visions of complicated mathematics, axioms, theorems, proofs, and lemmas, coupled with hypothetical applications based on data well-abstracted from reality. What the reader will find, however, is a straightforward, but practicable, approach to incorporating time series of data in strategic analysis. This approach was developed from situations faced by corporate strategists and researchers and is accessible to anyone who remembers only the barest essentials from a college course on probability and statistics.

Managers intuitively view the world in terms of the relative positions of competitors, suppliers, divisions, departments, etc. Extending that intuition to specific data over time and formalizing the approach is the essence of Ordinal Time Series Analysis. All that is required is to replace the absolute numbers traditionally used in time series analysis with the rank position of those numbers. What emerges when rankings rather than absolute numbers are employed are patterns of strategic behavior relevant to the products, firms, or other entities being analyzed.

The methodology presented here has been tested over a period of seven years with Ph.D. students, managers, and MBA students. Employing Ordinal Time Series Analysis as a methodology, Ph.D. students have been able to design and carry out original research within a span of a semester that has either made contributions to knowledge or shed new light on existing findings. Both of the latter two groups have been able to grasp the basic principles of Ordinal Time Series and to quickly apply them to product, firm, or industry analyses in a matter of a couple of hours. These applications have consistently yielded important strategic insights—even with not-so-reliable data.

There are aspects of thinking about the world in terms of time series of rankings that do require some adjustment from approaches to dealing with absolute numbers. While rankings are common-place in managerial environments, their use has been informally structured and limited to static or single-dimensional comparisons. The use of ranks over time as a tool for strategic analysis requires that this intuitive concept be placed in the same type of logical framework and process that is usually reserved for absolute (cardinal) data. Ordinal data are remarkably easy to manipulate, but can require some concentration before sensible interpretations of the resulting analysis can be generated. This is because thinking about and explicating relative positions over time in a consistent fashion requires that attention be paid to arrangements that involve simultaneous multiple shifts in the performance of a number of firms or other entities.

This book is designed to introduce the reader to the methodology of ordinal time series in an applications-based manner. The situations selected for illustration have been chosen to represent a range of levels of analysis, ranging from a product-level analyses, to firm level, to industry level, and even global analysis. Data used in these illustrations are drawn from publicly available sources and demonstrate the ability of the methodology to provide new and interesting strategic insights into corporate behavior using "generic" data.

The basic computational requirements of ordinal time series analysis generally can be fulfilled by existing spread-sheet or data base management programs. However, some of the statistical tests of significance and the computation of information statistics are probably better undertaken by specialized programs designed for that purpose.

This book grew out of a complex of motivations and circumstances. For five years as Associate Director of the IC^2 Institute at The University of Texas at Austin I had fostered and participated in the development of several large data bases. The particular data base I was developing was concerned with the behavior of the 1500 largest manufacturing and service companies in the U.S. from 1954 to the present. Specifically I was interested in determining how corporate transactions such as mergers, acquisitions, reorganizations, etc., affected corporate economic performance. As a long-time student of strategy, I was convinced that strategic management could not be understood through a disjointed series of cross-sectional analyses of five years of data at a time. The alternative was to develop data bases that covered spans of twenty-five years or more and included, in addition to the financial data in existing data bases, the set of transactions that constitute the initiators and outcomes of strategic implementations.

I began the development of such a data base in 1976 and in the summer of 1981 was still attempting to computerize the remaining, and key, third of the data—that relating to mergers, acquisitions, and other transactions. The financial performance data had been loaded, as had the annual rankings of the largest 500 manufacturing firms and the top 50 service firms in a number of industries as published by *Fortune*. When the

Institute Director, George Kozmetsky, made it clear that some tangible output from the project was expected by the end of the summer, my options were limited—the financial data were not unique and would have to be supplemented by additional information to yield substantive output, and the transactions data base was not ready. That left only the time series of rankings of the *Fortune* 500 manufacturing and service firms as candidates for analysis.

In the process of waiting for the data base to be computerized, I had been giving some serious thought to the problem of methodologies to be used in analyzing time series data. A little library research convinced me that existing techniques were laden with mathematical complexities and required many onerous assumptions about the nature of the data being analyzed. I wanted something that would yield strategic insights, but would work with a minimum of assumptions on generally available data, and not involve a high level of mathematical complexity to be implemented.

The confluence of necessity and availability led me to examine a time series of the *Fortune* rankings of the top 50 transportation companies in the period 1960 to 1978. The significance of the patterns contained in that initial crude analysis provided the intellectual impetus for the development of Ordinal Time Series Analysis.

The production of a book, in contrast to publication of an article, requires the participation and support of a relatively large number of individuals. As a consequence, I would like to thank several people. For my co-authors on individual chapters, in addition to my thanks for the intellectual companionship, there is compensation in the form of satisfaction in seeing their work in print.

I am grateful to the IC^2 Institute for providing support over the years, and for a quiet office where much of this book was written. I especially want to thank the Institute Director, George Kozmetsky, for delivering the ultimatum that spurred the development of Ordinal Time Series Analysis, and also for insisting that the results appear in the form of a book, rather than just as a series of articles. Thanks also go to Ray Smilor, Executive Director of the Institute, who handled the contractual arrangements—not once, but several times after the first publisher became a casualty of the merger and acquisitions wave of the 1980s. Linda Teague of the IC^2 staff has earned special recognition for her efforts in managing the production of this volume—in addition to carrying out her regular Institute duties. Dean Robert Witt of the Graduate School of Business of the University of Texas at Austin is due acknowledgement both for support provided and for keeping a straight face when I maintained that I could both be Chair of the Management Department and complete this book.

I owe a particular debt of gratitude to Bill Cooper, Professor of Accounting, Management, and Management Science and Information Systems and Centennial Research Fellow at the IC^2 Institute, who, for the second time, saw me through two major undertakings. Two decades ago when we were both at the Graduate School of Industrial Administration at Carnegie Mellon University, he as Professor and I as Ph.D. candidate, Bill set the standards for research and edited my dissertation. He did an encore with respect to this book, by serving as editor of the series of books of which this work is a part. I am grateful for his comments, criticisms, and suggestions on several drafts of the manuscript and for the general intellectual and moral support he provided.

Finally, while I have tried to take pains to prevent my work from interfering with my family life, I have not always been able to meet that goal. To the degree I have not been successful in that regard, and beyond, I owe special thanks to my wife, Elizabeth, and to my son, Chad, and daughter, Tia, for the support they gave me and the patience they have exhibited during the long process.

ORDINAL
TIME SERIES
ANALYSIS

1

Introduction

Timothy W. Ruefli
Chester L. Wilson

The situations confronted by practicing strategy or policy analysts or by researchers in the areas of strategy and policy often involve a number of organizational entities that interact in a performance space involving a number of input dimensions and outcome measures. For example, in performing an analysis of the competitive situation in an industry, anywhere from five to several hundred firms might be considered along the dimensions of operating revenues, net income, number of employees, return on equity (ROE), assets, and research and development (R&D) expenditures. A policy analysis might well involve all 50 states, or the top 100 Standard Metropolitan Statistical Areas, or all 200 counties in a state, and might measure these entities on the dimensions of population, per capita income, infant mortality, per capita health care resources, life expectancy, and education level. Given the dynamic nature of strategy and policy problems, data for such analyses might cover years, or even decades. Cross-sectional analyses, whose results have restricted applicability, dominate the methodological approach in these areas because of the difficulties inherent in traditional longitudinal studies (see, for example, Kimberley 1980, or Miller and Friesen, 1982).

Further complicating strategy/policy analyses are the problems associated with the quality of data (especially in terms of their definition and comparability) concerning levels of performance of organizations. Organizations usually report data that reflect their status as given by their current accounting methods and policies. Since accounting methods and decision practices differ from organization to organization, performance data may not be exactly comparable from one organization to another. For example, one firm may have used a LIFO (Last In, First Out) accounting method for inventory while another used FIFO (First In, First Out); the first may have had a conservative approach to writing off losses while the second had a more liberal approach. Such differences may or may not affect the outcome of a strategic analysis, depending on how they are incorporated into the data analysis. In the analysis, however, these and other differences should either be accounted for in an explicit fashion, or data analysis techniques that are not sensitive to these perturbations should be employed.

Even given the availability of longitudinal data of usable quality, significant problems remain. Data that are comparable from one organization to the next in a given year, may not be directly comparable for the same organization from one year to the next. One common reason for this is that price levels change over time and allowances must be made in the data for inflation or deflation. Although this is easily done given an appropriate price index, the problem is determining just what is the appropriate price index. Price indices are usually generated across entire segments of an economy and may not truly reflect the economic conditions of a particular industrial segment (see, e.g., Mansfield, 1987). Also restricting the intertemporal comparison of organizational performance are business and economic cycles that are not well reflected in price indices. In comparing month-to-month performance for a firm with a seasonal product, for instance, some allowance should be made for the seasonality of the data. The same is true for organizations that have longer-term cycles affecting them. While quantitative techniques have been developed to address various aspects of eliminating trends from data, (see, e.g. Hadley, 1969, chapter 8; Granger and Hatanaka, 1964) even if all subsidiary problems are not present the application of these techniques represents a substantial undertaking. More troublesome are one-of-a-kind external impacts on an industry. Changes in government policy can have differential effects on industries and on firms within those industries. Deregulation of an industry may favorably affect some firms while harming others. Nor are such effects limited to firms in the same industry; firms in competing and complementary industries may also be affected.

Other circumstances that can arise to confound the intertemporal comparability of data include changes in organizational accounting practices, changes in capital structures, and other similar temporal decisions within the entities being analyzed. If allowance is to be made for such circumstances, data transformations can become idiosyncratic to individual firms and entail a laborious computational process even if only a small number of organizations is sampled.

Beyond the problems associated with data comparability, there are possible complications associated with matching data analysis techniques to the characteristics of the data. For example, given data that are comparable over time and across organizations, the appropriateness of a particular model will depend, in part, on the nature of the underlying distributional form of the data. Commonly used regression models, for example, assume that the data are normally distributed. The models used in parametric statistics can be particularly restrictive in their assumptions, and application of these techniques in cases where the assumptions fail can yield a situation where the technique works for the analyst, but the results of the analysis do not work in the real world.

There is no known set of statistical techniques that avoids all of the problems mentioned above. Particular techniques usually imply trade-offs of one set of problems for another for given levels of power, precision, or confidence of results. The next sections of this chapter develop in a more formal fashion the problems and alternatives associated with analysis of multidimensional, multiorganizational, longitudinal data, and will report a methodology that addresses the problems in a fashion that is especially appropriate to applications in the areas of strategy and policy.

AN EXAMPLE

To motivate this discussion, we examine an example of a single firm measured along two performance dimensions. Assume that an analyst wishes to examine the competitive position of Pan American Airlines against the largest airlines with respect to operating revenue and net income. Specifically, assume that the comparison is to be made between Pan Am and: (1) all other competitors and, (2) the average performer for each performance measure. Further assume that the cardinal data on the operating revenues and net income (in current dollars) of the top nine airlines are available. Figure 1.1 presents the cardinal data for Pan Am.

Before presenting the ordinal data for Pan Am, conventions regarding some aspects of the presentation and interpretation of ordinal data in graphical form need to be established. An ordinal transformation assigns the rank of "one" to the best performer, the rank of "two" to the next best, and so forth. Since most of the commercially available software packages for graphics presentation are designed to present cardinal data, the scale of their vertical axis is set so that the minimum value must be less than the maximum value as in Figure 1.2. For ordinal data this means that the first rank, the position of the best performer, would be located at the bottom of the vertical axis, the next best performer would be located just above the first, and so on. To have the graphs oriented in the customary fashion, so that movements away from the horizontal axis represent improvements in rank position, while movements towards the horizontal axis worsening of rank position, requires the vertical scale to be inverted. Not all software packages have this ability as yet. However, one software package for IBM compatible personal computers that has this capability is Microsoft Excel, and there were indications that Microsoft Chart was planning to introduce the capability.

Figure 1.1. Pan American Airlines Cardinal Data

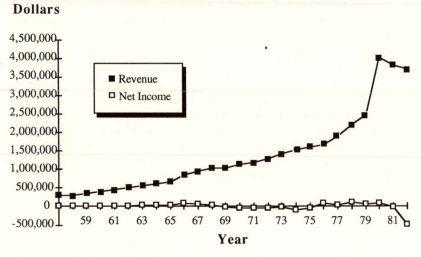

Figure 1.2. Cardinal Analysis Space

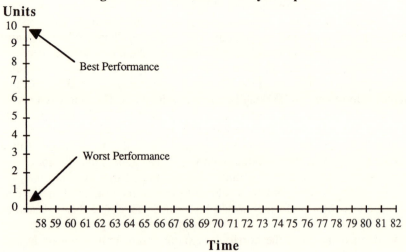

Other possible solutions to this situation are to multiply all rank numbers by minus one and then ignore the minus signs on the graphs, or accept the existing scale convention and reorient our thinking. We have chosen to use the flexibility of Microsoft Excel; therefore in graphs such as

Figure 1.3 showing the rank position of organizations where the horizontal axis represents time, improved performance is indicated by a movement towards the physical top of the graph and worsening performance is indicated by movement towards the bottom of the graph. The arrows in Figure 1.3 reinforce this point.

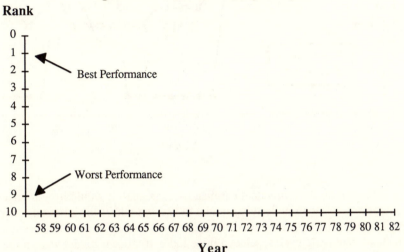

Figure 1.3. Ordinal Analysis Space

Figure 1.4 presents the ordinal data on operating revenue and net income for Pan Am. To obtain this graph, the cardinal operating revenue and net income data for the nine largest airlines were ranked in each year and then the rankings for Pan Am were plotted. The first point to notice is that in Figure 1.1, because of the magnitude of the difference between operating revenue and net income, the net income data were compressed into a narrow band around the horizontal axis. In Figure 1.4, because operating revenue and net income share the same ranking scale, no such scale discrepancy occurs.

It can be seen in Figure 1.4 that Pan Am's rank position started at the highest rank in 1957, dropped to third, and returned to the second position. With the exception of a drop to third in 1965, Pan Am stayed in second until 1969, when a worsening trend to fourth and then fifth place occurred. Pan Am returned to third position in 1980 (as a result of the acquisition of National Airlines), but worsened to fifth again by 1982. Since the average rank of the top nine airlines is the fifth rank, the position of Pan Am with respect to the average performer in terms of rank is easy to discern without the need for further computation.

Figure 1.4. Pan American Airlines Ordinal Data

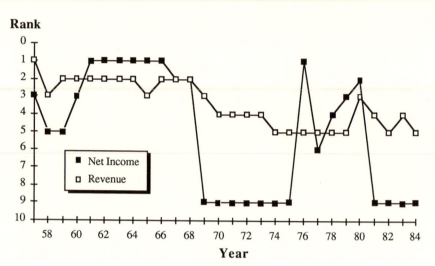

To present the equivalent cardinal data, an analyst would have to make assumptions about an underlying model to use and adjust for inflation, select a price index (if a linear model was chosen), and adjust for the possible effects of economic cycles, select a price index if a linear model was chosen, and adjust the data to constant dollars. Figure 1.5 shows the results of this process for a reduced set consisting of the top six airlines for the period 1957 to 1982. The addition of more firms or the inclusion of another dimension of performance overly complicates the presentation, so the reference set for the cardinal data for this example has been reduced to the top six airlines in terms of their operating revenue.

To be completely analogous with the ordinal process, the average performance in each year for each dimension should first be computed. Then the differences between Pan Am's revenue and net income and the revenue and net income of each of the other five firms, and of the average firm, should then be computed and plotted. This immediately presents a problem of scaling. Because the magnitudes of revenue and net income are so different, either two scales or two graphs are required if lower magnitude differences are not to be rendered unobservable. Since both the use of two dimensions and the plotting of all six differences for even one dimension would result in a largely unreadable graph, Figure 1.6 shows only the differences between the revenues of each of the top five firms, the average revenue of the top nine firms and Pan Am's revenues, deflated by the wholesale price index in all cases. Since this is somewhat confusing, Figure 1.7 shows only the top firm and the average in relation to Pan Am. The graph shows that Pan Am had an increasing trend against the average for the first decade, came down to the average in 1969 and then had a decreasing trend for the next decade. Revenues increased sharply above the average in 1980 (with the acquisition of National) and then began to decrease again. With respect to the top firm, Pan Am lost ground slowly until 1965, experienced a sharp worsening in 1966 to 1969, was stable from 1969 to 1971, generally declined in the period from 1971 to 1979, had a nonrecurrent improvement in 1980, and declined after that point.

Figure 1.5. Deflated Cardinal Revenues—Pan Am and Top Six Airlines

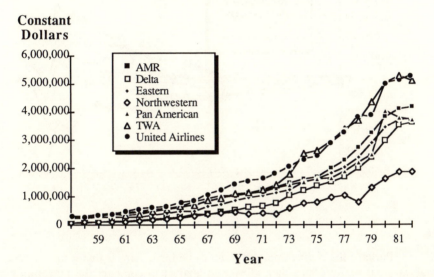

Comparing the cardinal and ordinal interpretations of revenue position, we find that the slight cardinal worsening in 1958 (barely perceptible in the cardinal graph, Figure 1.6) cost Pan Am two rank positions. From the inherent logic of the rankings, an analyst knows, without seeing further data, that this is because two lower-ranked competitors improved their performance sufficiently to surpass Pan Am. Without plotting the data, the cardinal analysis does not reveal the relationship of Pan Am's performance to any other firms. The ordinal analysis, however, indicates that the sharp cardinal drop in 1969 cost Pan Am only one rank position (because the two larger competitors also lost or did not gain sufficiently), while the cardinal improvement from 1969 to 1970 cost another rank position (because the competition improved more).

The decline in cardinal data from 1971 to 1979 cost Pan Am only one rank position (because the competition was also having problems). Finally, the cardinal improvement from the 1980 acquisition gained Pan Am two rank positions, which were lost by cardinal declines in the next two years.

Figure 1.6. Deflated Cardinal Revenue Differences—Pan Am and Top Six Airlines

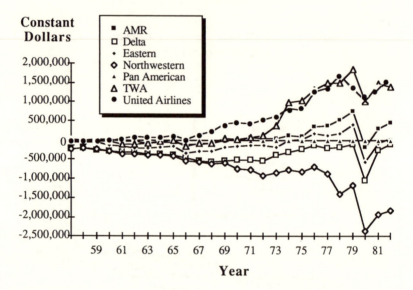

Perhaps the most important point to be made here is that a time series of cardinal performance data allows an analyst to compare the performing entity only against its own history. Ordinal time series data on the same performance dimension for the same entity requires the analyst to compare the entity not only against its own performance, but against the performance of all of the other entities against which the entity is ranked.

EVALUATION

Thus, even with more assumptions and computations, the cardinal analysis does not clearly indicate the competitive effects of cardinal shifts, which are evident on an ordinal graph. To show competitive effects in cardinal terms would require the presentation of additional data. From the point of view of a corporate strategist, the competitive effects may well be the most important—at least initially. On the other hand, in our example, the ordinal analysis obscured the absolute direction of some of the revenue movements as well the absolute differences between Pan Am and the leading firm.

Figure 1.7. Deflated Cardinal Revenue Differences—Pan Am and Top and Average Airlines

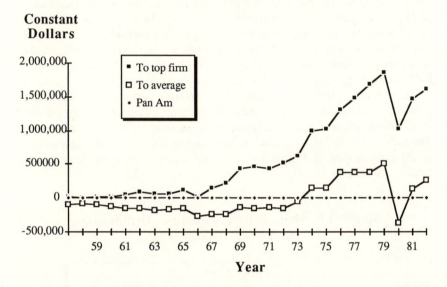

The simple Pan Am example allows us to make several comparisons between cardinal and ordinal analysis. The cardinal analysis required a more restrictive assumption about the nature of the model relating the observed and "actual" data than did the ordinal analysis (linear versus simply increasing). It required a further assumption about the appropriate price index to use. Considerably more computations were needed in the cardinal case to achieve an analogous result to the ordinal model. The interpretation of the result of the cardinal analysis in terms of competitive analysis was also more difficult. While it was clear that Pan Am was above the cardinal average and by what amount, given the error due to model and parameter specification and data collection, it was not clear how Pan Am measured up competitively. Even if the underlying data distributions were identified and the standard deviations for each year were calculated, Pan Am's competitive position would not be clear without additional data. The ordinal analysis showed Pan Am's position *vis a vis* the other large airlines, but it did not indicate the magnitude of the distance in dollar terms. However, the ordinal analysis showed that at one time when Pan Am was making cardinal gains, it was losing competitive position in the market.

Finally, it is evident from this two-dimensional example that graphing together the cardinal values of multiple dimensions of competitive performance makes discernment and analysis difficult; because multiple scales are required to show net income and return on equity on the same graph with operating revenue, and so forth. On the other hand, since ordinal analysis uses the same integer scale for all dimensions, presentation of even five performance dimensions is relatively easy, thus facilitating visual analysis. To illustrate this point, Figure 1.8 presents ordinal data for Pan Am on the dimensions of operating revenue, net income, assets, number of employees, and return on equity, ranked against other large airlines. Relations among levels of performance on the five measures over time can be seen clearly—all in the context of the relative performance of the other nine airline companies. Presentation of the same information using cardinal data would involve the generation of a substantial number of graphs, comparison among which would be awkward at best. Further, interpretation of the ordinal data in Figure 1.8 can have a direct strategic character (for details, see chapter 4).

Figure 1.8. Pan American Airlines Ordinal Data on Several Dimensions

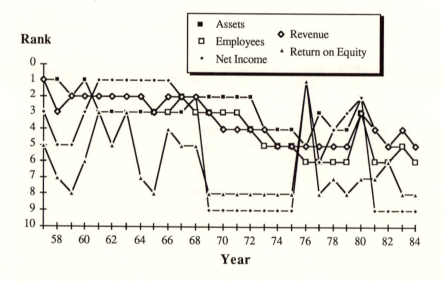

In discussing the ubiquitousness of cardinal analysis in policy/strategy research, Hatten (1979, p. 452), after discussing cost as the reason for the paucity of ordinal data in such research, goes on to observe:

> On the other hand, the reason may lie not in the costs and problems of collecting nominal and ordinal data, so much as the apparent availability of interval data which allows the use of the most advanced analytical tools. It may even be because "higher" scaled data are considered more "respectable." If this is the case, it should be noted that usually, the more precise the measurement (of a concept), the less certain we can be of what it is we have measured, as the Heisenberg principle warns us, e.g., "What single variable best measures scale of production?"

The importance of the ordinal time series approach is that it allows a corporate strategist a relatively simple way to analyze and present longitudinal data on a number of firms, measured along multiple performance dimensions, without making restrictive assumptions about underlying relationships among the observations, and without engaging in a multitude of computations. As Brockett and Kemperman (1980, p. 111) have shown in other circumstances, the data can even be somewhat "dirty," yet the ranking approach can still yield some useful results where cardinal analysis might be nearly impossible or misleading.

TYPES OF APPLICATIONS

Motivation

In its most general form, ordinal time series analysis (OTSA) has a wide range of potential applications. Particularly appropriate are situations where multidimensional data on a number of entities have been gathered over time; where the underlying data distributions are not likely to be normal; where the data are assumed to be somewhat "dirty"; where the data processing resources (including time) are limited; and where the researcher or decision-maker is interested in the broader aspects of the behavior of the entities in question.

The criteria outlined above are applicable to a number of areas of the social and management sciences, including psychology, geography, social work, economics, and business. The strategy and policy areas of management fully exemplify these qualifications. From the wide range of possible use in the strategy/policy area we have selected some representative applications for this book. These applications were chosen to demonstrate the flexibility of ordinal time series analysis and the type of results it generates. Some of the applications were chosen because they have been undertaken previously using a methodology based on cardinal analysis; the ordinal analysis presented here can then be contrasted with the cardinal analysis. Other applications do not have contrasting cardinal analyses available, but have been selected to demonstrate the range and types of applications of ordinal time series analysis.

Overview

The next two chapters will develop the statistics employed by ordinal time series analysis. Chapter 2 will present three and illustrate their use in analyzing industry behavior. Based on ordinal data, chapter 3 will develop information statistics that will allow the characterization of the behavior of a set of entities over time. Chapter 4 will present an application of ordinal time series analysis to the analysis of the largest firms in the transportation industry over the period from 1957 to 1984. Chapter 5 will demonstrate how ordinal time series analysis can complement an intuitive management analysis by presenting an ordinal analysis of the groups of firms selected by Peters and Waterman in their book *In Search of Excellence* (1982). The following chapter will look at one of the long-standing issues in corporate strategy, the relations among strategy, structure, and corporate performance. The classic study by Rumelt (1974) will be replicated using ordinal time series analysis, which will show how ordinal analysis can complement and clarify cardinal analysis.

Chapter 7 will step inside a firm to address the problem of product strategy. Ordinal time series analysis will be applied to data on software products to demonstrate the types of information the analysis produces at this micro level. The following chapter will jump to the macro level of world trade to undertake an analysis of world exports for 159 countries and the various trade groups that comprise the world economic community. Finally, chapter 9 will shift the context to combine a subset of world trade and corporate strategy and demonstrate how ordinal time series analysis can identify strategies of groups of firms in the U.S. and Japanese microelectronics industries.

2

Data Considerations and Rank Statistics

Timothy W. Ruefli
Chester L. Wilson

This chapter will present a general mathematical context for comparing ordinal and cardinal analysis. It will then discuss the nature of the data formats and transformations that are required for ordinal time series analysis, and will describe the rank statistics that form the basis for the ordinal analysis. The development of the data considerations and the rank statistics will be presented in general form and will initially be illustrated by examples utilizing a limited number of entities at only one level of analysis and along only one performance dimension. In subsequent sections of the chapter, the analysis will be extended to include larger numbers of entities at multiple hierarchical levels and along multiple performance dimensions.

ORDINAL VERSUS CARDINAL ANALYSIS

Let us assume that the data for a strategic analysis are in the form of observations of performance for a set of N firms on K performance dimensions over M years. Let $y_{i,t,j}$ be the observed performance of the ith firm in year t along the jth performance dimension, and let $x_{i,t,j}$ be the "true" performance level if proper allowance could be made for inflation, seasonality, sampling error, and so on. It is the true performance upon which an analyst would prefer to base conclusions; however, only the observed data are available. Analysis using this observed performance data is what we shall term "cardinal analysis." More precisely stated, by cardinal analysis we shall mean methodologies employing nominal, interval, or ratio scales of measurement, that is, everything but ordinal scales (Stevens, 1946). Thus analyses using frequency counts (twelve firms are profitable, three are not), meaningful distance measures (Firm D's revenues are $1,250,000 greater than Firm K's), or meaningful ratios (Firm D is three times as profitable as Firm K), would be classed as cardinal analyses.

Theoretically, existing statistical techniques using the cardinal data can be employed to obtain estimates for the $x_{i,t,j}$. The first step in this process is to assume that the relationship between the observations and the true values can be expressed in functional form:

$$X_{i,t,j} = f(Y_{i,t,j}) \tag{2.1}$$

where $X_{i,t,j}$ is the estimated true value to be obtained from the observed $Y_{i,t,j}$ via some suitably specified functional form for the model. Since there is not always enough data of high quality to determine the true functional form, this latter step usually requires assumptions that will significantly affect the nature of the results of the ensuing analysis. For example, one common solution is to assume that the underlying function is linear:

$$X_{i,t,j} = b_{i,t,j}Y_{i,t,j} + c_{i,t,j} + w_{i,t,j} \tag{2.2}$$

where $b_{i,t,j}$ is a price or price index possibly varying for entity i and dimension j in each period t, while $c_{i,t,j}$ represents a possible bias, and $w_{i,t,j}$ is random error term (with mean of zero).

Each of the factors in equation 2.2 should be a source of concern for an analyst. The determination of an appropriate price index for a firm or group of firms is a nontrivial problem and can introduce error in the equations. The problem is compounded if we wish to compare $X_{i,t,j}$ to $X_{k,t,j}$ (the performance of two different entities along the same dimension in the same time period). The two entities may be subject to different economic influences and thus require different indexes to adjust their performance levels. For example, one firm may be a manufacturer, for which a raw materials or commodity price index should be used, while the other firm may be a retailer, for which a wholesale price index should be employed.

There is also a problem in comparing the performance of a firm, $X_{i,t,j}$ (in an inclusive or exclusive manner), to a measure of the aggregate performance of the rest of its subgroup, or its industry, at time t. The cardinal analysis approach might compute an average $X_{i,t,j}$ for the reference group and then state the observed $X_{i,t,j}$ within a specified number of standard deviations from the mean. Even if an underlying statistical distribution is assumed to hold, the resulting statement of $X_{i,t,j}$ in units of mean to standard deviation relations does not unambiguously locate the position of the firm relative to its competition.

An analogous problem arises if an analyst wishes to compare a firm's performance on dimension j with its performance on dimension k in the same time period (that is, compare $X_{i,t,j}$ to $X_{i,t,k}$) using cardinal analysis. The usual solution is to form a ratio of the two cardinal performance levels for each firm in the reference group, compute a mean, and place the ratio for firm i within so many standard deviations of the mean (see, e.g., Byrnes, 1985, p. 89). In both of the last-mentioned situations, assumptions about the underlying distribution must be made in order to transform the cardinal data to ratio data. Further complications arise if the analyst wishes to test whether or not subsets of firms have been differentially affected by various events, or when it is desirable to compare three or more dimensions of performance at a point in time.

Although cardinal analysis techniques can be used to analyze longitudinal data on multiple firms on multiple performance dimensions, such techniques often require significant numbers of assumptions (starting with an assumption of the underlying relationship, as in equation 2.2 above). Cardinal analysis employs even more complicated mathematical transformations if nonlinear relationships or possible differential effects are involved. These difficulties we conjecture to be among the prime reasons that there are not more longitudinal studies of firm performance in the literature.

Ordinal time series analysis addresses these problems by making the simple assumption that the $X_{i,t,j}$ are merely a monotonic function (either increasing or decreasing) of the $Y_{i,j,t}$ and transforming the $X_{i,t,j}$ to their rank $R_{i,t,j}$ against all other entities in the set of N firms at time t. The firm with the "best" cardinal performance level, which may mean largest or smallest, depending on the performance dimension, receives a rank of one on that dimension, the next best performer a rank of two and so on. The assumption that the $X_{i,t,j}$ are a monotonic function of the $Y_{i,j,t}$ is the weakest possible assumption that retains any usefulness (Brockett and Kemperman, 1980, p.107), and the transformation from cardinal to ordinal data is the only one that gives the same values for the observations as for the actuals regardless of the true relationship (see, e.g., Hollander and Wolfe, 1973 or Hajek and Sidak, 1967 for a general context or Brockett and Kemperman, 1980 for a specific application).

A special virtue of the rank transformation, in addition to its simplicity, is that comparisons across time can be made directly without additional discount factors. Also, comparisons between firms at a point in time can be made without the extensive computation required by models of the kind involved in cardinal analysis, as described in the case of Pan Am in chapter 1. Further, with the rank statistics developed below, an individual firm can be related to various industry subgroups without requiring the special distributional assumptions of cardinal analysis.

The use of ranks also facilitates the comparison of a firm's performance along two or more performance dimensions at time t. In using ordinal data, comparisons are not restricted to dimensions taken two at a time: the relative positioning of the ranks allows direct comparisons. For example, if a firm has a net income rank and an operating revenue rank higher than its rank by number of employees, then relative to the other firms against which it is ranked it is more profitable on a per employee basis, and its employees are more productive in terms of sales. Since the rank transformation generates for each performance dimension in each year a closed set consisting of the first N integers, for one firm to have a higher rank on one dimension relative to another dimension, one or more other firms must have the relationship reversed. The closed property of the rank set also provides access to a number of statistics useful in characterizing the behavior of various groups and subgroups of the entities being studied as will be seen below. This property provides another benefit of ordinal analysis. Since all performance dimensions are transformed into the same set of N integers in each year, the results for different performance dimensions can be presented in graphical form on the same scale. This aids an analyst both in interpreting multidimensional data and in explaining the results to others in a direct and simple manner.

DATA FORMAT

The Nature of Ordinal Data

Historically, when data analysis for management strategy and policy is performed, the data are of two types: cardinal data, that is, absolute numerical levels of performance or ratio data, that is, ratios of cardinal performance data. Ordinal time series methodology utilizes a third kind of data, ordinal data. These data are in the form of rankings of organization or product performance over time for each entity and for each of the selected performance dimensions. The best performer on a particular dimension is given a ranking of one, the second best is given a ranking of two, and so on. Examples of dimensions of performance that are fruitful in an ordinal time series approach to competitive or market analysis of industry include the standard measures of operating revenue, net income, number of employees, assets, and return on equity. They may also include such dimensions as passenger-seat-miles, product quality, R&D expenditures, occupancy rate, and so forth.

As was indicated in chapter 1, ordinal time series analysis can start with the same absolute numerical performance data as does cardinal analysis. But instead of the various transformations used in cardinal analysis, ordinal time series analysis makes only the simple transformation of ordering the entities being analyzed along each performance dimension for each year for which there are data. Given that the original data on entity performance are in cardinal form (that is, absolute numerical levels of performance) they must be transformed to yield ordinal rankings; the entities must be ordered (for example, sorted or indexed) each year along each dimension, and assigned ranks based on their performance. The statistics developed below are generated directly from the ordinal data. The only variation on this simple transformation occurs when the criterion for ranking is a ratio, for example, return on equity. In this case the ratios of the cardinal data are computed and then the entities are ranked by this ratio.

In presenting this development, the basic entities of analysis are assumed to be firms, and examples from that context will be used to illustrate the development. The reader should keep in mind that the methodology is equally applicable to situations where the basic entities to be analyzed are governmental bodies, products, sub-units of a firm or agency, or geographic regions. To emphasize this, wherever possible the generic term "entity" will be used in reference to the basic object of analysis.

The analysis of industry behavior using ordinal time series data has some characteristics that may disturb analysts experienced in cardinal data analysis. First, in deriving ordinal rankings from cardinal data some information is obviously filtered out, obscuring some of the details of the behavior of the entities being studied. For example, Table 2.1 shows the cardinal and ordinal performance data for three firms, A, B, and C. As the data show, Firm C increased significantly in cardinal performance from 1980 to 1981, but its rank remained the same, whereas Firm B actually worsened its cardinal performance level in the same time period, but retained its rank position. It is the apparent seriousness of the loss of these detailed data that has dissuaded analysts from using ordinal data in time series form.

Table 2.1. Net Income Data

Firm	1980 Cardinal	1980 Ordinal	1981 Cardinal	1981 Ordinal	1982 Cardinal	1982 Ordinal
A	753,278	1	634,222	1	507,828	2
B	569,801	2	499,117	2	479,001	3
C	237,664	3	475,231	3	600,554	1

Advantages of Ordinal Data

Many of the advantages of ordinal time series analysis stem from the transformation of cardinal to ordinal data and the concomitant "information loss." While it is true that some detailed information is filtered out in the rank transformation, it is also true that much of the short-term business cycle and midterm economic cycle noise is filtered out by the same process. Ordinal time series analysis reveals longer-term trends in industry and market behavior, as well as those behaviors that are the result of a group of entities having been affected in a differential fashion. For example, ordinal time series analysis will not reveal (and that in itself may be informative) the effects of a raw material price increase or a recession that equally affects all organizations or products being analyzed. It will, however, make evident the effects of such a price increase or, say, a change in public policy or a period of inflation that has negative impacts on some firms or products and not on others.

For example, in Table 2.1 the cardinal data show the effects of a one-year inflationary period in 1981-1982, followed by a one-year deflationary period. The ordinal data are not affected by the price changes, since all the firms were affected proportionally. Furthermore, this example indicates that the most pernicious problem of cardinal ayalysis, determining the proper discount rate to use in making intertemporal comparisons of performance, is eliminated by ordinal time series analysis. This is accomplished by making the assumption that the ith rank in time t is equivalent to the ith rank in all other time periods for the purpose of the comparison. The reasonableness of this assumption may depend on the underlying structure of the industry or market. Being in third position, for example, when there are four large dominant firms in an industry is not necessarily equivalent to being third when there is only one dominant firm in the industry, or when there are no dominant firms in the industry. An analyst must allow for such structural shifts when interpreting the results of an ordinal analysis.

Second, ordinal data require that well-known parametric statistical techniques be abandoned for lesser-known nonparametric techniques. However, the use of ordinal data avoids unrealistic parametric assumptions, and nonparametric techniques have the advantage of ease of computation. Given the obviousness and virtues of the use of ordinal rankings, it might be supposed that they have had wide application. Yet an extensive literature review by the authors revealed only two remotely similar uses of ordinal time series, the application to health reporting systems by Brockett and Kemperman (1980) and its use as a measure of turnover in the banking industry by Heggestad and Rhoades (1976) and Rhoades and Rutz (1981).

Problems Arising from Ordinal Data

The use of ordinal data, while reducing the number of assumptions and the complexity of computation does not free ordinal time series analysis from all data problems. Most of these problems are also faced in cardinal analysis but a few are unique to ordinal analysis. One of the problems for both methods concerns the selection of the population for analysis. It is very rarely the case that a population of organizations or products is stable over long periods of time, or that data on the population are complete for the period of analysis. More frequently, analysis must be undertaken on incomplete sets of entities. For example, while it would be desirable to perform an industry analysis utilizing data from all of the firms in an industry, very often the analysis must be performed with data from only the largest firms in the industry. It is often the case that data are available only for the largest public firms in an industry; this creates scale and sample biases that might generate problems if a substantial portion of industry activity is attributable to a large number of small or privately held firms. Since firms are often classified as being in an industry on the basis of their revenues, single-product or service firms are lumped together with near-conglomerates.

Moreover, a firm may be classified as being in an industry if more than, say, 50% of its operating revenues came from industry-related activities, and if total revenues place the firm in the top N firms in the industry. Rankings along the other dimensions selected for analysis such as net income, assets, and return on equity, are contingent on the firm being in the top N along the dimension of revenue. Thus there may be firms that have net income or other performance figures that would place them in the top group by that measure, but because their revenue figures are not high enough, they are not listed. In general this occurs when the population is determined by criteria along one or more defining dimensions measuring heterogeneous activity. This results in a comparability problem because of commingled factors.

Problems also arise with respect to the dynamics of the population being studied. Data for organizations are often collected period by period. To perform time series analysis the data must be organized longitudinally by organization. Therefore organizational identities must be traced over the time span of the analysis, including information on mergers, acquisitions, and name changes. Conventions must be adopted to account for these events. For name changes, the simplest convention is to continue the time series of data, but under the new name. Mergers of ranked firms with firms outside the population should be treated not as a new entity but as a continuation of the previously ranked firm. In the event of a merger between two previously ranked firms, the entities prior to the merger can be considered to have been dropped from the rankings following the merger, and the resulting entity can be treated as a newly ranked firm. Alternatively, the merger can be treated as consisting of a surviving entity and an absorbed entity, in which case only one of the firms would drop from the rankings.

In addition to the problems mentioned above, there are some data problems that are specific to ordinal analysis. Up to this point, we have assumed that each firm has a unique rank, that is, the number of ranks n, generated by the mapping is equal to the number of firms, N. In cardinal analysis, the number of firms for which there are data may change from period to period, the only adjustment that is made in the analysis is to change the parameter associated with population size in the statistics. In ordinal analysis, to have access to the some of the measures of relative uncertainty, it is generally desirable to have a constant number of firms in each time period, even if some of them are not naturally ranked. Because firms leave and enter the top n firms from year to year, and are not ranked when they are not in the top n a convention for assigning a rank to a firm for which there are no data must be adopted. One possibility is to assign an artificial rank of "$n+1$" to unranked firms. This is conservative with respect to the analysis of the unranked firms insofar as the actual rank of firms outside the top n is, in all but at most one case, greater than $n+1$. Engwall employs a similar artifice with his class 0 (Engwall, 1973, p. 26).

There are other alternatives to a convention of assigning a rank of $n+1$. One possibility would be to use a median assignment of $n+(N-n)/2$ to unranked firms. This is less conservative with respect to the artificially ranked firms than the $n+1$ convention, but is more accurate if the entities being assigned this rank are in existence during the entire period of the ranking, and are just not large enough to appear in the top n positions. Another convention for unranked firms that is equivalent to the previous convention under some circumstances is randomly to assign ranks $n+1$, $n+2$, and so forth to the unranked firms. Yet another possibility, appropriate if it is known that an entity does not exist before or subsequent to its appearance in the rankings, is to exclude such entities from the calculations. Thus if there are a total of N entities that appear at some time in the rankings, but in year t only n_t of them are ranked, while the other $N-n_t$ entitles are presumed to be nonexistent, then the ordinal time series analysis can be undertaken with a variable number of ranked entities in a given year. The statistics calculated for any year will then be with respect to n_t, and some adjustments may have to be made to meaningfully compare the statistics from one year to the next.

The problems cited above may, of course, vary from data source to data source and from analysis to analysis. It is possible to use predeveloped rankings that are reported by a number of business, government, and trade publications. *Fortune, Forbes, Inc.* and other publications publish annual rankings of a number of types of corporations, while *Softsel, Variety*, and other magazines report weekly rankings of products or services. In the section that follows, the *Fortune* rankings of the 50 largest transportation companies from 1957 to 1984 will be used to illustrate the nature of each statistic as it is presented. This particular set of rankings was chosen because of wide familiarity with the transportation industry, permitting the reader more easily to check the interpretation of the results of the ordinal analysis.

RANK STATISTICS AND ANALYSIS

Given a group of N entities ranked along K performance dimensions over a period of M years, let the rank of entity i in year t along dimension k be $r_{i,t,k}$. For the *Fortune* data, N is 108 firms in total, ranked over $M = 28$ years and ranked along $K = 5$ dimensions. Let S be an index set of a group of n firms that are a subset of the N firms. S could indicate the firms in some industry subgroup,(for example, railroads or airlines), or the top n firms, and so on. The firms in S could be selected by a priori criteria, by factor analysis, or by other techniques, such as cluster analysis. Then three rank statistics giving the position, direction, and volatility of any group S of firms in the rankings can be defined. These definitions are presented below and are illustrated by using the results of the analysis of the *Fortune* data.

Position

The Statistic. The position of a set S of entities in year t along dimension k is their average rank:

$$P(S)_{t,k} = \frac{\sum r_{i,t,k}}{n} \quad i \,\varepsilon\, S, |S| = n.$$

(2.3)

and $i \,\varepsilon\, S$ means that i is an element of the set S of ranked entities, and where the vertical lines indicate the number of items in the set S.

In this notation, summation over the index i can be in any order in which the set S is arranged. The value of $P(S)_{t,k}$ is called the position statistic for the set S of entities in year t along dimension k. It is the average rank of the set S and gives the relative position of a subgroup within an industry or market in each year along the selected dimension. While average rank has little meaning for the total group of entities (it is constant and equal to $N/2$), it does have relevance for subgroups of firms within the population.

Interpretation. Figure 2.1 shows the operating revenue rank positions for three subgroups of firms in the transportation industry for the period from 1957 to 1984. As mentioned in chapter 1, position graphs are constructed with average rank measured along the vertical or Y-axis such that the best rank is at the top of the graph, furthest from the X-axis. Therefore movements toward the X-axis represent worsening in rank position, while movements away from that axis represent improvements in rank performance. This is because the highest rank is the first rank, the next highest rank is the second rank, and so forth. The highest *rank positions* have the lowest *rank numbers*.

Figure 2.1. Operating Revenue Posititons—Transportation Mode Groups

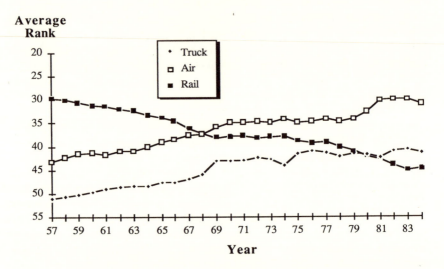

It is also important to note that the judgment of whether an increase in rank is desirable is dependent on the performance measure and the perspective and interests of the party making the judgment. For example, if firms are ranked on the basis of their net incomes, then being in the first position is presumably desirable, all other things equal, since the firm in that position has the largest net income. However, if firms are ranked by the number of industrial accidents per employee, then being ranked first is a dubious distinction that most firms would avoid if possible. If firms are ranked by number of employees, then the value of higher rank positions may vary with the observer. Those concerned primarily about providing jobs and reducing unemployment may view higher ranks in this case as more desirable. On the other hand, if the concern is for labor productivity, then lower rank by number of employees may be desirable if it does not adversely affect operating revenue and net income rankings.

An Example. With this in mind, we can turn again to Figure 2.1 and note that the average operating revenue rank position of the largest airlines has improved at varying rates, and with minor setbacks over the entire period from 1957 to 1984. The same holds true for the largest trucking firms. The largest railroads, on the other hand, show a trend of general worsening of average operating revenue position over the same period.

The pattern of changes in average rank are surprisingly smooth, especially considering the nature of the events having impact on the industry. During the period covered by Figure 2.1, airlines and trucking were deregulated, and all groups experienced the effects of the energy crisis. This latter event is the type of "noise" that ordinal analysis screens out. The energy crisis shows up in two ways in Figure 2.1. First, the pattern of changes in average rank position leveled off for all three groups in the period 1971 to 1977. Second, when in 1974 oil was embargoed by the Organization of Petroleum Exporting Countries (OPEC) and prices quadrupled, the revenue position of the trucking group worsened slightly, then recovered. The reason for this fluctuation is that trucking companies were more sensitive to the sharp change in supply and price than were the railroads and airlines. In the other years, the changes in supply and price affected all three groups more equally.

The foregoing illustrates that while the position statistic by itself provides information about the industry being analyzed, the interpretation of the patterns developed by the statistic may rely on information that is outside the scope of the ordinal analysis. This information might consist of a sequence of events in the history of the industry, or it might consist of cardinal analysis. Further, the discussion to this point has been on a one-dimensional basis; but the extension of the analysis to multiple dimensions is immediate, and can yield further conclusions derived from observations of the relations among positions along different dimensions. This extension will be undertaken later in this chapter.

Volatility

The Statistic. The volatility in rank shift of a set of entities, S, from year t-1 to t is given by:

$$V(S)_{t,k} = \frac{\Sigma |r_{i,t,k} - r_{i,t-1,k}|}{n} \quad i \, \varepsilon \, S, \, |S| = n.$$

$$(2.4)$$

The volatility, or average absolute rank shift, gives the gross amount of the rank change activity within the group, without regard to direction, and indicates how active the group is on average in terms of rank changes. For the entire set of entities, the minimum value for $V(S)$ is zero, achieved when each entity has the same rank in both years; the maximum value, assuming no artificial ranks, is $N/2$ if N is even and $(N^2-1)/2N$ if N is odd. For a single entity the maximum value of $V(S)$ is $N-1$. For any subset of entities, the maximum value of $V(S)$ is the maximal value of the class of n-permutations of N, which value is the sum of absolute differences in components of the permutations from the natural order.

Interpretation. Higher values of $V(S)$ indicate higher levels of average rank shift activity, which implies higher levels of positional turbulence in the set of entities. An analogue of this measure was used (see Rhoades, 1980 and Rhoades and Rutz, 1981) as a measure of the stability of a group of firms in an industry. Note that $V(S)$ measures the rank shift activity of a group of entities ranked relative to each other, not to any superset of entities.

An Example. Figure 2.2 graphs the revenue volatility of the three transportation mode groups. From this graph it can be observed that, with the exception of several anomalous spikes, the average firm in each group changed no more than one rank position until the early sixties; this level of activity increased over time until in the later years, the average firm changed two rank positions from year to year. This provides an analyst with a measure of the increasing change both internal and external in this industry. Two spikes in the volatility of the railroads in 1967 and 1969 signalled their participation in the reorganization of the northeastern railroads and in the wave of mergers and acquisitions during the late sixties. The 1975 spike in revenue volatility in trucking indicated the impacts that the oil embargo and price increases had on this mode group. The impact of the deregulation of the airlines in 1978 can be seen in the sharp increase in revenue volatility for this group in the post-1978 period. In this case volatility increased from an average of one rank shift in the period prior to deregulation to an average of three in subsequent years.

Analogous to the analysis of the position statistic, the volatility statistic itself provides information, but interpretation of this information depends, in part, on the analyst's knowledge of external events. Patterns in the statistic serve as invitations to further investigation to provide background motivation for interpreting the behavior of the statistic. The example provided here was one-dimensional, but the introduction of additional dimensions is straightforward and provides additional information in the form of relations among the various dimensions. This development will be undertaken in later sections of this chapter, and in the next chapter.

**Figure 2.2.   Operating Revenue Volatility—Transportation
Mode Groups**

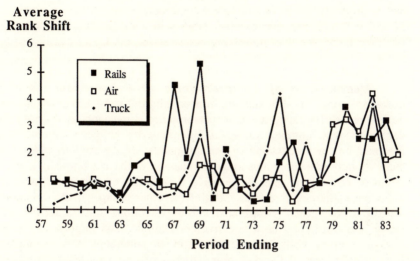

Direction

The Statistic.   The direction of the average rank shift of a set S of entities from year t-1 to year t is given by:

$$D(S)_{t,k} = \frac{\Sigma(r_{i,t,k} - r_{i,t-1,k})}{n} \quad i \, \varepsilon \, S, \, |S| = n.$$

(2.5)

Note that: $D(S)_{t,k} = P(S)_{t,k} - P(S)_{t-1.,k}$

The direction, or average signed rank shift, gives the average net change in rank, allowing negative and positive shifts to cancel out to the degree possible.   Since the directional rank shift is merely the change in the positional statistic, it is a second-order statistic.   If the statistic is computed for the entire population being studied it is equal to zero, since there are a finite number of ranks, and positive rank shifts must equal negative rank shifts in the aggregate.

Interpretation.   The direction statistic specifies the magnitude of the average improvement or worsening in rank for the set of entities along the selected dimension.   Positive values of $D(S)$ indicate a worsening in rank, while negative values indicate improvement in average rank. A zero value for $D(S)$ indicates that the positive and negative rank shifts for the individual entities canceled out. Note that $D(S)=0$ is not incompatible with $V(S)>>0$, that is, an entity can be in a turbulent environment and yet the set of entities of which it is a part can exhibit stability in average rank position, e.g., stratified industries with no mixing across strata, but high volatility within strata.

Measurement of Competitiveness or Cooperation. There is, however, a use for this statistic across subgroups. An analyst can use directional shifts along a single performance dimension to quantify the degree of rank competition or complementarity between subgroups of organizations or products along that dimension. In the obvious case where there are only two subgroups in the population, we have a zero-sum game in terms of rank shifts and the positive rank shifts of one group must be reflected in the negative rank shifts of the other group. If the directional statistic for one group is correlated with the directional statistic for the other group, the result will be a negative correlation. The importance of this statistic emerges when there are more than two subgroups in the population. In this latter case, if the direction statistics of two groups are correlated, then the coefficient of the slope will indicate the nature of rank competition or complementarity between the two groups in the environment established by the population and the significance level of the coefficient will be the degree of significance that is attached to that level of competition or complementarity.

For example, consider the case of two disjoint subgroups, A and B, ranked in a larger population. If the coefficient of correlation between $D(A)$ and $D(B)$ is negative and significant then the competition between A and B is relatively strong and significant; if the coefficient is positive and significant, then A and B can be regarded as being associated with respect to the dimension, and if the coefficient is not significant, then A and B can be regarded as being independent with respect to dimension k. The interpretation of this statistic will vary depending on the nature of the dimension k. If k represents the dimension of operating revenue then a negative correlation between $D(A)$ and $D(B)$ represents competition between A and B for market share. If k is the number of employees then the correlation indicates the degree to which the two groups of firms are cyclical or counter-cyclical with respect to each other in terms of employment.

An Example. For an example of the use of the direction statistic in this fashion, Figure 2.3 shows the revenue rank shifts of railroads, airlines and trucking groups. Since lower rank numbers (i.e, higher rank positions) indicate improvement in position, in the direction graph, negative values for

D(S) indicate improvements in rank position. It can be seen in Figure 2.3 that airlines and trucking moved together in terms of rank shift, with airlines leading trucking, and move opposite to railroads until 1969 or 1970. Empirical measures of competition, neutrality, or complementarity between subgroups can be obtained by computing correlation statistics of the relevant signed rank shift figures. Table 2.2 gives the Kendall Tau B correlation coefficients for the railroad, airline and trucking group directional rank shifts in operating revenue and the associated significance levels in the period 1960 to 1977. The interpretation of these statistics is that since there was a weak negative relation between the direction of average revenue rank shifts of the railroads and the airlines these two groups were not competing strongly for the same market. Similarly, the near-zero coefficient at a negligible level of significance between airline and trucking directional shifts indicates no market relation between these groups in the period examined. On the other hand the negative coefficient, significant at the 0.003 level, relating railroad and trucking directional shifts indicates that losses and gains in railroad rank position were associated with gains and losses, respectively, of the trucking group. This indicates a strong degree of market competition between these two groups and, in fact, gives an analyst a way of obtaining a quantitative measure of the level of competition.

Figure 2.3. Operating Revenue Direction—Transportation Mode Groups

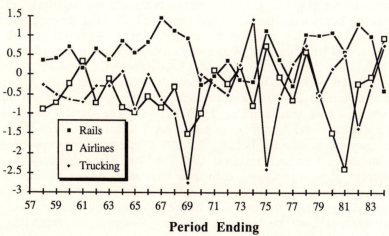

Table 2.2.   Kendall Tau B Correlation Coeffients and Significance Levels for Directed Rank Shifts 1960–1977

	Airlines	Trucking
Railroads	-0.142	-0.501
	(0.400)	(0.003)
Airlines	—	+0.006
	—	(0.972)

MULTIPLE DIMENSIONS

Thus far we have implicitly assumed an analysis process that is carried on one dimension at the time. Strategy and competitive analysis often involve the examination and comparison of multiple dimensions of performance. In this section we will examine how the analysis of multiple dimensions is undertaken in ordinal time series analysis.

Position on Multiple Dimensions

While each of the rank statistics can be computed on any number of dimensions, comparison of the position statistics across dimensions can provide the richest source of information for a strategic analyst. These position graphs also allow the analyst to make inferences about the relative performance of the factors of production in the different subgroups. This is possible because the number of rank positions is the same for each dimension and each year. Let us define the concept of rank equality as the base case that occurs when the rank of an entity on one dimension is equal to its rank on the other dimension(s). Consider the case where n firms are ranked and all exhibit rank equality. For simplicity consider the case of only two dimensions, say, where firms are ranked by number of employees and net income in each year as in Case I in Table 2.3. Now consider Case II where Firm A has a rank by number of employees that is four positions higher than its rank by net income. Because there are a finite number of rank positions, some other firm or firms must have employee ranks that total an equal number of positions lower than their total ranks by net income. In the example, Firm F has an employee rank that is four positions lower than its net income rank. In general, a firm exhibiting rank inequality on some dimensions must be balanced by one or more firms exhibiting rank inequality in the opposite direction on those same dimensions. Thus, in the case above, where a firm has an employee rank higher than its net income rank, such as Firm A, the implication is that relative to the other firms in the ranked population, this firm is probably earning relatively fewer dollars per employee. Additionally, because of the zero-sum nature of the rankings, it means that some other firm or firms are probably earning relatively more dollars per employee. An analyst can use this information on relative position along various dimensions to identify and evaluate entities and groups of entities that have favorable or unfavorable circumstances in terms of their relative productivity. The implication is qualified because it is possible that the inequality in ranks can exist and yet not have an effect on the ratio. In the extensive corporate data that have been analyzed to date, if the difference in ranks was greater than two positions, it was unlikely that the inference drawn above was incorrect.

Table 2.3. Rank Equality

Firm	Case I Employee Rank	Case I Net Income Rank	Case II Employee Rank	Case II Net Income Rank
A	7	7	3	7
B	2	2	2	2
C	9	9	9	9
D	5	5	5	5
E	11	11	11	11
F	3	3	7	3
G	6	6	6	6
H	4	4	4	4
I	8	8	8	8
J	10	10	10	10
K	1	1	1	1
L	12	12	12	12

The context for the qualification developed above is presented in the next section of this chapter. At this point, however, it is worth noting that an analysis of position statistics provides a good indication of situations where productivity or nonproductivity of resources exists. To verify these indications, the analyst must resort to cardinal analysis; but at least the analyst has an indication of where it is to be applied.

Ratios of Ranks and Ranks of Ratios

One of the transformations that is made in cardinal analysis to allow meaningful comparisons across firms and across time is the use of ratios of cardinal performance. While ordinal analysis does not need the ratio transformation to permit such comparisons, the information obtained by an ordinal analysis of performance ratios can be useful to an analyst. The ordinal analysis of ratios requires an additional step beyond the formation of the ratios from cardinal data to obtain the ranking of the firms by the ratio.

Given the positional analysis as outlined in the previous section, is there any further value in going beyond a cardinal analysis of ratios to an ordinal analysis, given that an additional transformation is required? It is important at this point to note that in the previous section we were discussing the relative position of average ranks, while here we are discussing the ranking of ratios. It can be shown that, under certain restrictive circumstances when dealing with a large group of entities that are assigned randomly to subgroups, there is a relationship between the ratio of the ranks and the rank of the ratios. However, in general it cannot be assumed that there is a relation between the two.

Thus an ordinal analysis of ratios does not duplicate information obtainable from an analysis of relative rank positions. The advantages of an ordinal analysis of ratios over a cardinal analysis are that the ordinal analysis carries with it the ease of presentation of the results, as discussed in chapter 1 and that ordinal analysis permits ease of meaningful comparisons across ratios. Although two ratio values in cardinal analysis can be compared from one firm to another and over time, the ratios have to be formed from the same dimensions in each case. Thus we can compare return on assets for Company A with return on assets for Company B, or for Company A in 1977 and in 1982, but it may be difficult to compare meaningfully return on assets for company A to return on sales for Company A in the same year. On the other hand, using ordinal analysis it is easy to compare the rank of return on assets for Company A with the rank of return on sales for Company A.

Table 2.4 illustrates the foregoing. In this hypothetical example comparing the cardinal ratios of net income (NI) to assets and net income to number of employees, the top part of the table shows that Firm A gets a better return on its assets than does Firm B. On the other hand, firm A gets a lower net income per employee than does Firm B. The ordinal analysis in the lower part of the figure provides a richer context for evaluating the position of the two firms and hence the basis for a more informative conclusion about the two firms. Here it can be seen that Firm B is the largest in the comparison set in terms of the primary measures. Further it can be seen that not only is firm A's return on asset position better than Firm B's, it is the third best in the comparison set. Firm A's net income per employee position is in line with its size rankings, but Firm B's net income per employee position is only one rank better, and is not in line with its size rankings. In a strategic analysis of these two companies it could be concluded that in the year measured, Firm B has sacrificed performance for size, while Firm A has achieved a relatively efficient use of its assets.

Table 2.4

Cardinal Data

Firm	NI	Assets	Employees	NI/Assets	NI/Employees
A	$100,000	$150,000,000	10	0.0667	$10,000 per
B	$200,000	$3,500,000	15	0.0571	$13,000 per

Ordinal Data

Firm	NI Rank	Asset Rank	Employee Rank	NI/Asset Rank	NI/Employees Rank
A	8	8	8	3	8
B	1	1	1	7	7

CONCLUSION

In this chapter we presented an overview of the nature of the data and the data transformations that are employed in an ordinal time series analysis. We also presented three rank statistics that can be employed in ordinal analysis, interpreted the statistics, illustrated their interpretation with an example involving one performance dimension. In the last section of the chapter we discussed some of the information that could be gained by an analyst from a comparative analysis of multiple performance dimensions in ordinal terms.

The statistics presented in this chapter measured performance at a point in time or from one point in time to the next. In the next chapter we will develop measures of the uncertainty associated with the rank shift process over a period of time encompassing multiple transitions. Having developed these measures, we will then discuss their use and interpretation in a strategic or competitive analysis.

3

Information Statistics

Timothy W. Ruefli
Chester L. Wilson

The rank statistics presented in the previous chapter are measures of group behavior at a point in time or from one point in time to the next. In strategy and policy analysis it is often desirable to have a measure of the relative uncertainty involved in rank shift activity of a group of entities over a number of periods. Such a measure would, for example, help identify which dimensions of performance stratified a group of firms or products most, and might indicate which dimensions were the focus of management control, and which were not controllable or were allowed to be uncontrolled. Ordinal time series analysis accomplishes this by using an information statistic that is a variation of the entropy measure (see Ashby, 1956, ch. 9; Theil & Fiebig, 1984) along each dimension of performance. The information statistic can also be regarded as a measure of the volatility over a period of time in a market, industry, or industry subgroup along each of the dimensions for which it is computed.

Information statistics have been applied in a number of management and marketing contexts (for example, Charnes, et al., 1983; Phillips, 1980); but there have been few applications in the strategy/policy area. Perhaps the most widely known application of a variation of the entropy measure is in industrial organization as a measure of market concentration (Hart, 1971; Scherer, 1980, pp. 58-59). This measure was also employed by Jacquemin and Berry (1979) as a measure of diversification, and was later used by Palepu (1985) in his study of diversification strategy and profit performance. In his dissertation, Carter (1979) used the entropy measure to derive a statistic for a brand switching process and thereby to determine the segmentation (if any) of a market.

TRANSITION MATRICES

Development

Given the rankings according to a performance measure k, of a set S, of n entities from a population of N entities over a period of m years, an uncertainty measure can be calculated for the rank shift process of those entities in that time period. If $n = N$, then the rankings of the entities can be used as they are. If $n < N$, that is, if S is a proper subset, the n entities must be reranked relative to each other so that the highest performer in each year is ranked first, the next best second, and so forth. The next step is to construct an incidence matrix, T_k, that has as elements $t_{i,j,k}$, where $t_{i,j,k}$ is the number of times that any firm in rank i in any year moved to group rank j in the next year. T_k can be converted to a matrix, p_k, of relative transition frequencies $p_{i,j,k}$ by setting $p_{i,j,k} = t_{i,j,k}/m$. Defined in this fashion, the transition matrix is doubly stochastic, that is, each row sum and each column sum is unity. Engwall used a matrix of this type in his models of industrial structure (Engwall, 1973, p. 26).

Examples

The upper left-hand sections of the transition matrices for the largest petroleum refining firms, ranked by assets and by net income are presented in Tables 3.1 and 3.2. In Table 3.1, the 1.0 in the upper left-hand corner of the matrix means that the refiner in the first rank stayed there for all periods. The .84 at the intersection of the second row and second column means that the firm in second position stayed in second position 84% of the time, while the .16 to the right of the .84 means that the rest of the time the second ranked firm dropped to the third rank.

The matrix for net income rank transitions has nonzero values fairly widely dispersed, while the asset matrix has its nonzero values clustered along the main diagonal. This is as expected. Net income rank would be expected to have changed over a wider range of possibilities than did assets.

One desirable property of an information statistic would be the ability to differentiate between rank transition processes, such as the two represented in Tables 3.1 and 3.2. This would allow an analyst to characterize and quantify different rank transition processes by their level of relative uncertainty. Before proceeding to the development of such statistics, we should note that the transition matrices themselves may reveal information of value to a strategic analyst.

Table 3.1. Transition Matrix:
Petroleum Refiners Ranked by Assets

Rank at T+1

		1	2	3	4	5	6	7	8	9	10	11	12	13	14	
	1	1.0	0	0	0	0	0	0	0	0	0	0	0	0	0	...
	2	0	.84	.16	0	0	0	0	0	0	0	0	0	0	0	...
	3	0	.04	.72	.20	.04	0	0	0	0	0	0	0	0	0	...
R	4	0	.12	.12	.72	.04	0	0	0	0	0	0	0	0	0	...
A	5	0	0	0	.08	.88	.04	0	0	0	0	0	0	0	0	...
N	6	0	0	0	0	.04	.96	0	0	0	0	0	0	0	0	...
K	7	0	0	0	0	0	0	.64	.28	.08	0	0	0	0	0	...
	8	0	0	0	0	0	0	.32	.44	.24	0	0	0	0	0	...
A	9	0	0	0	0	0	0	.04	.16	.64	.12	.04	0	0	0	...
T	10	0	0	0	0	0	0	0	.04	0	.72	.16	.08	0	0	...
	11	0	0	0	0	0	0	0	.04	0	.12	.60	.20	.04	0	...
T	12	0	0	0	0	0	0	0	0	0	0	.20	.56	.16	.08	...
	13	0	0	0	0	0	0	0	0	0	.04	0	.04	.52	.24	...
	14	0	0	0	0	0	0	0	0	0	0	0	.04	.20	.56	...

. . . .

. . . .

. . . .

Interpretation

We have already seen that the transition matrix, through the degree of dispersion of the nonzero entries, can indicate to the analyst the degree of relative uncertainty associated with the rank transitions. The transition matrix can also reveal information about the structure of the industry or market being examined. For example, in an industry dominated by a small group of firms, for example, the majors in the petroleum industry, the transition matrices should have a block-diagonal structure, especially along dimensions such as assets. This is because the top-ranked firms will trade places with each other, but will not usually move out of the top group, and no lower ranked firms will move up into the top group. The asset rank matrix in Table 3.1. shows strong block-diagonal structure. The top rank had no interaction with the rest, and firms in ranks two through six changed places with each other but did not change places with firms at ranks below the sixth. The ensuing discussion develops statistics to quantify differences between the types of processes that generated the two matrices in Table 3.1. and 3.2.

Table 3.2. Transition Matrix:
Petroleum Refiners Ranked by Net Income

Rank at T+1

		1	2	3	4	5	6	7	8	9	10	11	12	13	14	
	1	1.0	0	0	0	0	0	0	0	0	0	0	0	0	0	...
	2	0	.80	.12	.04	.04	0	0	0	0	0	0	0	0	0	...
	3	0	.12	.68	.12	0	.04	0	.04	0	0	0	0	0	0	...
R	4	0	.08	.16	.60	.12	.04	0	0	0	0	0	0	0	0	...
A	5	0	0	.04	.24	.68	.04	0	0	0	0	0	0	0	0	...
N	6	0	0	0	0	.12	.48	.32	.04	.04	0	0	0	0	0	...
K	7	0	0	0	0	0	.36	.56	.04	0	0	0	.04	0	0	...
	8	0	0	0	0	.04	.04	.04	.56	.16	.08	0	0	.04	0	...
A	9	0	0	0	0	0	0	.04	.16	.36	.12	.20	0	.04	0	...
T	10	0	0	0	0	0	0	0	.04	.08	.44	.20	.08	0	.08	...
	11	0	0	0	0	0	0	0	.04	.16	.20	.24	.12	.08	.04	...
T	12	0	0	0	0	0	0	.04	.04	.08	.08	.24	.28	.08	.08	...
	13	0	0	0	0	0	0	0	0	0	.04	.04	.12	.24	.16	...
	14	0	0	0	0	0	0	0	0	.04	0	.04	.16	.36	.24	...

INFORMATION STATISTICS

Development

Given a transition matrix P_k, we can generate a number of measures that give information about the level of uncertainty associated with the rank shift behavior of groups of entities. Consider the simple case and let the matrix P_k be q by q, then :

$$H(S)_k = ((\sum_i (\sum_j p_{i,j,k} \; ln p_{i,j,k}))/q/-ln(1/q).$$

(3.1)

where "ln" means the natural logarithm.

$H(S)_k$ is a measure of the relative amount of uncertainty associated with rank shifts of the group of entities along dimension k, based on the historical data used to generate the matrix, and normalized for the number of ranks used in the matrix. This interpretation will become clear as each of the terms in equation 3.1 is explained below.

In equation 3.1, the summation over j yields the "entropy" of a particular row of the matrix (Ashby, 1956, p. 174), and the total of those summations over i is the total of all of the row entropies. Dividing that total by q yields the average entropy, which is also called the entropy of the matrix (Ashby, 1956, p. 175). Since it is often desirable to be able to compare two rank shift processes that may involve a different number of ranked entities, the matrix for the entropy must be normalized. One way to do this is to divide the actual entropy calculated by the maximum possible entropy achievable in a process with an equivalent number of ranks. Maximum entropy occurs when there is an equal probability of moving from one rank to any other rank, that is, when the transition matrix entries are all $1/q$. In this case, the entropy would be: $-\Sigma\ 1/q\ [\ln(1/q)] = -\ln(1/q)$, hence the last term in equation 3.1 normalizes the expression (Ashby, 1956).

Since $\ln(1/q)$ is equal to $-\ln(q)$, equation 3.1 can be simplified and rearranged to yield equation 3.2:

$$H(S)_k = \frac{\sum_i(\sum_j p_{i,j,k}\ln\ p_{i,j,k})}{q\ \ln q}\ .$$

$$(3.2)$$

This is the form of the equation we will employ in the rest of the discussion.

Interpretation

$H(S)_k$ ranges from zero to one and can be interpreted as the fraction of the maximum possible uncertainty exhibited by the group of entities. If A and B are two sets of entities and $H(A)_k > H(B)_k$, then we can infer that there is less uncertainty associated with the rank shifts of group B along dimension k than there is associated with group A rank shifts. Horowitz and Horowitz (1968) call the normalized version of the entropy measure "relative entropy," and Theil and Fiebig call the unnormalized statistic a measure of uninformativeness (1984, p. 5); thus $H(S)_k$ could be interpreted as the *relative* uninformativeness of the rank transition process. The closer $H(S)_k$ is to one, the more random (uninformative) the rank transitions exhibited by the group of entities along the selected dimension. The measure in current use most analogous to $H(S)_k$ when the ranking dimension is return on equity is the average industry beta computed by some brokerage firms.

$H(S)_k$ can also be interpreted as a measure of the effects of competition among a group of entities. If $H(S)_k$ is equal to zero, the rank shift process yielding that statistic would have the shift from one rank position to the next fixed for all ranks positions for all years. In terms of the transition matrix, each row and each column would have a one and q-1 zeros in it. While there are $q!$ ways to generate such a matrix, the most likely way this would happen in an industry or market situation would be for the entities to remain in the same rank position for the entire period of study. Thus the only nonzero entries would be along the main diagonal, and they would all be ones. This would indicate an industry with a perfectly stable group of firms.

On the other hand, if $H(S)_k$ is equal to one, there is only one way for that to happen: the transition matrix must have entries that are all equal to $1/q$, indicating that no entity stayed in a rank for more than one year, and that all had an equal probability of moving to any other rank position from its current rank position. A group of entities exhibiting this behavior would most likely be close to the same cardinal size, and would be in a very dynamic environment. This would be the case for a group of firms in an industry that meets the classical economic definition of competition.

The two cases just described are, of course, the extremes but they serve to characterize the imputed limits of behavior of a group of entities, based on this information statistic. In industries that have been examined to date, the information statistic has varied from 0.10 (life insurance firms ranked by assets) to 0.80 (airline companies ranked by return on equity).

Substatistics

While the statistic developed from equation 3.2 can distinguish between stratified and nonstratified groups of entities, there are aspects of rank shift behavior that a function over the entire matrix cannot distinguish. Consider the case of the two transition matrices in Table 3.3. In these two cases, the matrices are obviously different, but $H(A)_k = H(B)_k$. The matrix for group A represents a situation where the average entity gradually increased its rank position to the highest level and then fell to the worst position (see Figure 3.1). The matrix for group B represents a situation where an entity jumped rapidly to the top position and then, over time, was gradually displaced (see Figure 3.2). A third possibility, arising when the transition matrix is symmetrical or nearly symmetrical, is illustrated in Figure 3.3, where the average entity rises slowly in the rankings and then, having peaked, slowly worsens in rank position. It is of interest to a strategic analyst to be able to distinguish whether firms in an industry (or products in a market), follow one or another of these patterns, and to have a statistic that measures the degree to which a process resembles a particular prototype process.

Because the entropy function is log-linear, it can be partitioned to give three other measures of relative uncertainty that can be associated with the above-mentioned patterns of behavior, namely, those relating to aggregate increases (worsening), maintenance (stability), and decreases (improvement) in rank. The upper entropy measure for relative uncertainty in the worsening of rank position is generated by summing over j for $j > i$ in the inner sum of function (3.2). See Figure 3.4 for the location of the transition probabilities constituting the upper entropy in a six-by-six matrix. The diagonal entropy is the statistic for relative uncertainty associated with maintenance of rank and is generated by computing the inner sum in equation 3.2 only for $j = i$ (see also Figure 3.4). The analogous set of lower entropy statistics for relative uncertainty associated with decreases (improvement) in rank position is generated by computing the inner summation of equation 3.2 for $j < i$. The relevant transition probabilities for the example are found in the triangle in the lower left of the matrix in Figure 3.4.

Table 3.3. Two Processes

		Rank T + 1							Rank T + 1			
		1	2	3	4	5			1	2	3	4	5
R	1	.6	0	0	0	.4	R	1	.6	.4	0	0	0
A	2	.4	.6	0	0	0	A	2	0	.6	.4	0	0
N	3	0	.4	.6	0	0	N	3	0	0	.6	.4	0
K	4	0	0	.4	.6	0	K	4	0	0	0	.6	.4
T	5	0	0	0	.4	.6	T	5	.4	0	0	0	.6

Group A

H(A) = 0.418

Group B

H(B) = 0.418

Figure 3.1. Upper, Diagonal, and Lower Entropies

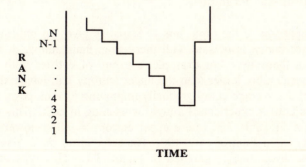

Figure 3.2. Lower Process over Time

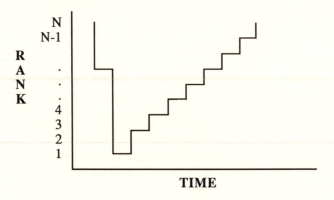

Figure 3.3. Balanced Process over Time

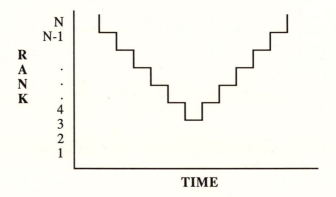

Substatistic Examples

Comparison of the three sets of statistics gives an indication of the relative uncertainty associated with increasing, maintaining, or decreasing rank within thegroup. For example, a group of entities with the lower entropy considerably larger than the upper entropy will have exhibited the behavior of the average entity gradually improving its rank position through many steps until it experienced a rapid worsening in rank. This is the case for Group A in Table 3.3, where upper entropy = 0.046, lower entropy = 0.182, and diagonal entropy = 0.190. The behavior of the average entity in this process over time is graphed in Figure 3.1. This type of behavior would be exhibited by firms in a market where firms with improved technological characteristics entered and gradually displaced existing firms of higher rank, and the firms with the oldest technology were forced out.

Figure 3.4. Partition of Transition Matrix

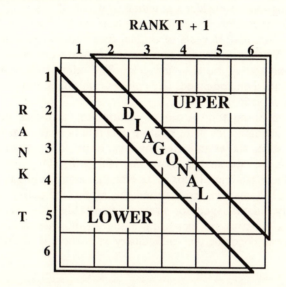

On the other hand, the subentropies for Group B are upper entropy = 0.182, lower entropy = 0.046, and diagonal entropy = 0.190, indicating that the average entity jumped to the top of the rankings and gradually worsened in position. This behavior over time is graphed in Figure 3.2. An example of this type of behavior would be exhibited by firms in a market characterized by a fad or fashion element. Firms with new products quickly captured the attention of consumers and then gradually declined in popularity as new fad products were introduced by other firms. The personal computer software products market treated in chapter 7 is an example of this type of market. These are extremes of behavior, especially for firms in an industry. More frequently encountered situations have upper entropy nearly equal to lower entropy indicating a process that behaves more symmetrically as depicted in Figure 3.3. The subentropies give the analyst an expectation of the average behavior of firms in an industry or industry subgroup in terms of improvement, maintenance, and worsening in rank.

TIME SERIES OF INFORMATION STATISTICS

Development

Information statistics can also be generated as a time series to indicate the patterns of change in uncertainty associated with a particular industry or industry subgroup. Consider a situation in which M years worth of data are available for N entities. To generate the time series of information statistics, we take the first $m < M$ years of ordinal data and compute the information statistics. We then roll the m-year period forward one year, dropping the first year and adding the $m +$ first year. The information statistics for this new period are then computed. This process continues until the data will not yield a new m-year period.

The resulting time series of information statistics indicates to an analyst the changing levels of relative uncertainty in the process over time. If the time series shows an increasing level of the information statistic along dimension k, then the analyst knows that rank shifts along this dimension are becoming more random. If this is the situation along only a few dimensions, then an analyst may have identified the aspects of performance that are increasingly mismanaged, or are unmanageable. If the levels of the information statistics are increasing along all dimensions of performance, the analyst can conclude that the industry as a whole is entering a period of turbulence.

Subprocesses

In addition to indicating the patterns of uncertainty in rank shifts over time, comparison of information statistics for different time periods can indicate changes in the underlying patterns of rank shift behavior. If the entropy measure for a subperiod is less than the entropy measure for the entire period, this is an indication that the underlying rank shift behavior of the entities in the group may have changed over time. This is so because if a period M encompasses two types of rank shift behavior then the entropy for the entire period will be based on a process that exhibits a wider variety of behavior, than either of the subprocesses. The individual processes are composed of rank shift behavior that is homogeneous, hence exhibits less variety, hence has a lower entropy. To illustrate this, consider the case of the two processes in Table 3.3. But instead of regarding them as being generated by two distinct groups of entities, A and B, let us consider them to have been generated by one group of entities at two sequential periods of time, A and B. Then if we compute the transition matrix for the entire time period $M = A+B$, the result is given in Table 3.4.

Table 3.4. Combined Processes

Rank T+1

R		1	2	3	4	5
A	1	.4	.3	0	0	.3
N	2	.3	.4	0	0	0
K	3	0	.3	.4	0	0
	4	0	0	.3	.4	0
T	5	0	0	0	.3	.4

Process $A + B$

$H(A+B)$ Total = 0.590
$H(A+B)$ Lower = 0.200
$H(A+B)$ Diagonal = 0.190
$H(A+B)$ Upper = 0.200

The entropies for the process represented by the matrix in Table 3.4. are:

Total   = 0.590
Diagonal = 0.190
Upper   = 0.200
Lower   = 0.200

The implication here is that by combining two processes that were both asymmetric, the result can be one process that is symmetric in the behavior of an average firm over time, but has a higher total entropy than either of the two individual processes.

We can generalize the above example. Let the period M be partitioned into two exhaustive and nonoverlapping subperiods A and B. There are then four possible cases to consider:

Case 1: $H(M) > H(A)$ and $H(M) > H(B)$
Case 2: $H(M) > H(A)$ and $H(M) < H(B)$
Case 3: $H(M) < H(A)$ and $H(M) > H(B)$
Case 4: $H(M) = H(A) = H(B)$

In case 1, the period M is composed of two different processes. In case 2, the period M started with one type of rank shift behavior, but transitions over time have become more random. Case 3 is just the opposite; here the process started in a period of relative random behavior and has settled down into a more certain pattern. This case can occur only because the underlying system being modeled is an open system. If the system is closed, then over time entropy for a closed process cannot decrease, and usually increases (Ashby, 1956, p. 136).

The fourth case, where all of the entropies are equal, would obtain if the nature of the underlying process remained exactly the same for the entire period, that is, if process A were identical to process B. Note that it is not possible for $H(M)$ to be smaller than both $H(A)$ and $H(B)$, because this would imply that some transitions that occurred in each of the two subperiods did not occur in the combined period—clearly a contradiction.

Data Requirements

Data requirements for generating the information statistics are generally more onerous than those associated with rank statistics. Since the frequency matrix is generated over a period of time, too short an interval will result in a weak characterization of the underlying process, and may result in poor predictions about the future; if the underlying rank shift behavior of the group of entities is changing over time, then too long a period will generate information statistics that are not relevant to the recent state of the process. Experience with data indicates that a decade's worth of data for large groups of entities is probably the least that should be used for either a subperiod or a full period.

If the situation is such that the number of entities is greater than the number of ranks assigned, then one of the conventions for assigning artificial ranks to the unranked firms must be followed. However, if the convention of assigning random ranks is followed, then these ranks must not be used in computing the information statistic, or the result will be biased in the favor of randomness. As far as the transition matrix is concerned, assigning $n+1$ as a rank or employing the midrank convention for unranked firms are equivalents. In both cases, an artificial row and column in the transition matrix must be created.

When transition matrices for subgroups of entities are generated in the situation where the number of entities is larger than the number of ranks assigned, then an additional step must be added to the process of reranking the entities in the subgroup. Although, for the entire population the number of unranked entities is constant for all years, for a subgroup it may vary. To allow for this, before the entities in the subgroup are reranked, the minimum number of entities with nonartificial ranks must be ascertained. Assume this number is x. Then in the reranking, for each year, all firms with a rank greater than x must be assigned an artificial subgroup rank according to the convention adopted.

APPLICATION AND INTERPRETATION

Information Statistics 1954-1982

Table 3.5 gives the results of computing the total, upper, diagonal, and lower entropies for the operating revenue of the top 50 transportation firms and for the railroad and airline subgroups over the period 1957-1982. The total relative uncertainties of revenue rank shifts for transportation firms as a whole and for railroads were nearly equal and about half of total possible uncertainty. The relative uncertainty of rank shifts for the airlines was much less than that for the other two groups, indicating that airline firms were much more stratified along the dimension of revenues. This implies that the relative market shares of the airline firms were relatively stable over the period examined. For the industry, upper entropy was slightly higher than lower entropy, indicating that the average firm took slightly fewer steps in worsening its rank position than it did in improving it. This situation was reversed for both the railroads and the airlines.

Table 3.5. Revenue Entropy Comparison: Transportation Industry 1957-1982

	Industry	Railroads	Airlines
Total Entropy	0.474	0.470	0.289
Lower Entropy	0.208	0.166	0.092
Diagonal Entropy	0.075	0.121	0.091
Upper Entropy	0.191	0.191	0.106

Time Series

Entropy measures can also be generated over a set of sequential time periods to yield for the industry and for the rail and airline groups, a time series that indicates changes in the relative amount of uncertainty associated with rank shifts. In this case a rolling 15-year period was used, that is, entropies were calculated for the first 15 years, then for year 2 through 16, and so on. Figure 3.5 graphs these figures for the top 50 transportation firms, and the railroad and airline subgroups. In the case of the transportation industry and the railroad subgroup it can be seen that the relative uncertainty gradually increased over the last decade, with the increase for the railroads being the greatest. The airlines exhibited a slight downward trend in relative uncertainty until 1977. From 1978 onward, the uncertainty associated with revenue rank shifts for the airlines increased substantially, but still remained far below that for the railroads, or for the transportation industry as a whole.

Figure 3.5. Entropy Time-Series: Fifteen-Year Operating Revenue Series

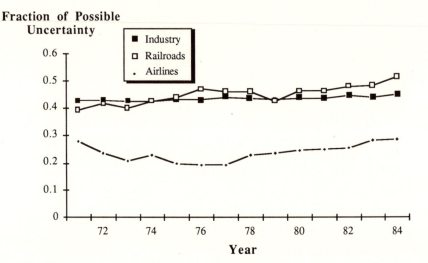

CONCLUSION

In this chapter we have presented the development of a set of information statistics that are designed to be of use in analyzing the uncertainty associated with the rank shift behavior of groups of entities over time. These statistics were derived from transition matrices which, by themselves, were shown to reveal useful information about the behavior of the entities being investigated. The information statistics are based on a variation of the entropy measure, and are interpreted as the percentage of total possible uncertainty associated with the rank shift behavior of a group of entities over a set time period. It was demonstrated that the primary information statistic could be decomposed to yield a set of substatistics that characterized the patterns of rank shift behavior more precisely. The chapter concluded with an application of the information statistics to the transportation industry along the dimension of operating revenue.

In the next chapter, we will pull together the threads of analysis of the largest firms in the U.S. transportation industry that have been used as examples in these first three chapters. The techniques for industry analysis will be extended to multiple dimensions of performance and applied to the transportation industry as a whole, as well as to the mode-based subgroups. The chapter will also demonstrate how ordinal time series analysis can be applied to the competitive analysis of individual firms, both in the context of the industry and in the context of their modal subgroups.

4

An Ordinal Time Series of the Transportation Industry: 1956 to 1984

Timothy W. Ruefli

In the two previous chapters a set of rank statistics and a set of information statistics were developed, and their use was illustrated by application to selected one dimensional examples from the transportation industry. This chapter will apply ordinal time series analysis in a fuller strategic analysis of the largest firms in the transportation industry. This approach will extend ordinal time series analysis to situations involving multidimensional performance measures, and will illustrate the process and value of using ordinal time series analysis in the strategic analysis of an industry.

The transportation industry has undergone substantial changes in the last quarter-century. These changes have been documented on a daily basis in the press, weekly in industry and news magazines, and over longer periods of time in scholarly books and journals (Cowing and Stevenson, 1981; Lieb, 1981; Altshuler, 1979; Spady, 1979; Temple, Barker, and Sloane, Inc., 1982; U. S. Department of Transportation, 1978). In this chapter we will look at the transportation industry from multiple perspectives involving the top 100 or so firms in the industry over the quarter century from 1957 to 1984. Deregulation impacted different segments of the transportation industry at different times and in different ways. The analysis presented here will focus on those differential effects and examine their implications for management, with some additional emphasis placed on the airlines, since their performance more clearly reflects the issues raised by deregulation. The analysis will be based on ordinal time series methodology to examine concretely the performance of firms and groups of firms from the perspective of the whole industry or from the perspective of subgroups within that industry. In particular we will compare the economic performance of the largest airline, trucking, and railroad companies, as mode groups and in terms of selected individual firms, with each other and with the performance of the largest firms in the transportation industry as a whole. The questions of concern include: Has deregulation given one transportation mode group an advantage or disadvantage over other groups? What individual firms' strategies have yielded better relative performance in the face of deregulation, and does this differ by mode or type?

There have been numerous studies of individual transportation companies, and of the railroad, trucking, and airline industries in general (for the latter, see particularly Byrnes, 1985; Freidlander and Spady, 1981; Taneja, 1979, 1980; and Mandell, 1979). For the most part, however, these approaches have relied on standard methodologies of data analysis and presentation. Although these studies are often detailed and revealing, they are beset with the problems of screening out the effects of short-term business cycle noise and of external events, such as the energy crisis. For the most part, they eschew comparisons across different segments of the transportation industry.

In this chapter we will use ordinal time series analysis to screen out the background noise of those external phenomena having no differential effects on the industry in question, which will permit immediate and meaningful cross-segment comparisons. The details of this methodology have been presented in the preceding chapters, and will not be repeated here; instead, we will be concerned with the new light the methodology can shed on the important problem of managing the impact of deregulation on individual firms and groups of firms.

METHODOLOGY

In analyzing a system as complex as that represented by the largest transportation companies, several problems must be faced. The problems involve making comparisons across multiple dimensions, multiple time periods, multiple firms, and multiple levels, all in a hierarchy of contexts; and the problem of screening out noise in the data (see Miller and Friesen, 1982). To manage these problems, we will analyze the rankings of firms and groups of firms over time. That is, we will take the performance data for each firm in each year along each dimension, and rank that firm against all other firms. This will permit us to compare the ranking of a firm based on revenue directly with its rank based on net income. We can also compare the ranks of two different firms based on their revenue; and we can compare the asset rank of a firm in one year with its asset rank in any other year without having to worry about the rate of inflation, and so forth. The comparisons will all be relative to the behaviors of the rest of the firms in the set being examined. We can also compare the rankings of a firm with rankings of other firms in its industry, or with just the firms in a subgroup.

From the ranks of individual firms we can generate aggregate rank statistics at the level of the industry as a whole and also for any subgroup in the industry. At any level, use of ranks gives us a direct benchmark against which to evaluate the performance of a firm or group of firms. Any changes that affect all firms in the same fashion, such as, inflation, will not show up in the analysis of the rankings, but any factors that affect firms differently, such as, the reduction of airline regulations will, if effective and if not offset by other factors, show up in the change of rankings of airlines relative to other types of transportation.

DATA

In keeping with the ordinal time series methodology outlined in the second and third chapters, the approach here utilizes input data in the form of rankings of firm performance over time for each of the selected performance dimensions. The data we will use are the rankings developed by *Fortune* magazine for the transportation industry for the period from 1957 to 1984. The particular dimensions of rankings examined include operating revenue, net income (NI), return on equity (ROE), assets, and number of employees. The employee rankings are available only from 1965 to 1984.

As with any data, the *Fortune* rankings have some limitations that should be noted. Firms are included in the *Fortune* transportation file if they are publicly listed U.S. firms and if more than 50% of their operating revenues come from transportation-related activities. Rankings along the other dimensions selected for analysis, net income, assets, and return on equity, are contingent on the firm being in the top 50 along the dimension of revenue. Thus there may be firms that have net income or other performance figures that would place them in the top 50 for that measure, but because their revenue figures are not high enough, they are not listed. Since firms are classified as being in an industry on the basis of their revenues, single product or service firms are lumped together with near-conglomerates. Also, since only the largest firms in the industry are ranked by *Fortune*, that portion of industry activity attributable to the number of small, growing, and potentially important firms is not incorporated directly into the analysis unless and until those firms are in the top 50 firms. Thus this analysis is from the point of view of the largest incumbents in the industry, and should be interpreted from that perspective.

Two conventions should be noted at the outset. One convention is that mergers of ranked transportation firms with firms outside the top 50 do not result in a new entity, and are treated as a continuation of the previously-ranked firm for the purposes of the analysis. In the event of a merger between two previously ranked firms, the entities prior to the merger are considered to have been dropped from the rankings following the merger and the resulting entity is treated as a newly ranked firm. Another convention is used when firms leave, or before they enter the top 50. Because they are not ranked when they are not in the top 50, a convention of assigning an artificial rank of "51" to unranked firms was adopted. This is felt to be a conservative practice since the actual rank of firms outside the top 50 is, in all but at most one case, greater than 51.

INDUSTRY RESULTS

In order to place the evaluation of the impact of deregulation on the largest transportation companies in perspective, we will first analyze the rank shift behavior of the top 50 transportation firms as a group. We will then decompose this group into subgroups based on transportation modes, and analyze the performance of selected subgroups. Following that we will focus on representative individual firms in the railroad and trucking subgroups and evaluate their performance in relation to the top 50 transportation firms. The analysis will conclude with an examination of selected airline companies.

Transportation Firms

Volatility. Average rank position is a meaningless measure for the industry as a whole, since it is a constant for each year; rank shift volatility is, however, a useful measure at the industry level. The increasing turbulence in the transportation industry in the past 25 years can be clearly seen in Figure 4.1., where the industry's volatility (measured by the average absolute level of rank shifts from one year to the next) is graphed. From 1958 through the middle 1960s volatility levels were stable across all dimensions, with the average firm shifting one position or less on operating revenue and asset rankings, two positions on NI rankings, and four positions or less on ROE rankings. In the later sixties, as the figure shows, volatility rose on all dimensions, peaking in 1969 with the economy-wide merger and acquisition wave and the reorganization of the eastern railroads. After a settling down period in the early 1970s, volatility levels began a general long-term increase, which continues to the present. Recent volatility levels are double those of a quarter-century ago, with volatility in return on equity spiking to very high levels in 1981 and 1983. This graphic depiction of the impact of deregulation and increased economic uncertainty on the industry suggests that the management environment of the firms in the industry is likely to be significantly different than it was just a decade ago.

Information Statistics. The top section of Table 4.1 shows the uncertainty associated with the rank shifts along the various dimensions of performance for the transportation industry. The levels reported are percentages of the level of uncertainty that would exist if rank changes were a totally random process. The results are not all as might be expected. Return on equity shifts are most uncertain, followed by net income shifts, operating revenue, and assets, with shifts based on the number of employees, somewhat surprisingly, are the most certain (that is, least likely to occur). The implication is that the firms in the transportation industry tend to adjust their work-forces in a more consistent way than they adjust asset levels or market share. Only in the case of ROE rank shifts are the lower and upper entropy measures far apart. This means that, for large transportation firms as a group, the average firm tends to improve its ROE rank in relatively few steps and then gradually worsens over a period of time.

Figure 4.1. Transportation Industry Volatility

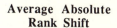

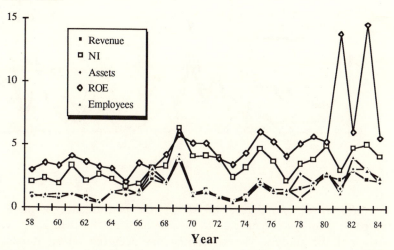

We will now examine and contrast the behavior of four transportation industry subgroups, railroads, airlines, trucking, and pipelines in the context of the historical general increase in the rank instability of the top transportation firms.

Railroads

Volatility. The contribution of the top railroad firms to the volatility of the top transportation firms can be assessed from Figure 4.2. Here it can be seen that the railroads were major contributors to the spike in rank shift activity in 1969, and to ROE activity in 1981 and 1983; other than that, however, railroad firms were not as volatile in their activity as the average transportation firm. In the post-1970 period, the activity levels of the various dimensions move more in concert with each other, with a rising trend in the last decade.

Figure 4.2. Railroad Volatility

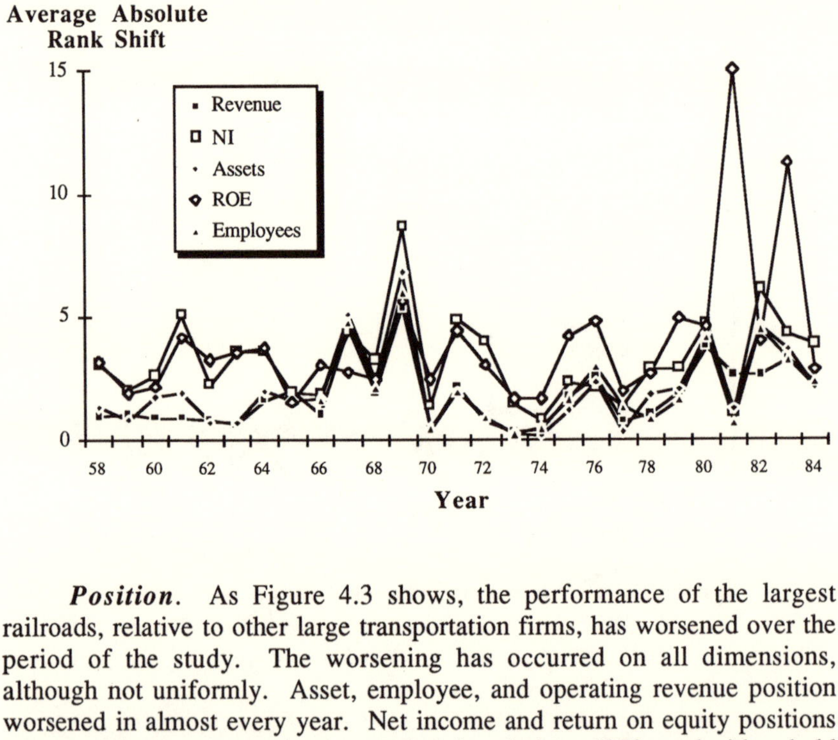

Average Absolute Rank Shift

Position. As Figure 4.3 shows, the performance of the largest railroads, relative to other large transportation firms, has worsened over the period of the study. The worsening has occurred on all dimensions, although not uniformly. Asset, employee, and operating revenue position worsened in almost every year. Net income and return on equity positions improved in the reorganization period just before 1970, and either held steady or improved slightly during the energy crisis. Return on equity had the worst position in all but two years and exhibits a much more pronounced cyclic pattern than did the other dimensions. The other two improvement periods in ROE position, in 1960-1961 and 1979-1981 followed legislation aimed at helping the railroads.

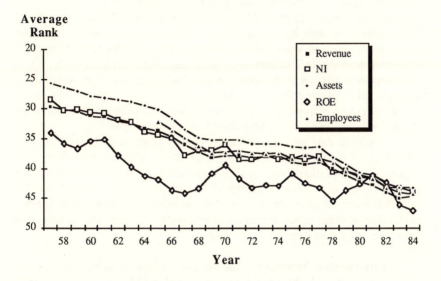

Figure 4.3. Railroad Position

Table 4.1. Entropy Comparison:
Transportation Industry, 1957-1982

	Operating Revenue (1)	NI (1)	Employees (2)	ROE (1)	Assets (1)
Transportation Industry					
Total Entropy	0.474	0.626	0.424	0.660	0.456
Lower Entropy	0.208	0.271	0.183	0.258	0.193
Diagonal Entropy	0.075	0.051	0.078	0.044	0.080
Upper Entropy	0.191	0.304	0.163	0.358	0.183
Railroad Subgroup					
Total Entropy	0.470	0.623	0.434	0.708	0.442
Lower Entropy	0.166	0.215	0.139	0.254	0.158
Diagonal Entropy	0.121	0.135	0.124	0.097	0.117
Upper Entropy	0.191	0.274	0.172	0.357	0.167
Airline Subgroup					
Total Entropy	0.289	0.718	0.300	0.796	0.398
Lower Entropy	0.092	0.252	0.086	0.258	0.120
Diagonal Entropy	0.091	0.121	0.094	0.113	0.118
Upper Entropy	0.106	0.346	0.120	0.425	0.160

(1) 1957-1982
(2) 1965-1982

Measurement of labor productivity in the transportation industry has presented major methodological problems (Lieb, 1981, p. 279). The methodology used here provides a ready indication of relative productivity. The relation of rank by number of employees to the rankings on other dimensions gives an indication of the relative productivity of labor. For example, ranking by number of employees that is higher than that of operating revenue, as is the case for railroads, indicates a relatively poor average sales per employee in comparison to other firms. The higher average rank position of number of employees when compared to net income also indicates a relatively low profit per employee.

The rank data also show that the energy crisis in the early 1970s had little impact on the railroads relative to other transportation firms. As Figure 4.3 shows, there was no significant shift in average rank position in the period of the sharp increases in the price of oil. This means that railroads were no more or less sensitive to price increases or shortages of fuel supply than other transportation modes—given the government allocation programs in place at the time.

Information Statistics. The second section of Table 4.1 gives the results of computing the total, upper, diagonal, and lower entropies for the railroad subgroup over the period 1957-1984. As can be seen, the railroads followed the pattern of the transportation industry as a whole in terms of the relative uncertainty of the rank shifts on all dimensions during the period.

For railroads, the entropy of maintaining rank is higher or about equal to that for airlines on all dimensions except return on equity, indicating that in general, the uncertainty associated with staying in rank position is greater for railroads than it is for airlines. Also for railroads, the lower and upper entropies are relatively balanced (the latter only slightly larger than the former), indicating that on average the uncertainty associated with improving rank is about the same as that associated with worsening in rank. This implies that for railroads, the number of steps (or years) associated with improving rank is only slightly smaller than the number of steps associated with worsening rank position.

Airlines

Volatility. The top airline firms showed a substantially different pattern of rank shift activity than the railroads or the top transportation firms as a whole. Airlines made only a modest contribution to the spike in rank shift activity in all transportations in 1969 (see Figure 4.1), but did have a sizable spike of their own on the dimensions of net income and return on equity in 1970 (Figure 4.4). This was a result of adverse airline industry conditions in that period (as indicated by the nominal increase in operating revenue and asset rank shift activity), rather than a result of merger and acquisition or reorganization (which would have generated shifts in all dimensions). Notice that operating revenue and asset rank shifts remained at a consistently low level until 1977. As deregulation occurred, rank shifts on these two dimensions began to increase sharply, quadrupling by 1982 and improving somewhat in the last two periods. At the same time, net income and return on equity activity continued their cyclic pattern around an increasing trend line originating in 1964.

Figure 4.4. Airline Volatility

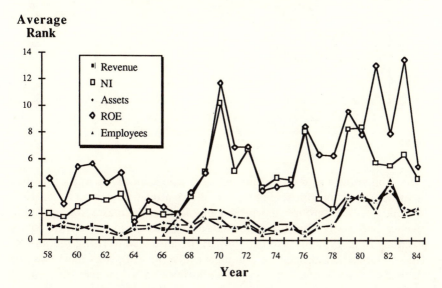

Position. The average rank position of the airline companies steadily improved in the period from 1957 to 1982, as Figure 4.5 shows. Improvement was relatively uniform on operating revenue and asset dimensions; net income and return on equity followed the cyclic pattern in the post-1964 period, as noted above. The effects of the rate freeze from 1962 to 1968 can be seen clearly in the ordinal data. For the first four years of the freeze, the average return on equity dramatically improved position, and then worsened somewhat in the last three years of the period. Net income position, on the other hand, improved in position in all but the last year of the freeze. The net effect of the freeze was to leave the airlines in a relatively better position than before. With the rates unfrozen in 1968, the airline return on equity and net income positions returned to their improving trend until 1972. The last cycle on these two dimensions peaked in 1982, followed by two years of relative improvement.

Figure 4.5. Airline Position

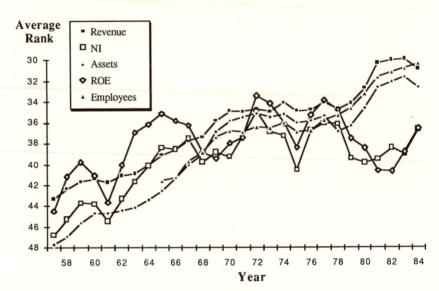

The airlines as a group showed more effects of the energy crisis than other transportation firms. Figure 4.5. shows a relatively smooth transition in rank position through the period of oil price increases for operating revenue and assets; but the worsening of net income and return on equity positions from 1972 to 1976 can, in part, be attributed to rising fuel prices. This indicates that airlines were more sensitive to fuel prices than were the railroads. This is not surprising since airlines have low fuel efficiencies compared to other transportation modes (Lieb, 1981, p. 336).

It is also interesting to compare the relative position of average rank by number of employees for the airlines and railroads. Note that in Figure 4.5, with the exception of the last year, average employee rank for the airlines was worse than average revenue rank. The interpretation is that airlines have had favorable employee productivity in terms of revenue generated when compared to other transportation firms. The data indicate that this advantage moved to a parity position in 1978 (when average revenue rank equaled average employee rank), and was reversed in 1984.

Information Statistics. The third section of Table 4.1 gives the results of computing the total, upper, diagonal, and lower entropies, for the top fifty airline subgroups over the period 1957-1984. These statistics show that for the airlines, and in contrast to the railroads or the transportation industry as a whole, rank by operating revenue was more stable than rank by employees; both are more stable than assets, and much more stable than the net income or return on equity dimensions. Note also that total entropies for return on equity and for net income for the airlines were higher, respectively, than those for railroads or for the industry as a whole. The relatively higher uncertainties associated with the dimensions other than operating revenues indicate that the airline industry is not stratified by size per se. Thus the low level of uncertainty associated with operating revenue should indicate to an analyst that management initiative was being directed toward achieving relative stability on this dimension. This provides evidence that market share was one of the competitive foci of management control in this industry.

In contrast to the railroads, the levels of uncertainty associated with rank shifts on the various profitability dimensions (Table 4.1) did not follow the industry pattern. Return on equity and net income were the two most uncertain measures, both at levels well above the industry average. Asset shifts were next in uncertainty, followed by employee rank shifts. For the airlines, rank shifts on operating revenue performance were the most certain, indicating that airlines were relatively stable with respect to market share. This implies that airlines have more of an emphasis on market share strategy in their corporate decision-making than did the other transportation modes. According to the data presented here, airline managers, in comparison with managers of other transportation firms accepted wider swings in relative levels of net income, return on equity, assets, and even levels of their workforces in order to stabilize market share. Recent higher levels of market share stability indicate that the focus on this strategic dimension increased as deregulation took effect.

For the airlines on the other hand, upper entropies are generally significantly greater than lower entropies, indicating that on average firms improved their ranks through a relatively fewer number of larger steps in fewer years and worsened in rank relatively more slowly, i.e., in a larger number of steps over a longer period of time. To a strategist in the airline industry this should indicate that, if industry experience is to be followed, the way to improve rank position is not to play a waiting game and make a series of small moves, but to make a small number of larger moves and, having succeeded, to defend the firm's position.

Trucking

Volatility. The pattern of volatility of rank shifts in the trucking subgroup is shown in Figure 4.6. In the first decade studied, operating revenue, asset, and net income shifts were low and comparable; only return on equity showed moderate levels of volatility. This was, of course, a period of substantial regulation in the trucking industry. Beginning in 1967, volatility on all dimensions increased, with return on equity and net income volatility doing so sharply. This increase peaked in 1975, and was a major contributor to the peak in transportation volatility in that period. After a brief lull in 1976, the aggregate rank shift activity on all dimensions resumed its upward trend. Notice that return on equity and net income volatilities moved together and, to an even greater degree, so did operating revenue and asset volatilities.

Figure 4.6.   Trucking Volatility

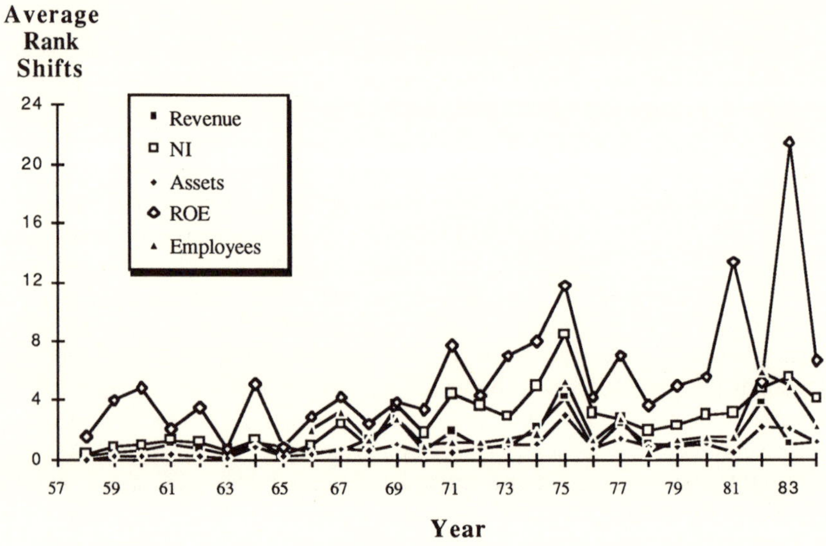

Position. Figure 4.7 shows that the average rank position of the trucking group improved on all dimensions until 1971, with return on equity position leading the way. The onset of the energy crisis reversed the improving trend in net income and return on equity, and even adversely affected average operating revenue position in 1973 and 1974. Even though return on equity position deteriorated from 1972 to 1982, it was still far below the average revenue position, indicating favorable performance on this dimension relative to other transportation firms. Relative employee productivity did not fare so well, as shown by the high employee rank position. Deregulation, potential and actual (in 1980), of this subgroup led to a stabilizing of the revenue and asset rank positions and was followed by improvements in financial performance rankings.

Figure 4.7. Trucking Position

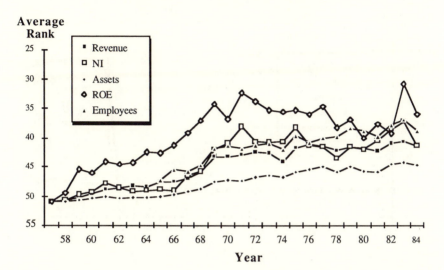

Information Statistics. In one or more years of the rankings, there were fewer than two trucking firms in the top 50 firms. Consequently, information statistics could not be computed for this group.

Pipelines

Perhaps the clearest case of deregulation having a varied effect on a group of transportation companies is that of the pipelines. The horizontal line at rank 51 from 1957 to 1978 in Figure 4.8. means that in that period pipelines were not ranked in the top 50 transportation firms. When the Natural Gas Regulatory Act of 1978 deregulated the pipelines, they quickly took entrepreneurial advantage of the opportunity to expand and combine. As a result, the largest of them on average jumped from out of the rankings in one year to the midpoint in the rankings the next year.

The pipeline firms' low average ranking by number of employees, compared to average rankings on all other dimensions, shows substantial relative employee productivity, as might be expected in a capital-intensive business. This latter situation is indicated by the relatively high average ranking based on assets. Return on equity rankings performed spectacularly in the first three years after deregulation and, like net income position, began to gradually worsen.

Figure 4.8. Pipeline Position

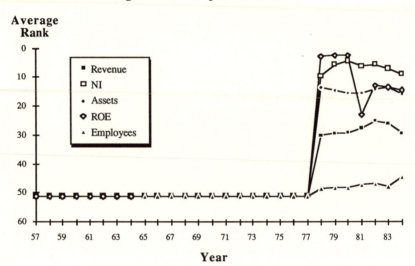

Time Series of Information Statistics

As an additional source of information for a strategic analyst, entropy measures can be generated over time to yield a time series that indicates the relative amount of uncertainty associated with rank shifts for the industry, and for the railroad and airline subgroups, along each dimension. In this case a rolling 15-year period was used for each dimension. Figure 4.9 graphs these figures for the top 50 transportation firms, while Figure 4.10 and 4.11 report analogous results for the railroad and airline subgroups, respectively. In the case of the transportation industry and the railroad subgroup it can be seen that the relative uncertainty gradually increased over the last decade along all dimensions. The airlines, while having a higher average entropy for net income and return on equity, and a lower average entropy for revenue and assets than the industry or railroads, exhibited a slight downward trend in the measure of uncertainty for the first two performance dimensions. This is further evidence to support the contention that the performance dimensions for railroads are more in agreement, whereas for airlines, operating revenue rank (i.e., market share), especially more recently, provided a more stable base for management action. Figure 4.12 supports this contention by showing the percent change in entropies for the railroads moves in concert. The equivalent graph for the airlines (Figure 4.13.) shows entropy changes for net income and return on equity as almost independent of revenue and asset entropy changes.

Figure 4.9. Entropy Time Series—Transportation Industry

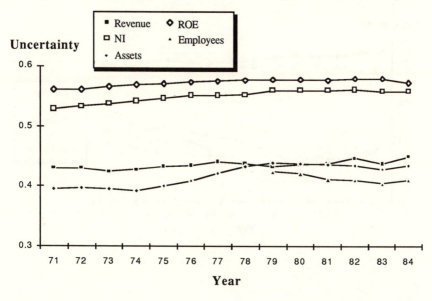

Figure 4.10. Entropy Time Series—Railroads

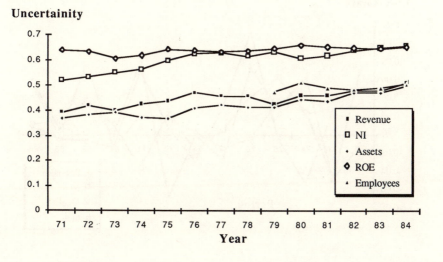

Figure 4.11. Entropy Time Series—Airlines

Uncertainty

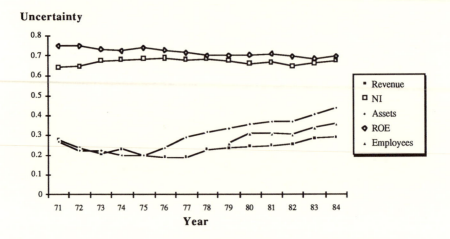

Figure 4.12. Change in Entropies—Railroads

Percent Difference in Uncertainty

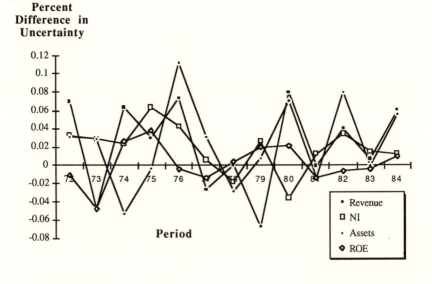

**Figure 4.13. Entropy Time Series Differences
Largest Airline Firms**

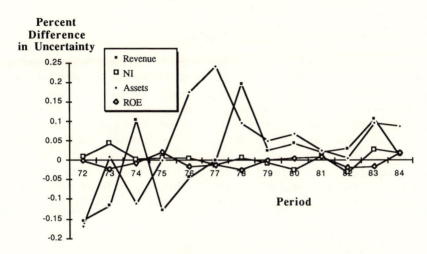

Comparison and Implications

The key deregulatory events in the transportation industry were: (1) the Natural Gas Deregulatory Act of 1976; (2) the Railroad Revitalization and Regulatory Reform Act of 1976; (3) the Airline Deregulation Act of 1978; and (4) the Motor Carrier Act of 1980. (The effects of the end of Civil Aeronautics Board controls over airline rates in 1983 are too recent to be evaluated.) While the shift in the rank performance of the pipelines in the rankings can be traced directly to deregulation in 1976, the shift in the relative fortunes of the railroads, airlines and trucking companies over the period studied was due to more than the effects of deregulation. The rapid improvement in airline technology relative to that of railroads, the shift in travel patterns, the near-completion of the federal interstate highway system, and the increase in the production of items of high value relative to weight have played major roles in the performance shifts noted here.

The clear effects of deregulation on these subgroups can best be seen in the last years of the period studied here in the uncertainty deregulation imposed on the trends generated by the aforementioned external forces. That is, without deregulatory acts, we would expect the trends of airline and trucking improvement and railroad worsening in performance have continued. In this period there is no indication that the rate of technological change increased, but the levels of rank shift and the associated uncertainties increased substantially. These latter uncertainties show the clear effects of the turbulence brought about by deregulation. Thus, for these three groups, deregulation did not affect the relative positions of the subgroups so much as it affected industry volatility and within-group positions of individual firms. This will be seen more clearly in the ensuing analysis.

ANALYSIS OF INDIVIDUAL FIRMS

Having established industry and subgroup patterns of behavior during the period of deregulation, it is now possible to use the rank analysis methodology to analyze and compare individual firms' responses to deregulation. The transformation to ordinal data also suppresses short-term noise in firm behavior. Comparison at the firm level can be made to both the industry level and the subindustry level, with strategic elements being identified in both contexts. We turn now to an examination of the rank performance of two railroad companies, three trucking firms, and five airlines. These firms will be examined in the context of their performance relative to all other large transportation companies, except where noted.

Railroads

Two dominant patterns emerge in the analysis of railroad firm rank behavior. The most commonstrategy in this industry over the past quarter century has been to stay predominantly in the railroad business and grow horizontally by absorbing other firms, or to be absorbed. A second strategy has been to keep the railroad business as a base, but to diversify into other businesses. The two railroad companies analyzed below are representative of these two strategies.

Chicago-Milwaukee Railroad. Of the two dominant patterns exhibited by railroad companies over the past quarter century, the Chicago-Milwaukee pattern of rank behavior exemplifies the type of firm that stayed largely in the railroad business. As Figure 4.14 demonstrates, return on equity position leads a pattern of worsening rank positions. Operating revenue showed a relatively steady decline in rank position, with rapid worsening in the period from 1976 to 1980, when it leveled off. Both asset and employee positions lay below the other rank positions, indicating relatively poor productivity on both human factors and capital. Net income position followed return on equity and dropped from the rankings in 1978.

Southern Pacific Railroad. The second dominant rank pattern exhibited by railroad companies in the period studied is illustrated by Southern Pacific's rank positions (Figure 4.15). Southern Pacific, like Santa Fe Industries, Rio Grande Industries and others, diversified away from the railroad business, but, still derived more than 50% of its operating revenue from transportation. For Southern Pacific and firms like it, return on equity rank by itself worsened over the period in a cyclic fashion, and was more poorly positioned than the ranks on all other dimensions. All other dimensions were comparably ranked until a gradual divergence and slight worsening in position took place in the last 12 to 15 years. A merger in 1983 dropped Southern Pacific as an individual entity from the rankings.

Figure 4.14. Chicago-Milwaukee Railroad Ordinal Performance

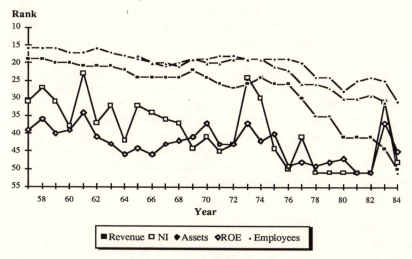

Figure 4.15. Southern Pacific Railroad Ordinal Performance

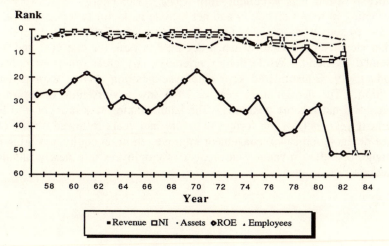

Trucking

Analysis of the rank behavior of the trucking industry yielded no strategy groupings similar to those found in the railroad industry. A pattern did, however, emerge in that successful trucking firms were found to have brought, or to be in the process of bringing their rank positions on the various dimensions into agreement. That is, if a successful trucking firm was in the ith position in terms of revenue in 1984, its ranking on the other dimensions (with the exception of assets, which were always lower ranked) were likely to be near the ith position also. Since the firms in the top 50 are there because of their operating revenue size, an interpretation of this behavior is that the managers of these firms responded to the uncertainty in their environment by reducing their strategic options and the scope of their firm's activities to be proportional to their revenue position. This implies that the firm established a balanced position in a market that would allow management to better cope with the environmental and industry uncertainty. The three firms selected all exhibit this behavior at some time in the period examined. Consolidated Freightways and Roadway Express were selected because they represent mainstream trucking firms, while United Parcel Service was included to show the effects of being in a high-growth segment of trucking.

Consolidated Freightways. Consolidated Freightways' improvement in rank performance (Figure 4.16) exceeded the industry as a whole on all dimensions, except for return on equity in six years and net income in one year. This firm showed the high asset productivity associated with trucking and, except for poor returns in 1960 and 1961, the return on equity position was excellent until 1972. The energy crisis forced a weakening in return on equity and net income ranks for two years, but both recovered somewhat in 1974. Operating revenue for Consolidated improved rather steadily until 1980, when it declined in rank for one year and then resumed its trend. While not experiencing any great relative employee productivity, Consolidated kept employee position in line with revenue position. The deregulatory year of 1980 saw a worsening of return on equity and net income positions. The latter ranking was brought into line the next year, but for the former two very bad years followed. The years since deregulation saw management improve return on equity and bring net income, operating revenue and number of employees into nearly identical positions.

Figure 4.16. Consolidated Freightways Ordinal Performance

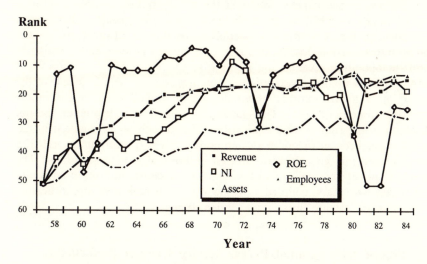

Roadway Express. Roadway Express appeared in the top 50 revenue rankings in 1960, as shown in Figure 4.17. The outstanding return on equity position of this firm in its first four years in the rankings is evident. However, since 1963 this position has gradually eroded. The pattern of rank behavior is much smoother for Roadway than it was for Consolidated (Figure 4.16). Only a slight worsening in all but asset position occurred during the energy shortage. Roadway's management brought rank position into alignment on all dimensions except assets through the 1970's. When deregulation legislation was passed in 1980, the firm was in a good position and good shape to take advantage of the situation.

Figure 4.17. Roadway Express Ordinal Performance

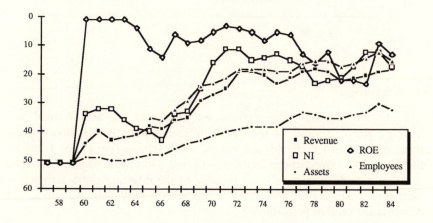

United Parcel Service. Consolidated Freightways and Roadway Express are in the same segment of the transportation business. United Parcel Service (UPS) is in a different strategic group and its rank performance (Figure 4.18) has consequently been quite different. Below the top 50 transportation firms until 1975, UPS entered at the eighth position in terms of operating revenue and in the first position in terms of number of employees. While the revenue position improved over the last decade of the study, the rank by number of employees continued to show the labor-intensive strategy of UPS. The uncertainty caused by deregulation did not show up in the rank positions of UPS. The growth of its segment of the business has been sufficient to swamp noise caused by uncertainty, and UPS has managed this growth well—at least in terms of its rank positions. The nearly identical rank positions of revenue, net income, and return on equity in the last two years, coupled with the very high rank position, indicate a well-balanced, mature firm with a service strategy.

Figure 4.18. United Parcel Service Ordinal Performance

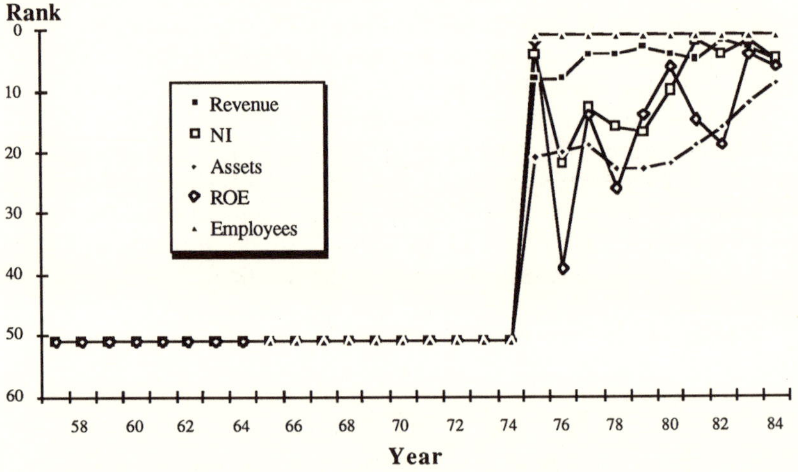

Airlines

In the previous two sections we examined selected railroad and trucking firms in terms of their performance relative to the other top 50 transportation firms. In this section we will examine five airline firms on that basis. The five airlines analyzed—United, Northwest, Delta, American and Pan American, were chosen because of the differing characteristics of their rank performance and the differing effects of impending and actual deregulation on that performance.

United Airlines. Figure 4.19 shows, for example, that in relation to the top 50 transportation firms, United Airlines was a leader in the airline subgroup's improvement in operating revenue and asset rankings, and that United followed the subgroup pattern of stabilizing these two performance dimensions in the period after 1969. Unlike the other airlines analyzed here, United engaged in acquisitions outside the airline industry, to the point where 90% of its revenues were non-airline in 1982. In the period from 1957 to 1969, United had moderate fluctuations in return on equity and net income. Beginning in 1970, when it acquired Western International Hotels concurrently with losing key Hawaiian routes (Byrnes, 1985, p. 38), United experienced wide fluctuations in return on equity and net income. The second large adverse shift in these two measures coincided with the acquisition of GAB in 1975. An improvement in both measures coincided with a change in the investment tax credit laws in 1977 (Byrnes, 1985, p. 87). The third major worsening coincided with the formal implementation of deregulation in 1978. Byrnes (1985, p. 122) states that United was one of the airlines that saw its prospects improve with deregulation. In fact, according to the methodology employed here, United's performance did not begin to improve until 1982, and did not approach pre-1969 levels of net income performance until 1984. Even then, return on equity position was still poor.

Figure 4.19. United Airlines (UAL) Ordinal Performance

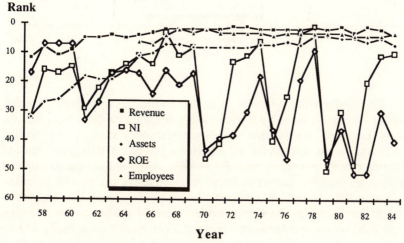

Northwest Airlines. Northwest Airlines in contrast to United, as shown in Figure 4.20, made greater gains in asset and revenue rankings relative to the top transportation firms, and in the period from 1969 to 1979 brought those two rankings to near equality. In the last five years of the study, revenue position improved relative to asset position, signaling improved use of assets on the part of Northwest's management. In the period up to 1970, Northwest had an excellent return on equity position, and until the last few years of the data enjoyed better net income and return on equity rankings and lower fluctuations in those rankings than United Airlines. Relative to the transportation industry, Northwest showed good employee productivity: its average rank on this dimension was lower than its revenue position in all periods where there were data for both.

Figure 4.20. Northwest Airlines Ordinal Performance

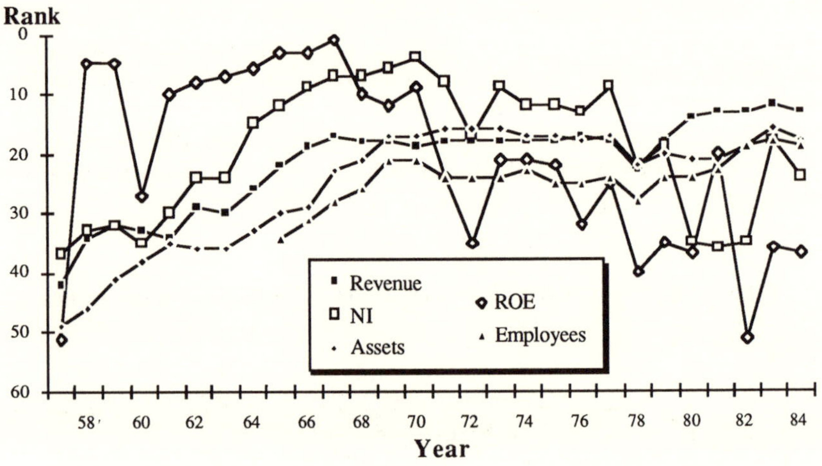

To highlight the different view that ordinal methodology provides, consider statements made by Byrnes (1985) based on cardinal data analysis. Byrnes describes "a profitable, slow-growth strategy such as Northwest's" (p. 45), and claims that "Delta and Northwest prospered throughout most of the deregulatory transition period" (p. 68). The analysis based on rank positions eliminates short-term noise from business cycles and inflation, shows only effects that are differential, and yields a view that suggests a different interpretation than provided by standard analysis. For example, Figure 4.20 shows that between 1964 and 1974 Northwest actually had no relative growth, and that it endured worsening relative profitability from 1969 to 1984.

Delta Airlines. Figure 4.21 shows that, like Northwest, Delta Airlines experienced steady improvement relative to other transportation firms on most ranked dimensions from 1957 to 1976. Asset and employee positions prior to 1975 indicate relative high productivity of these factors. Return on equity position was excellent until 1975 and net income position was favorable until 1979, but as deregulation took effect and the industry became more turbulent, return on equity and net income positions worsened for several years and improved only in the last year examined. The passage from Byrnes cited just above concerning Delta's "prosperity" during deregulation is contradicted by this pattern. The essential point here is that Delta's rank positions were aligned in the late seventies so that even though profitability fell as deregulation went into effect, the airline was able to recover quickly by 1984.

Figure 4.21. Delta Airlines Ordinal Performance

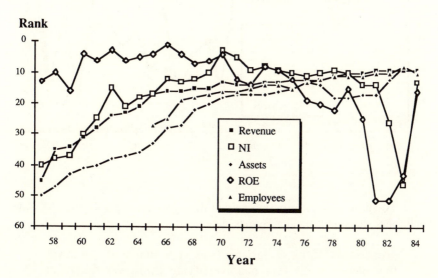

American Airlines. At the outset of the period studied here, American Airlines already had a well-established position in the transportation industry (Figure 4.22). Except for a substantial worsening in return on equity and net income positions in the early sixties, those positions improved until 1969. In the period 1969-1976, American embarked on a series of diversification moves that are graphically reflected in the poor return on equity and net income positions in those years. Improvement in these positions was not seen until American reduced its diversification in the last part of the seventies. The other three dimensions of performance improved slightly or remained the same until, at the end of the period, they were generally in agreement in terms of their rank position, indicating that management responded to the uncertainty of deregulation by balancing market performance and resource utilization. With the onset of deregulation, American's return on equity and net income positions, which had improved markedly, worsened (as was the case for the preceding airlines examined), but were brought back up in 1983 and 1984.

Figure 4.22. American Airlines Ordinal Performance

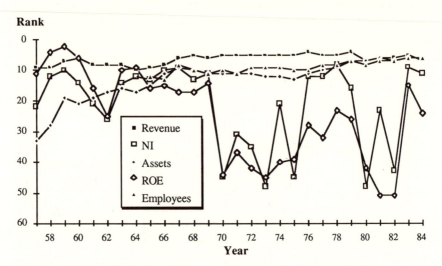

To show how information gained through rank analysis complements traditional analysis, consider Byrnes statement:

"American's earnings variance was very similar to, or lower than those of the four nondiversifying firms, yet American diversified actively. in the period immediately preceding American's major entry into the hotel business, it ranked second in earnings stability. In the following periods, spanning 1969 to 1978, it had only moderate variance, but it substantially increased its diversification. Therefore, earnings variance does not seem to have been an important motivation for American's diversification."

Figure 4.22 indicates that before 1969, American did have low variance on return on its equity position, but at worse (and worsening) rank positions than airlines such as Delta and Northwest (Figures 4.20 and 4.21).

In the post-1970 period, American did have moderate variance in ROE, but at much worse (though improving) rankings than the nondiversifying airlines. Thus Byrnes is correct as far as he goes; the rest of the story is that Americans worsening earnings position in the industry probably was an important motivating factor for diversification, and desire for improvement in its position for earnings and net income probably fueled further diversification.

Pan American. The rank positions of Pan American over time in relation to the top 50 transportation companies (Figure 4.23) provides a graphic illustration of the impacts of deregulation and management's reaction. Up until 1969 Pan American was making rank position gains on all dimensions. When the Civil Aeronautics Board made the transpacific awards in that year and Pan American diversified, the impact on return on equity and net income positions was immediate and disastrous, as the graph shows. In contrast, Byrnes (1985, p. 50), referring to absolute levels of returns, reports "Pan American's diversification raised its returns, which benefited both society and the airline." Pan American's operating revenue, asset, and employee positions began to slowly erode in the 1970s, to be reversed only slightly and temporarily in 1980 with the purchase of National Airlines. The other two performance dimensions did not improve until the company made a substantial sale of assets in 1976, but the effect was only temporary. The purchase of National accelerated the decline in net income rank, followed by similar behavior in return on equity rank.

Figure 4.23. Pan American Airlines Position in Transportation Industry

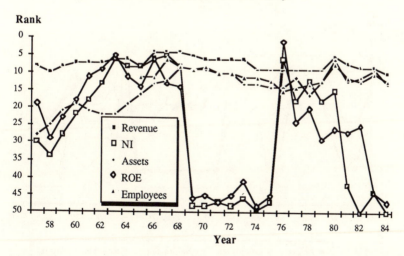

Pan Am in Relation to its Mode Group. Strategic analysis often calls for the evaluation of firm performance in a variety of contexts against differing reference groups. Ordinal time series analysis easily accommodates this. The airline rankings just presented were with reference to the other top 50 transportation firms; it is also useful to examine the position of a firm with respect to only those firms in its mode group. In the case of Pan Am, its position with respect to other airlines can be examined. To recast the strategic perspective to the level of the mode group, all that is necessary is to generate a simple reranking among airlines only from the larger set of rankings of the top firms in the transportation industry. Figure 4.24 shows Pan Am's position in terms of assets, return on equity, and number of employees with respect to the top nine airline firms. Several items of strategic interest can be observed in this presentation. In the first decade plotted, for instance, Pan Am's returns were consistently lower ranked than its other dimensions—indicating relatively poor performance even though its net income position was the best in the period 1961 to 1966. The effect of the loss of some of its transPacific routes in 1968 showed up dramatically in the drop in net income and return positions, followed by the slower decline in operating revenue, employees and assets. The continued poor performance of the NI and ROE dimensions can be traced to Pan Am's diversification strategy. The sharp improvement in only NI and ROE in 1976 was a result of the sale of assets (such as the Pan Am building), whereas the sharp improvement on all dimensions in 1980 signals the acquisition of National Airlines. This also illustrates how ordinal time series analysis reveals the effects of acquisition and sale of assets.

Figure 4.24. Pan American Airlines Position in Airline Industry

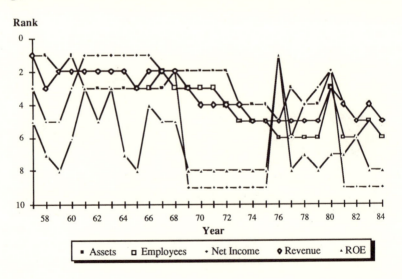

Implications

While the analysis of individual firms presented above was based on only the position statistic, similar comparisons can be made between individual firms with respect to the volatility and directional measures, giving an analyst a view of the longer term behavior of the firm relative to the groups of firms that make up its environment. Alternative views could be generated by reranking on the basis of geographic location, customer groups, or along other relevant strategic groupings.

As was hypothesized earlier in this chapter, analysis of individual firms in the transportation industry reveals that deregulation, while not altering the change in relative positions of the various modes of transportation (with the exception of pipelines), does alter the positions of individual firms within the mode groups. The analysis shows strikingly different patterns of response to the changing conditions in the transportation industry over the past quarter century.

In the airline industry, attempts at diversification in the late sixties and early seventies to buffer the effects of impending deregulation destabilized the profitability of airlines following this strategy. When deregulation became a fact in the late seventies, the profitability of all airlines, regardless of the strategy adopted, was destabilized. The data presented here imply that the managerial response to deregulation in this industry was to attempt to maintain market share and asset rank stability. The evidence further indicates that stability in market share and assets was paid for by instability in return on equity and net income. Recent data imply that while instability of this type still exists in this industry, some firms are bringing their performance into a balanced position and have prepared to cope in the new environment.

This situation is also the case for the firms in the trucking industry. Deregulation affected the relative profitability of a number of firms, but those in fast-growing market niches, like United Parcel Service, and those who have balanced their performance, like Roadway Express, have been able to maintain their relative profitability. In the railroad industry, on the other hand, if deregulation had any effects, they are not noticeable in the analysis presented here. Individual railroad companies continue their relative decline in performance on all dimensions in a comparatively smooth fashion. Apparently the maturity of the subindustry mitigates differential effects due to deregulation, and even strategic differences such as diversification or nondiversification do not appear to have a substantial effect.

CONCLUSIONS

This chapter has extended and combined the methodology developed in the previous two chapters and has presented an analysis of the impacts of deregulation on the transportation industry in general and on the railroad, trucking, and airline industries in particular from a new perspective. We have examined the situation in the transportation industry in a highly relative fashion by using the rank position data of the firms in the industry. The multiple perspectives generated here have revealed that deregulation altered the pattern of change among the major transportation modes only in the case of pipelines, but has not affected the relations among railroads, airlines, and trucking modes in a similar fashion. The major impact of deregulation for these three modal groups was to raise the levels of volatility and uncertainty within the groups. Thus, the impact of deregulation shows most clearly in the differential behavior of individual firms as opposed to groups of firms. Analysis of individual railroads showed similar results for different diversification strategies. Analysis of individual airlines indicated that profitability was hurt both by diversification and by deregulation, and analysis of trucking firms showed that growth strategies could swamp the effects of deregulation.

Two interesting patterns that have been noted, but not fully explained here, are: (1) declines in return on equity position tend to lead the decline on all other dimensions for groups of firms; and (2) the better managed firms tend in times of environmental turbulence to bring the performance rankings on all dimensions into agreement, conditioned on the capital intensity of the industry subgroup. Further study is required to ascertain if the observed relationships can be generalized, perhaps to the point that they can be used for managerial analysis and/or prediction.

Although the ordinal time series methodology is robust and comparatively easy to apply, and has been shown to reveal strategic insights into the behaviors of groups of firms, it should also be noted that the methodology is not proposed as a panacea for the strategic decision problem. So complex a problem requires multiple approaches, including those based on cardinal analysis, because each reveal a facet of the strategic situation; ordinal time series analysis is only one of the methodologies that can be employed by a strategy analyst. The material presented in this chapter suggests that the appropriate position for ordinal time series analysis in industry or competitive analysis is as the initial form of data analysis. It is especially useful in developing categories of strategic behavior and in identifying broad industry trends, the details of which can be filled in by more conventional analytic and ad hoc techniques. The findings of the ordinal analysis will tell the analyst much about the competing firms, and will suggest areas that require further data analysis. Cardinal methods can then be employed to develop information that was lost in the transformation to rankings. Finally, as the figures in this chapter suggest, an ordinal format is particularly suitable when it is desirable to display longitudinal data on a number of dimensions in a concise form for presentation to senior executives.

5

Excellent Companies: An Ordinal Time Series Approach

Timothy W. Ruefli
Rob L. Jones

In the years following the publication of Thomas Peters and Robert Waterman's *In Search of Excellence* in 1982, there has been a good deal of discussion about the book and its conclusions about management and excellent performance. Some critics have questioned Peters and Waterman's rejection of a rational approach to management; others have cited post-publication performance of some of the selected firms to cast doubt on the claim of excellence for these firms and, hence, to call into question the findings of the book. Still others have rejected the universality of some of the prescriptions (e.g., keeping close to the customer) on the more general grounds of known management problems in dealing with implementation of such prescriptions.

In the first part of their book, Peters and Waterman explicitly reject the "rational model" approach to evaluating firms and take an admittedly qualitative approach—supplemented by some general financial criteria—to identifying excellent firms. In spite of the implicit challenge in this approach, a search of the literature revealed only one semicomprehensive attempt at a rational analysis of Peters and Waterman's effort. In order to evaluate Peters and Waterman's excellent firms on a comparative basis, extensive data from *Fortune* for a sample of Peters and Waterman's firms was evaluated using ordinal time series analysis. The data cover both the period in which the firms were selected, and the period subsequent to their selection with an intent to examine the underlying information upon which Peters and Waterman made their selection. The results of this analysis shed some light on the appropriateness of designating these firms as excellent and on the validity of some of Peters and Waterman's conclusions regarding "excellent" firms.

IN SEARCH OF EXCELLENCE METHODOLOGY

Peters and Waterman initially identified 62 firms as possible excellent firms (see Table 5.1). These were chosen by consensus of opinion among "an informed group of observers of the business scene" (Peters and Waterman, 1982, p. 19). No further information on the criteria was provided, other than that the sample was limited to very large firms. The authors' concern was "with how big companies stay alive, well and innovative." (p. 22). The authors grouped the 62 firms into the following industry categories (pp. 19, 22):

1. High Technology
2. Consumer Goods
3. General Industrial
4. Service Companies
5. Project Management
6. Resource Based

The original group was then screened on financial performance using the following measures (pp. 23-25):

1. Compound asset growth
2. Compound equity growth
3. Average ratio of market value to book value
4. Average return on total capital
5. Average return on equity
6. Average return on sales

In order to qualify as a top performer, the firm "must have been in the top half of its industry on at least four out of six of these measures over the full twenty-year period" (p. 23). A second screen was made on innovativeness, using opinions of "industry experts."

This process yielded 43 firms meeting all of the criteria for excellence (see Table 5.1, underlined firms). The authors then noted commonalities of management practices in these firms and characterized the firms by the following attributes (pp. 13-15):

1. A bias for action
2. Close to the customer
3. Autonomy and entrepreneurship
4. Productivity through people
5. Hands on, value driven
6. Stick to the knitting
7. Simple form, lean staff
8. Simultaneous loose-tight properties

Table 5.1. Peters and Waterman's Sample

High Technology

Allen-Bradley	Hughes Aircraft	Schlumberger
Amdahl	United Technologies	TRW**
Wang Labs	Texas Instruments*	IBM*
Data General*	Western Electric **	Intel*
Digital Equipment*	Lockheed	NCR**
Emerson Electric*	National Semiconductror*	Xerox**
General Electric	Hewlett-Packard*	Rockwell**
Gould**	Westinghouse**	Raychem

Consumer Goods

Blue Bell**	Bristol-Meyers*	Atari
Eastman Kodak*	Chesebrough-Pond's*	Avon*
Frito-Lay (Pepsico)	Levi Strauss*	Mars
General Foods**	Polaroid**	Maytag*
Johnson & Johnson*	Revlon*	Merck*
Procter & Gamble*	Tupperware	

General Industrial

Caterpillar Tractor*	McDermott**	
Dana Corporation*	3M*	
Ingersoll-Rand**	General Motors**	

Service

Delta Airlines	Disney Productions	K-Mart
Marriott	McDonalds	Wal-Mart
American Airlines		

Project Management

Bechtel	Fluor	Boeing*

Resource-Based

Exxon**	DuPont*
Arco**	Standard Oil (Indiana)/Amoco*
Dow Chemical*	

Underlined firms meet all criteria for excellence
*indicates a firm in the reduced sample in this study
**indicates firms added to achieve expanded sample

While the above attributes were not universally present, according to Peters and Waterman they served to differentiate the selected firms from other less successful companies. These attributes are the prescriptions for excellence offered by the authors to those who would be excellent.

EVALUATION

In spite of the considerable attention attracted by *In Search of Excellence*, a review of the literature revealed little in the way of historical validations of the claim of Peters and Waterman's 43 firms to excellence. In part this may have been because of the dependence of the study on qualitative judgments, but also because of the formidable problems of doing longitudinal studies of firms (see Kimberly, 1976, 1980, and Miller and Friesen, 1982).

In November, 1984, *Business Week* did a cover story on the firms identified in *In Search of Excellence* and identified several of the chosen firms that had fallen on hard times. In particular, Revlon, Atari, Hewlett-Packard, Levi Strauss, Texas Instruments, and Digital Equipment Corporation were cited as evidence that the analysis of and the guidelines for excellence were flawed. In a review of *In Search of Excellence*, Carroll (1983) raised a broader set of questions, in addition to pointing to specific firms' recent problems. He discussed Peters and Waterman's rejection of the rational model of managing and their attempts to articulate a new theory of management. While Carroll did describe Peters and Waterman's sampling methodology, his criticisms of it were limited to questioning why Schlumberger was included while all other European firms were intentionally omitted. Carroll also observed, "Without so stating, Peters and Waterman are suggesting that these lessons are more reliably isolated through a process of identifying common denominators in excellent companies than through other analytic techniques."

Of the other literature that reviewed Peters and Waterman's findings, only a study by Bettis and Mahajan (1985) used an analytic model as its primary methodology. Bettis and Mahajan examined the risk/return performance of a group of diversified firms that had an intersection with the *In Search of Excellence* sample. Their general conclusion was that "the perception of best run companies used in the McKinsey study did not adequately consider risk in evaluating performance. Alternatively, excellence as defined by the study may omit risk as a consideration. In either case the absence of risk would seem to introduce a significant simplification." The analysis presented below will qualify this finding.

DATA FOR ORDINAL TIME SERIES ANALYSIS

The data used in this study were the rankings complied by *Fortune* for the largest 500 firms, ranked by operating revenue, for the period from 1954 to 1984. The dimensions used were operating revenue, net income (NI), assets, and number of employees. Since not all of the 43 firms that meet all standards for excellence in *In Search of Excellence* are in the

Fortune 500, a subset of these firms was used in this study. Comparable data were not available for six service firms, and no data were available for seven firms that were private, foreign, or subsidiaries of other firms, so these firms were omitted. Five other firms were omitted for lack of data on other grounds (e.g., the firm did not appear in the *Fortune* 500 until 1980 or after). Therefore, there were 25 firms in our analysis in five of the six industry categories, as indicated by the single-starred firms in Table 5.1. This sample is well-dispersed across Peters and Waterman's industry categories, and while no measure of statistical significance can be generated, the results presented here are indicative of the similarities and differences to be found in the larger sample of 43.

Some of the firms in our sample were not in the *Fortune* 500 for one or more years. In these cases an artificial rank of 501 was assigned to these firms. Since this convention was employed largely in the early years of the study when a few of the firms were not yet large enough to enter the 500, it was felt that the results obtained employing this convention were conservatively biased, and then only for the first decade of the study.

From the set of statistics developed for ordinal time series analysis, two statistics, position and volatility, as described in chapter 2, were selected for this analysis. The results of this analysis are presented in the next section.

RESULTS

The results of the analysis are depicted in Figures 5.1 to 5.10. The position graphs are configured so that the highest rank (best performance) is at the top of the vertical axis and the lowest rank (worst performance) is at the bottom of the axis. Therefore improvements in relative performance result in upward shifts, while worse performance yields downward shifts. The results reported here are for the subsample of 25 firms, and subsets of that group.

Results for Entire Sub-sample

Figure 5.1 shows that entire sample of 25 firms exhibited consistent improvement in average rank across the dimensions of operating revenue, assets and employment (with the exception of operating revenue in 1957). Net income in a number of years showed a worsening for a one-year period and in 1981 through 1983 showed the only multiyear decline in average rank in the thirty-year period. The average rank for net income for the entire sample was better than the ranks to other dimensions by an average of 40 rank positions in the period from 1954 to 1972. In the period from 1973 to 1980 net income was better than the others by an average of 20 rank positions. This indicates that the sample firms enjoyed better profitability than other *Fortune* firms in the period up to 1980. After 1980, relative profitability for the sample firms worsened, but then began to recover in the last year. The sources of this problem will be identified below.

Figure 5.1. All Firms Meeting Excellence
Criteria—Position in *Fortune* 500

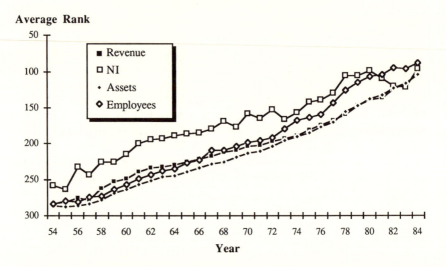

Based on ordinal data for the period from 1954 to 1979, the average firm in the *Fortune* 500 in 1960 *lost* at least 130 rank positions on each dimension by 1979. Thus the performance of the subsample of Peters and Waterman's firms is impressive in that the average firm *gained* approximately 125 rank positions in the same period on all dimensions considered. This is a net gain of 255 positions against the average of the cohort, and is indicative of outstanding performance by these firms. Thus the ordinal data support Peters and Waterman's contention that, as a group, these firms were excellent performers in the period up to 1980.

There still remains the problem, noted by several critics, of poor performance by selected firms in the post-1980 period. As was noted above, the ordinal data show worsening in the net income position from 1981 to 1983 for the sample group. Compared to the rest of the *Fortune* 500, this is indeed poor performance, but here we need to note that by 1980 the firms in the sample had grown quite large and were approaching the upper limits of the rankings. In this case, a more pertinent analysis would be to compare the performance of the excellent firms with the average of other firms in the top 200 in 1980. Table 5.2 compares the performance of Peters and

Waterman's firms with the average of the *Fortune* 200 in 1980. These results indicate that in the period from 1980 to 1984 the largest 200 firms did not perform well on average when compared to the rest of the *Fortune* 500, and that Peters and Waterman's sample fared considerably better than did the average very large firm.

Table 5.2.   Average Rank Position Change Comparison:
1980 to 1984

| | Average of *Fortune* 200 in 1980 | | Sample of Excellent Firms | |
Period	Net Income	Operating Revenue	Net Income	Operating Revenue
1980-1981	Lost 9	Lost 5	Lost 11	Gained 3
1981-1982	Lost 55	Lost 3	Lost 10	Gained 9
1982-1983	Gained 5	Lost 10	Lost 1	Gained 9
1983-1984	Gained 9	Gained 0	Gained 26	Gained 9
Net 1980-1984	Lost 50	Lost 18	Gained 4	Gained 30

Figure 5.2.   All Firms Meeting Excellence Criteria—Volatility

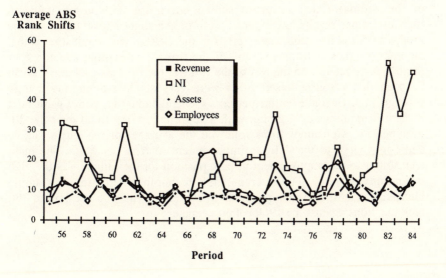

Figure 5.2 shows the volatility of the sample along the four dimensions in terms of their average absolute rank shift. Here higher levels of the statistic imply more activity. From this figure it can be noted that in the early, middle, and late parts of the period studied, net income rank shift activity was relatively high, with intervening periods of moderate activity. The last and highest level of net income volatility came after the completion of Peters and Waterman's study. Employee volatility showed a somewhat shorter cyclic trend that leveled out in the last seven years. Overall, net income volatility was the highest, as might be expected, but employee volatility was the next highest. The dynamics of operating revenue and assets were relatively the same throughout the period, with a slight increasing trend.

Results by Performance Dimension

To examine the sources of change in the sample, position statistics can be calculated for each of the industry groups of firms identified by Peters and Waterman. The statistics can then be compared by dimension across groups, and by group across dimensions. We will first review the results by performance dimension and then examine the results for four industry groups; the project management group will be omitted since we have data for only one firm.

The results by groups for operating revenue and assets show almost identical patterns, as can be seen in Figures 5.3 and 5.4. Notice that ability of the ordinal times series to screen out noise without complicated transformations results in the depiction of only a slight impact on any of the groups of firms from the energy crisis in the 1970s. The implication is that the energy crisis did not give any of the firms a substantial advantage or disadvantage relative to the rest of the firms in the *Fortune* rankings. It can be seen that resource-based firms were very stable maintaining a high average rank over the entire period. General industrial firms were next highest in rankings as a group, with a slight improving trend over the 30-year period. Consumer firms followed the average for the entire sample and contributed to the definite improvement in rank position. The main contributor to the improvement in rank position for the sample was the high technology group. The average high technology firm in our sample improved at least 250 rank positions in 30 years. This is a net gain of 380 rank positions against the 1960 cohort average.

**Figure 5.3.   All Firms Meeting Excellence
Criteria—Asset Position**

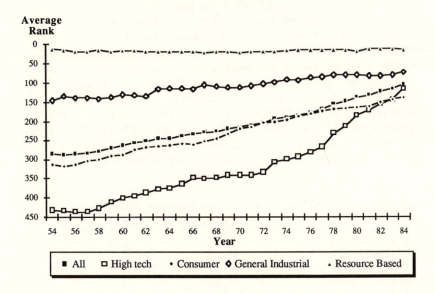

**Figure 5.4.   All Firms Meeting Excellence
Criteria—Operating Revenue Position**

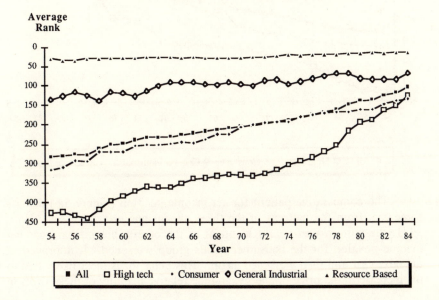

When the comparative rankings for number of employees are examined (Figure 5.5), they show a pattern similar to those for revenue and assets. However, resource-based firms experienced a slight worsening in rank position, indicating that as a group they employed fewer individuals relative to the rest of the *Fortune* 500 over the last 30 years. General industrial firms increased their relative levels of employment in the first decade, but then leveled out, while consumer goods firms showed a more substantial increase in relative number of employees. The greatest increase in relative employment levels was generated by the high technology firms. Their relative increase in number of employees was especially steep in the period 1976 to 1979. (Note that this does not imply that these firms are necessarily adding employees in an absolute sense; it could be that they were merely losing employees at a significantly slower rate than other firms.)

Figure 5.5. All Firms Meeting Excellence Criteria—Employee Position

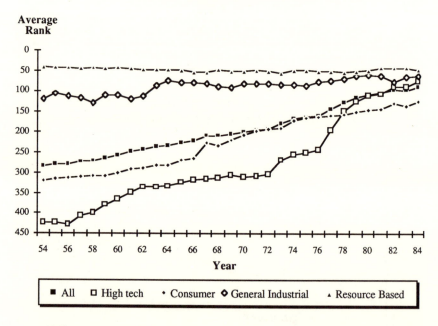

The comparative pattern for net income position (Figure 5.6) departs somewhat from the patterns of the three dimensions just discussed. Until 1971, the pattern was nearly identical to the others, but in that year net income position for the consumer goods group worsened. It improved in the next year and then worsened again. This behavior is most likely tied to the increase in the price of energy, and the relative inability of these firms to pass the increase along to the consumer. Resource-based firms showed little impact from the energy shortage on net income position, in part because their aggregate position was so high that it could not go much higher. General industrial firms, which had a level net income position until 1978, began a worsening trend that was halted in 1981, only to sharply again worsen in 1982, followed by improvements in the last two years. High technology firms generally improved until 1980, and then worsened their position for three years, but recovered in 1984 nearly to the old trend line.

Figure 5.6. All Firms Meeting Excellence Criteria—Net Income Position

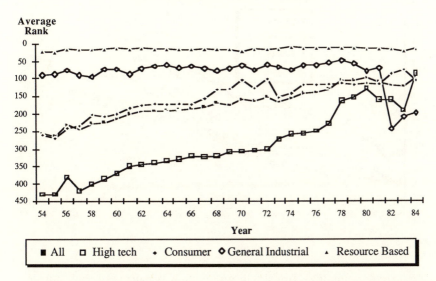

This comparative analysis along each dimension has shown that the groups of firms in the sample behaved quite differently relative to the *Fortune* 500 and to other over the period examined. This raises a question as to whether different types of excellent management might be called for in each of these groups of firms, depending on their position. To provide support for this remark we will next examine each of the four industry groups along all four dimensions.

Results for Industry Subgroups

Figure 5.7 shows the average rank position of the consumer goods group. The outstanding feature of this graph is the extremely favorable position of net income relative to the other dimensions over the entire period. The implication is that this group was comparatively more profitable than the average *Fortune* 500 firm and, as shall be seen, relatively more profitable than any of the other groups. The other key development to notice here is the way employee position became higher than asset and operating revenue positions, indicating that compared to the rest of the *Fortune* 500, the number of employees was being changed in this group disproportionate to growth in assets and operating revenue.

Figure 5.7. Consumer Goods Firms—Position on All Dimensions

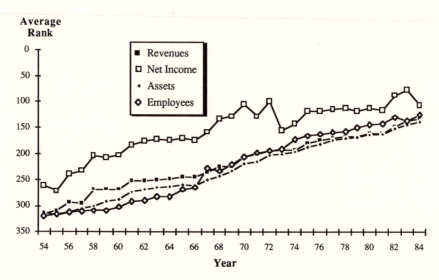

High technology firms as a group show a pattern of rank positions (Figure 5.8) that differed from the consumer goods firms. Through 1980, operating revenue and asset positions were associated with each other, as were net income and employee positions. In 1981, net income position worsened and departed from employee position, but returned in 1984. The worsening of net income position was a contributor to the decline in this statistic for the entire sample. The growing importance of human resources to the high technology group of firms is indicated by the constantly improving employee position and its increasing distance from the other dimensions.

Figure 5.8. High Technology Firms—Position on All Dimensions

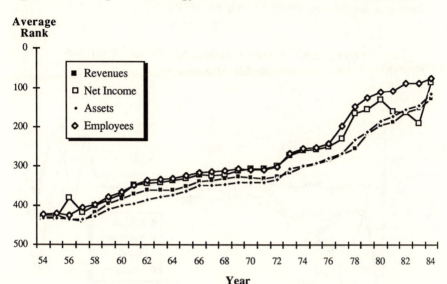

Figure 5.9 shows that until 1979, general industrial firms had a favorable net income position relative to the other dimensions (though not as favorable as consumer goods firms). Operating revenue position was associated more with employee position than amont the previous two industry groups. However, this changed in 1980, when operating revenue position and asset position became nearly identical and continued that way. The historically low asset position indicated a relatively favorable level of capital productivity, until the last five years. As was noted in the comparative analysis, 1982 was obviously a bad year for these general industrial firms; the average firm in the sample lost 140 rank positions in net income. As of 1984, net income position had not yet recovered to its former level.

The outstanding feature of the resource-based firms (Figure 5.10) is the low average rank by employees in comparison to the positions of the other dimensions. This is in line with the high capital intensity associated with the industry. The data indicate that relative employee productivity grew over time, in that the rank by employees declined relative to net income and operating revenue ranks. Asset position was relatively high, as expected, and was related in position to net income. The higher position of assets relative to net income in the last four years indicates the comparatively poorer profitability of assets in this group for that period. In this graph, the impact of the energy crisis can be more clearly seen. The worsening trend in net income position, which began in 1960, peaked in 1970 and then net income position improved until 1974. Following a few years of stability, there was another worsening trend until 1983.

Figure 5.9. General Industrial Firms—Position on All Dimensions

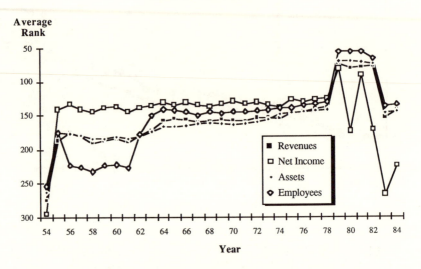

Figure 5.10. Resource-Based Firms—Position on All Dimensions

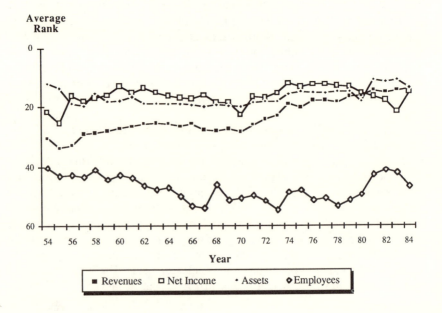

Results for Expanded Sample

To test the significance of having met all the criteria for excellence, ordinal time series data for an expanded set of firms was examined. To the 25 firms meeting all criteria for excellence for which there were comparable data was added a set of 15 firms of the original 62 that did not meet all criteria for excellence, but for which there were data (see Table 5.1, double-starred firms). The analysis outlined above was rerun on this expanded set, and the results were substantially the same as reported above— except for the case of general industrial firms, which showed increasingly heterogeneous behavior. The implications of this are twofold. First, with the exception of general industrial firms, meeting all the criteria for excellence does not materially improve the performance of the firms on the dimensions considered. Second, in light of the distinct performance of the general industrial firms meeting all criteria for excellence, and the further differences generated by the addition of those general industrial firms in the original 62 that did not meet all criteria, we must conclude that firms in this category are by nature more heterogeneous than those in the other industrial groups.

To further compare Peters and Waterman's implicit methodology with a more analytic approach, alternate approaches to generating a sample of potential excellent firms were investigated. Examining the data patterns generated by ordinal time series analysis suggested two possible selection criteria. The first considered stability as an objective, and used as a screen the criteria of minimum variance in rank performance in the period from 1960 to 1979, along the four dimensions, for the largest 200 firms in 1980. Using these criteria a set of 44 candidate firms was generated; of these, 16 were among the 40 of Peters and Waterman's original sample for which there were data. More importantly, the screen yielded 28 additional firms, that had performed, on average, as well as Peters and Waterman's firms. Although Bettis and Mahajan (1985) concluded that risk considerations did not enter into Peters and Waterman's criteria, the appearance of these 16 firms in a set screened by minimum variance would indicate that some implicit measure of risk was being employed. The reason for the discrepancy in findings is most likely due to the risk concept being selectively employed by Peters and Waterman.

The second selection procedure used growth as an objective, and ranked the largest 200 firms in 1979 by improvement in rank position in the period from 1960 to 1979. Of the top 42 firms selected by this criteria, 10 were in the 40 in Peters and Waterman's sample for which there were data. Combined, the two simple screens suggested here would select 16 out of Peters and Waterman's 25 firms that meet all standards for excellence and for which there were data.

The point in examining these alternative screens is not to replicate Peters and Waterman's selection methodology but to suggest that there are rational, analytic approaches that are relatively easy to apply and that can capture much of the essence of Peters and Waterman's more intuitive approach. Further, the analytic selection procedures provide the reader with a basis for evaluation of both the selection process and the resulting prescriptions. This is especially important if the prescriptions turn out to be sensitive to the nature of the original sample.

CONCLUSIONS

It was the stated intention of this chapter to reexamine the bases for Peters and Waterman's selection of excellent firms, and to do so using an analytic technique. Having done this, we can draw several conclusions. The ordinal time series analysis of the subsample of 25 and the expanded sample of 40 of Peters and Waterman's excellent companies does indeed show what can be considered overall excellent performance in the period from 1960 to 1980. In the period beyond 1980, the ordinal data show weakening in the net income position of the entire group for two years, with a subsequent recovery. The data also show that this performance is comparatively better than the performance of the average firm in the *Fortune* 200 in 1980. Thus in singling out individual firms' poor performance in an absolute sense, Peters and Waterman's critics are, to some extent, taking specifics out of context. Further, the data show that the net income position failure to recover to the original trend line position was largely due to the relatively poor performance of one of the industrial subgroups—general industrial firms. On the grounds of the results summarized here, relative to the other firms in the *Fortune* 500 in the period from 1954 to 1984, Peters and Waterman appear to be justified in the designation of their set of firms as "excellent."

While providing support for the results of Peters and Waterman's selection process, the results presented above call into question the generic nature of their prescriptions for excellence. The significant differences in the patterns of rank behavior in the different industry groups suggest that the groups faced significantly different management situations. The resource-based firms, for example, had high rank position throughout the period studied on all dimensions except number of employees. This implies a focus on capital productivity in the group, and means that individual management teams must have the same focus or lose competitive position. High technology firms, on the other hand, increased the relative number of their employees. Therefore the prescription to seek "productivity through people" means two different things to these two groups of firms. For one group it means seeking productivity through people by leveraging their output through increased capital intensity, while for the other it means seeking productivity through people by developing new ideas. This implication of the industry-specific nature of prescriptions is reinforced by the significantly different performance of the general industrial firms in recent years.

The main conclusion to be drawn here is that while the prescriptions for excellence generated by Peters and Waterman may be valid for most of the groups of firms they investigated, they are not necessarily valid for all groups—and that where they are valid, they are not necessarily valid in the same way. That is, differing patterns of industry performance revealed by the ordinal time series analysis suggest that prescriptions for excellence should be more specific to each industry to allow for the differences in internal and external environments. Alternatively, the general prescriptions of Peters and Waterman must be interpreted and implemented in an industry-specific fashion, and thus, should not necessarily be taken at face value.

A final philosophical conclusion is that Peters and Waterman's rejection of the value of rational approaches in management goes too far. The application of such an approach here has, we hope, demonstrated the complementarity of intuitive and rational approaches. Peters and Waterman's intuitive findings inspired this rational analysis of their study; our rational methodology was able to refine their analysis, supporting some points and calling others into question. These findings will, we hope, stimulate further thinking, both intuitive and rational, into the characteristics of management excellence and the conditions under which excellence prevails.

6

Strategy, Structure and Corporate Performance: An Ordinal Time Series Analysis

Timothy W. Ruefli
Donde Ashmos

Two issues that have frequently appeared in the corporate strategy literature in recent years are those of diversification strategy and organization structure, and the relation of each to economic performance. Numerous researchers have explored the types of diversification strategies pursued by successful companies, and the types of organizational structure that provide the largest corporate economic gains (Chandler, 1962; Wrigley, 1970; Rumelt 1974; Pitts, 1977; Salter and Weinhold, 1979; Bettis, 1981; Christensen and Montgomery, 1981; Dundas and Richardson, 1982; Montgomery, 1982; Rumelt, 1982; Bettis and Mahajan, 1985; and Palepu, 1985). While the substantial shift in American industry from the U-form or functional type of organization structure to the M-form or product structure has been well documented (Rumelt, 1974; Williamson, 1975), significant questions about the relationship between structure and corporate performance remain. Likewise, there has been a considerable amount of research on the topic of diversification; but there is little agreement on the amount or type of diversification that is most profitable for the typical business firm. The strategy of diversifying through acquisitions maintains its popularity, as diversification activity among firms has steadily increased in recent years, albeit not as dramatically as in the period of the late 1960s. However, diversification remains a phenomenon that in many ways is still poorly understood.

Perhaps the study that provides the best starting place for an empirical study of the relationship between various diversification strategies and organizational structure on the one hand, and economic performance on the other is that by Rumelt (1974). His finding that economic performance is more related to the type of diversification than to the amount of diversification raised serious questions about the wisdom of corporate diversification into unrelated areas of business. This finding, when viewed in the light of the substantial decline in the number of single-business companies between 1950 and 1970 (Rumelt, 1974, p. 50) offered normative appeal to corporate strategists considering acquisition as an attractive investment alternative.

The purpose of this chapter is to explore further the issues of diversification strategy and organization structure by reexamining the performance of the firms that Rumelt studied in his 1974 work, using an alternate methodology based on ordinal time series analysis. The reason for reexamining Rumelt's findings and extending his study is that he relied heavily on decade averages of groups of firms' financial indicators in cardinal form. His use of cardinal data and the averaging process may have hidden group behavior that is made more evident through the use of a methodology that fills in the details obscured by those averages. Utilizing the same set of firms, classified in the same categories developed by Rumelt, this chapter examines the performance of these groups of firms in terms of statistics based on the relative rankings of the firms in the *Fortune* 500 along four dimensions—net income, assets, operating revenue, and number of employees—in each year from 1954 to 1979. The use of ordinal time series analysis allows us to examine performance on a year-to-year basis, yet screens out short-term "noise" (see chapter 2). The results presented here confirm some of Rumelt's findings and those of subsequent confirming studies, but challenge others.

The remainder of the chapter is organized into six sections, the first of which provides a summary of the pertinent literature and outlines Rumelt's methodology and significant findings. The next section discusses the data employed in the analysis. In the fourth section, the findings of this study in regard to the relation of strategy choice to corporate performance are given; the fifth section presents analogous material when firms are classified by type of organization structure. In both cases our findings are compared with those of Rumelt. Major implications of the findings are discussed in the last section, along with possible explanations for those findings and some concluding remarks.

LITERATURE REVIEW

Introduction

There are two classic empirical studies of corporate strategy, organization structure and firm performance that are direct major precursors of Rumelt's work. The first is that of Chandler (1962), which analyzed the relations among strategy, structure and performance for 70 U.S. corporations. Chandler observed progressive stages in strategy development and concluded that unless diversifying firms adopted a divisionalized structure that economic performance would suffer. The second major precursor to Rumelt's study was that of Wrigley (1970), which built on Chandler's study and analyzed a sample of 100 firms drawn from the *Fortune* 500 in 1967. Wrigley used qualitative judgments to identify four strategy categories, and documented the pervasiveness of diversification and divisionalized structure among the largest manufacturing and mining companies. Wrigley's 1967 sample served as a basis for the group of firms in Rumelt's 1969 sample. Rumelt's study, which will now be examined, not only expanded on the notions of strategy and structure explored by Chandler and Wrigley, but added the important component of economic performance for use in comparing organizational structures and corporate strategies. It is this aspect of his study that is of particular interest in the present study.

Rumelt's Methodology

Rumelt selected three samples of 100 firms each from the 500 largest industrial firms in each of the years 1949, 1959, and 1969. The samples for the latter two periods were drawn from the *Fortune* list of the 500 largest industrial firms, while the 1949 sample was drawn from a Federal Trade Commission report list of the largest 500 firms classified by size of assets. Because of multiple appearances of firms in samples and some minor data problems Rumelt ended up with 246 firms in the sample. Building on the earlier work of Chandler (1962) and Wrigley (1970), Rumelt went beyond the previously developed measurement technique of "specialization ratio" (the proportion of a firm's annual revenues attributable to its largest discrete market activity), and added to it vertical and related ratios as factors in categorizing the firms in his sample according to different diversification strategies (Rumelt, 1974, ch. 1). Firms were similarly classified according to organization structure. The categorization of structure was based on annual reports and previous research by Chandler (1962); Stieglitz and Wilkerson (1968); White (1963); Kern (1964); and on other publicly available information.

Economic performance was estimated along several financial dimensions based on annual data collected by Standard and Poors. Only those firms which stayed in a strategy or structure category for the whole decade being analyzed were used as a basis for the results attributed to that category. Since firms were classified only every decade, it is not clear that their maintenance of that category or their position in the *Fortune* 500 was verified for each of the nine intervening years. The annual data were aggregated into decade averages for each firm for the periods 1949-1959 and 1959-1969. These averages were further aggregated over the firms in each strategy or structure category to yield a performance measure for each of the strategy and each of the structure groups.

Rumelt's Categories and Findings

Definitions. Based on the methodology outlined above, Rumelt expanded on Wrigley's four strategy classifications and generated nine strategy classifications for the firms in his samples:

(a)   Single Business—firms that are basically committed to a single business.

Dominant Businesses—firms that have diversified to some extent, but still obtain most of their revenues from a single business. Four types of dominant businesses include:

(b)   Dominant-Vertical—vertically integrated firms.
(c)   Dominant-Constrained—nonvertical dominant business firms that have diversified by building on some particular strength, skill, or resource associated with the original dominant activity.
(d)   Dominant-Linked—nonvertical dominant business firms where most diversified activities are not linked to the dominant business, but each is somehow related to some of the firm's other activities.
(e)   Dominant-Unrelated—nonvertical dominant business firms in which most diversified activities are not related to the dominant business.

Related Businesses—non-vertically integrated firms that are diversified but without a dominant line of business, and in which diversification has been accomplished primarily by relating new activities to old activities. Two types of related businesses are:

(f)   Related-Constrained—related business firms that have diversified chiefly by relating new businesses to a specific central skill or resource and in which each activity is somehow related to almost all of the firm's other activities.
(g)   Related-Linked—related business firms that have diversified by relating new businesses to some strength or skill already possessed, but not always to the same strength or skill.

Unrelated Businesses—non-vertical firms that have diversified without regard to relationships between new businesses and current activities. Two types of related businesses are:

(h)   Unrelated-Passive—unrelated business firms that do not qualify as acquisitive conglomerates.

(i)   Acquisitive-Conglomerates—unrelated businesses firms that have aggressive programs for the acquisition of new unrelated businesses.

In addition to categorizing the firms in his sample according to strategy type, Rumelt also classified them by type of organizational structure. The five structural classifications he used are:

(a)   Functional—major subunits are defined in terms of the business functions or stages in the manufacturing process.

(b)   Functional with Subsidiaries—an organization that is basically functional but which has one or more separate product divisions.

(c)   Product Division—an organization that consists of a central office and a group of operating divisions, each having the responsibility and resources needed to engineer, produce, and market a product or set of products.

(d)   Geographic Division—an organization that consists of a central office and a group of operating divisions, each having the responsibility and resources needed to engineer, produce, and market a product or set of products in a different geographic area.

(e)   Holding Company—an association of firms or divisions commonly owned by a parent corporation.

Strategy Findings.   While numerous findings of interest were presented in Rumelt's study it is the major findings relating strategy to performance that are of interest here as follows:

(a)   Dominant-Constrained and Related-Constrained groups were unquestionably the best performers.

(b)   Dominant-Vertical and Unrelated-Passive groups were the lowest performers.

(c)   Among the dominant business firms, the Dominant-Vertical groups were low-performing while the Dominant-Constrained were among the highest performing.

(d)   Among related business firms, the Related-Constrained subgroup was high performing, while Related-Linked firms were average or slightly below average.

(e)   Among the unrelated business firms, the Unrelated-Passive subgroup was among the poorest performing; the Acquisitive-Conglomerate group was average in profitability and substantially above average in growth.

(f)   The system of classification revealed differences in financial results and policies that were not discernible if simple measures of diversity were employed to discriminate among firms.

(g)   Performance differences among the strategic categories were more closely linked to the way in which the firm related new businesses to old than to overall diversity.

Structure Findings. Of the many results regarding organization structure, the two involving the relation of structure to performance are of interest here, as follows:

(a)   The Product Division firms, in general, outperformed the Functional and Functional-with-Subsidiaries firms.

(b)   The two types of functional firms did not display similar patterns of performance. The Functional-with-Subsidiaries types had relatively low rates of sales growth but high growth rates in earnings, while for the Functional firms the opposite was true.

Other Related Studies

Rumelt's work is significant not only for the comprehensiveness and importance of its findings, but also for the numerous replications and partial replications it spawned. These include: Montgomery (1979, 1982): Bettis (1981); Christensen and Montgomery (1981);   Bettis and Hall (1982); Chandrasekaran (1982);   Nathanson and Casino (1982);   Rumelt (1982); Bettis and Mahajan (1985); and Palepu (1985). Much of the research since Rumelt is summarized in Palepu and will not be reviewed again here.

The Bettis and Mahajan study used a sample of 79 firms cross-classified by risk category and by three of Rumelt's strategy categories. The study suggests that risk/return is a factor that cuts across diversification categories and affects corporate performance. While risk/return will not be used as a factor in this study, the general approach used by Bettis and Mahajan of examining Rumelt's sample from a different perspective and a different methodology is analogous to the approach described in this chapter.

In another recent study, Palepu (1985) used the entropy measure used by Jacquemin and Berry (1979) and others (e.g., Scherer, 1980) to measure the total, related, and unrelated diversification of a sample of 30 firms from the food processing industry for the period from 1969 to 1979. Using a five-year moving average of return on sales as the measure of performance, Palepu found that there was no significant cross-sectional difference between the profitability of high versus low diversifiers or between related versus nonrelated diversifiers. He did find that the growth rate of the profitability of the related diversifiers was higher than the growth rate of the profitability of the nondiversifiers, thus putting him in general agreement with Rumelt.

While there are other studies that bear on the topic of the relation of strategy and structure to corporate performance, the aforementioned studies are the most relevant. The next section will present an overview of the data that were used in the present study and some of the methodological considerations involved in employing that data.

DATA

Introduction

Data for the analysis presented here were drawn from the *Fortune* rankings of the top 500 manufacturing companies in the United States in each year from 1954 to 1979, augmented by information concerning major corporate transactions over the same period. Rankings used in this analysis, in addition to operating revenue ranking, were those for net income (NI), assets, and number of employees. Firms are included in the *Fortune* manufacturing file if they are publicly listed, if they are U.S.-based, if 50% of their operating revenue is from mining or manufacturing, and if their operating revenues make them one of the largest 500 firms by this measure. There are, therefore, some limitations inherent in the data being used. Since firms are classified as being in the *Fortune* 500 on the basis of their revenue rankings, their rankings along the other dimensions selected for analysis— net income, assets, and number of employees—are contingent on the firm being in the top 500 along the dimension of revenue. Thus there may be firms that have net income or other performance figures that would place them in the top 500 by that measure, but because their revenue figures are not high enough, they are not included.

Operational Methodology

Rumelt's sample of 246 firms served as the basis for the sample used in this study. Rankings over time could not be found for 7 of those firms, giving a base of 239 firms. Since Rumelt used decade intervals in his analysis, we did not have his classification data for each of the 26 years of our analysis. Therefore, we decided that for this initial analysis, firms would be classified into the strategy and structure categories assigned to them by Rumelt for 1969. Thus our results are to be interpreted as revealing the behavior of a group of firms was classified in 1969. Precedence for this approach is provided, in part, by other studies replicating Rumelt's study and by Rumelt himself. Bettis (1981), Christensen and Montgomery (1981), Montgomery (1982), and Bettis and Mahajan (1985) appear also to have used Rumelt's 1969 classifications. Further, Rumelt used the 1969 classifications for the Acquisitive Conglomerate group in the original study. He also found that mean financial values for the two decades differed only by a constant amount, therefore he did not report values for the earlier decade.

Table 6.1 shows the number of firms in each of the strategy categories in 1969, plus the miscellaneous category. This latter, not much discussed by Rumelt, contains firms that for a variety of reasons did not maintain their strategy throughout the decade.

Table 6.1. Number of Firms in Each Group

Single Business	14
Dominant-Vertical	33
Dominant-Constrained	16
Dominant-Linked	10
Dominant-Unrelated	3
Related-Constrained	46
Related-Linked	44
Unrelated-Passive	18
Acquisitive-Conglomerate	14
Miscellaneous	<u>41</u>
Total	239

One other convention was required by the nature of the data and the ordinal time series methodology. Up to this point in the exposition, we have been implicitly assuming that each firm had a unique rank and stayed in the *Fortune* rankings in each year. Because firms leave and enter the top 500 from year to year, they are not ranked when they are not in the top 500. The alternatives to dealing with this situation are either to limit the analysis to those firms that appear in the *Fortune* 500 each year or to adopt a convention of assigning a hypothetical rank to unranked firms. Rumelt did not constrain his firms to be in the top 500 when he used financial data to construct his decade averages. Thus, although it is not made explicit in Rumelt's study, there are financial data from firms which were outside the *Fortune* 500 for part of the decade in which averages were computed. Following this approach our analysis reflects the influence of a firm even if it is not in the top 500. We accomplish this by assigning a rank of "501" on all dimensions to all firms not listed in the *Fortune* 500 in that year. This was felt to be conservative with respect to the analysis, insofar as the actual rank of firms outside the top 500, but in the top 1,000 is, in all but at most one case, greater than 501. This is not the case, however, for firms that have not been formed or that have been merged into other firms in a particular year. These latter firms are also assigned a rank of 501 on the grounds that unless they are a dominant part of the sample the conservativeness of the 501 convention more than compensates for the artificiality.

Figures 6.1 and 6.2 show the number of firms in each strategy category that are ranked in the *Fortune* 500 in each year of the study. From these graphs it can be seen that the effect of the firms outside the *Fortune* 500 is greatest in the early and late years of the study. The effects of this convention are minimized if they affect all subgroups in the sample relatively equally. To guard against the possibility that the adopted convention introduced a substantial bias, we also performed the analysis using only firms that were ranked in the *Fortune* 500. In this case, the performance rankings of the various strategy groups were found to be identical to the rankings when all firms were included and the 501 convention was employed, and our major conclusions were found to be the same. The next section of the chapter will examine the results of applying the ordinal time series methodology to the *Fortune* rank data.

Figure 6.1. Number of Firms in the *Fortune* 500: Rumelt's First Four Strategy Categories

Number of Firms

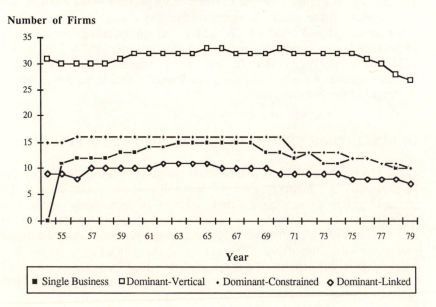

■ Single Business   □ Dominant-Vertical   • Dominant-Constrained   ◇ Dominant-Linked

**Figure 6.2. Number of Firms in the *Fortune* 500:
Rumelt's Second Five Strategy Categories**

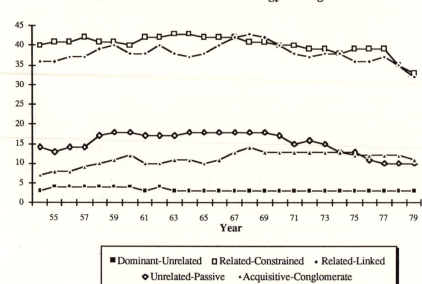

In this vein, it is worth inquiring about the representativeness of the average firm in Rumelt's sample in terms of its position in the *Fortune* 500 in key years. If the sample is representative, the average rank of the firms in the sample should be 250.5. When the average operating revenue ranks of the sample are computed, however, the positions are: 1954 = 200, 1959 = 217, 1969 = 198, 1979 = 184. In all cases the sample average rank is better than the average of the 500, implying that Rumelt's sample has a bias toward the larger of the *Fortune* firms.

ORDINAL TIME SERIES ANALYSIS—STRATEGY FINDINGS

The results of the multidimensional analysis of ordinal time series can be presented in a number of ways. We will first present an analysis by strategic groups comparing the rank behavior of each group on the four dimensions of net income, operating revenue, assets and number of employees. Following that we will examine the performance of all of the groups on each dimension. The ability of the methodology to produce results that reveal patterns of performance over time by strategy group and by performance dimension adds a depth and richness that were lacking in previous studies.

Analysis By Strategy Group

For each of the nine strategy groups we will first present the position of the group in terms of its average rank in the *Fortune* 500 on each dimension for each of the 26 years in the study period, then show its rank volatility from year to year, and then, for selected groups, examine the direction of its average rank shifts on each dimension. Following the rank statistics, we will present the information statistics for each group. The groups will be presented in the order of their appearance in Table 6.1.

Single Business. The rank performance of the Single Business strategy group is graphed along all four dimensions in Figures 6.3 and 6.4. (Note that in the graphs of average rank position the lower rank positions at the bottom of the graphs indicate smaller absolute levels of performance.) The performance of the group was worse than the average of the *Fortune* 500 for each year on the two output dimensions of operating revenue and net income. The mid-1950s to the early 1960s was a period of substantial improvement in rank, followed by an equally steep worsening until the early 1970s, due in part to firms dropping out of the *Fortune* 500 rankings and receiving a ranking of 501 (see Figure 6.1). Employee rank and asset rank tended to move together; they were lower than operating revenue in all years, and lower than net income in the period from 1957 to 1976, indicating favorable sales and net income productivity for assets and employees.

Figure 6.3. Single Business Strategy Firms—Position

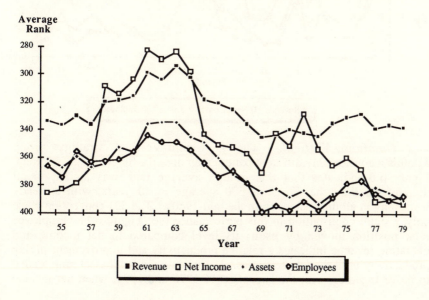

Figure 6.4 shows that net income volatility for the Single Business group was high relative to the other dimensions, and especially so in the last decade when, after spiking from 1967 to 1969, employee volatility followed the pattern of operating revenue and assets.

The information statistics for this group (Table 6.2) indicate that, within the group, rank movements based on operating revenue, assets, and employees were all at approximately one-third of maximum possible uncertainty, while rank changes based on net income position were over two-thirds of the maximum. All are significantly different from a point distribution at the .05 level, and the net income rank shifts are significant at the .001 level. (The entropy statistic is chi-square distributed according to : $X^2 = M(n\text{-}1)H/\ln(M)$ with $n\text{-}1$ degrees of freedom, where M is the number of transitions observed and n is the number of ranks.) Examination of the lower and upper entropy statistics indicates that on all dimensions, shifts to improved positions involved fewer steps than did shifts to worse positions.

Figure 6.4. Single Business Strategy—Volatility

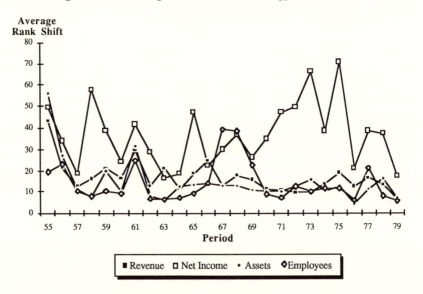

Dominant-Vertical. The Dominant-Vertical strategy group exhibits a considerably different pattern than does the Single Business group. Figure 6.5 indicates that this group's average rank was higher on all dimensions than the *Fortune* 500 average in all years, with a steady worsening in all dimensions from the mid-1960s. The 501 convention made only a small contribution to this performance (see Figure 6.1). Employee rank position moved by itself; its level compared to net income and operating revenue indicates a relative productivity and improvement in that productivity until the late seventies. Net income rank and asset rank tended to move together, with the exception of 1970 and 1971, when net income worsened. Operating revenue rank held the best position with the exception of a few years from 1969 to 1972.

Table 6.2. Information Statistic Comparison: Rumelt's Strategy Categories

	Operating Revenue	NI	Assets	Employees
Single Business (10)				
Total Entropy	0.386+	0.681***	0.367*	0.352*
Lower Entropy	0.124	0.257	0.108	0.110
Diagonal Entropy	0.108	0.142	0.106	0.096
Upper Entropy	0.154	0.282	0.153	0.146
Dominant-Vertical (27)				
Total Entropy	0.384***	0.506***	0.312***	0.337***
Lower Entropy	0.151	0.156	0.115	0.124
Diagonal Entropy	0.092	0.089	0.082	0.085
Upper Entropy	0.141	0.213	0.116	0.128
Dominant-Constrained (10)				
Total Entropy	0.283	0.453**	0.236	0.326
Lower Entropy	0.098	0.156	0.081	0.117
Diagonal Entropy	0.078	0.117	0.074	0.088
Upper Entropy	0.106	0.179	0.081	0.121
Dominant-Linked (7)				
Total Entropy	0.393	0.672***	0.363	0.375
Lower Entropy	0.135	0.240	0.125	0.131
Diagonal Entropy	0.110	0.164	0.108	0.106
Upper Entropy	0.148	0.268	0.129	0.138
Dominant-Unrelated (3)				
Total Entropy	0.153	0.153	0.153	0.102
Lower Entropy	0.039	0.039	0.039	0.039
Diagonal Entropy	0.036	0.036	0.036	0.024
Upper Entropy	0.078	0.078	0.078	0.039
Related-Constrained (33)				
Total Entropy	0.458***	0.514***	0.440***	0.512***
Lower Entropy	0.187	0.205	0.172	0.201
Diagonal Entropy	0.087	0.077	0.089	0.082
Upper Entropy	0.185	0.232	0.178	0.229
Related-Linked (32)				
Total Entropy	0.409***	0.546***	0.406***	0.448***
Lower Entropy	0.161	0.231	0.156	0.175
Diagonal Entropy	0.084	0.078	0.086	0.085
Upper Entropy	0.164	0.238	0.164	0.187
Unrelated-Passive (10)				
Total Entropy	0.424**	0.664***	0.492**	0.510**
Lower Entropy	0.149	0.225	0.158	0.168
Diagonal Entropy	0.116	0.138	0.130	0.127
Upper Entropy	0.164	0.238	0.164	0.187
Acquisitive-Conglomerate (7)				
Total Entropy	0.409	0.648***	.552**	0.393
Lower Entropy	0.129	0.203	0.170	0.129
Diagonal Entropy	1.121	0.168	0.152	0.117
Upper Entropy	0.159	0.276	0.230	0.147

Significance levels (difference from point distribution):

* .05   + .02   ** .01   *** .001

Figure 6.5. Dominant Vertical Strategy—Average Rank Position

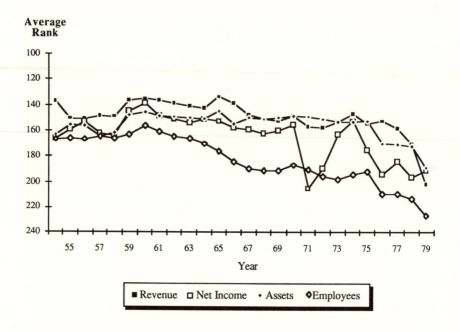

The volatility along the various dimensions is shown in Figure 6.6 The notable thing here is the departure of the net income volatility levels from the other three dimensions after 1969, and the lessening independence of operating revenue in the same period. This is indicative of the increased uncertainty faced by this group in the last decade of the study.

Information statistics for this group (Table 6.2) show that rank shifts based on net income involved about one-half of the possible uncertainty, and thatshifts based on operating revenue were somewhat more uncertain than those based on assets and employees. All are significant at the .001 level. Improving and worsening shifts were about equal in number of steps for all dimensions, except for operating revenue, which had marginally more steps associated with improving position than with worsening.

Figure 6.6.   Dominant Vertical Strategy—Volatility

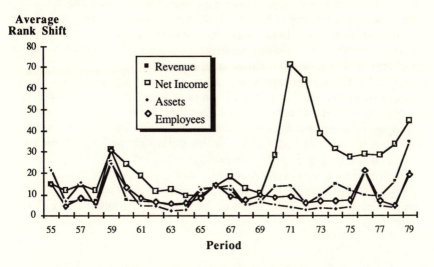

Figure 6.7.   Dominant Constrained Strategy

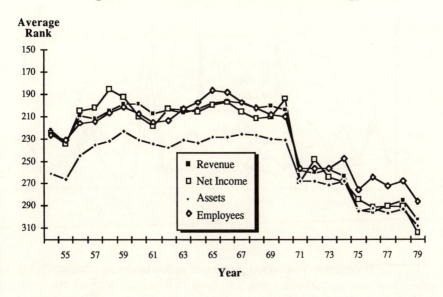

Dominant-Constrained.   The rank performance of the Dominant-Constrained group can be divided into two periods, 1954 to 1970 and 1971 to 1979, as is evident in Figure 6.7. In the first period, operating revenue rank and employee rank tended to move together and to a lesser degree, to move with net income rank. Asset rank was lower, indicating relatively high asset productivity. In this first period the performance of the Dominant-Constrained firms was, on average better than the average *Fortune* 500 firm. The shift in performance from 1970 to 1971 was due in some part to a net of three firms dropping out of the *Fortune* 500 (see Figure 6.1), but was probably due more to a performance shift for the Dominant-Constrained firms. This is supported by the group's average rank behavior in the second period where asset rank moved into agreement and employee rank moved higher indicating a decline in relative employee productivity. Overall performance in this period showed a negative trend and was worse than average for the *Fortune* 500.

Volatility levels were relatively stable at moderate levels for all dimensions until a spike in 1971 as a result of a number of firms in this group exiting the top 500, followed by a lesser departure in 1975 (see Figure 6.8).

Figure 6.8. Dominant Constrained Strategy—Volatility

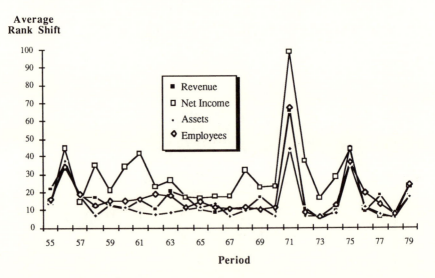

The Dominant-Constrained group had substantially lower uncertainty associated with operating revenue and asset rank shifts than with employee rank shifts, and these in turn were lower in uncertainty than shifts associated with net income. Only the latter shifts are significant and at the .001 level. In all cases upper entropies were nearly equal to lower entropies, indicating an equal number of steps were associated with improvements and worsenings in rank positions.

Dominant-Linked. The Dominant-Linked strategy group exhibited average performance on the dimensions of operating revenue, assets, and employees during the 1960s, coupled with good net income position and relatively poorer performance in the 1950s and 1970s as demonstrated in Figure 6.9. The first three dimensions mentioned above tended to move together, while net income was more variable. The effects of firms leaving the *Fortune* 500 contributed to, but did not explain all of the performance decline in later years. The high net income volatility was accompanied by increased association of rank shift activity on the other dimensions (Figure 6.10), possibly indicating attempts on the part of management to control performance on these dimensions.

Figure 6.9.   Dominant Linked Strategy—Average Rank Position

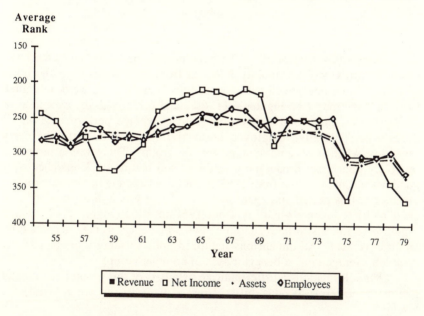

Information statistics for this group (see Table 6.2) are nearly the same as those for the Single Business group, with an equivalent interpretation. However, only the net income statistic is at a significant level.

Figure 6.10. Dominant Linked Strategy—Volatility

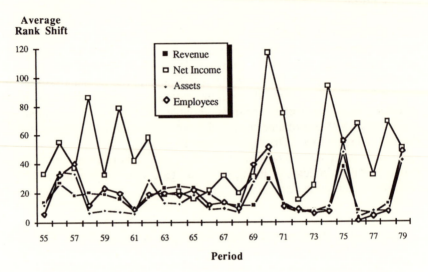

Dominant-Unrelated. The results for the Dominant-Unrelated group of firms, while markedly different from the behaviors of the other groups, must be interpreted with reservations because there were only three firms in this group (see Figures 6.11, 6.12 and 6.13) With the exception of the first year, the group showed better than average performance on all dimensions. Relative employee productivity was good until the early seventies, when it became average for the group. There was a period of relatively poor asset productivity in the period before 1963, matched by a good net income position from 1955 to 1960. Assets and net income moved together in this period and again in 1962. There was a three-year spike in asset and net income volatility from 1961 to 1963 (Figure 6.12), which Figure 6.13 reveals to be made up of two worsenings in rank separated by an improvement. All dimensions stabilized in the ensuing years to a nearly common average rank, a behavior seen in no other group.

The information statistics indicate members of this group had minimal interaction in terms of rank shifts. None of the statistics are at significant levels.

Figure 6.11. Dominant-Unrelated Strategy—Average Rank Position

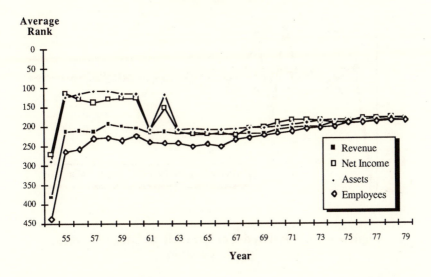

Figure 6.12. Dominant-Unrelated Strategy—Volatility

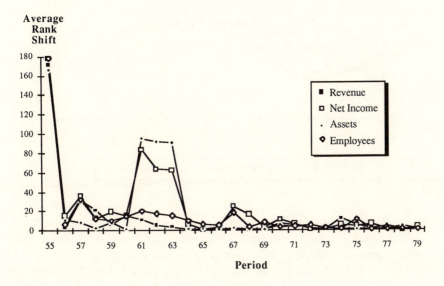

Figure 6.13. Dominant-Unrelated Strategy—Direction

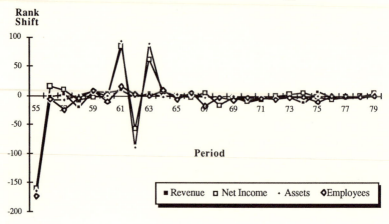

Figure 6.14. Related-Constrained Strategy—Average Rank Position

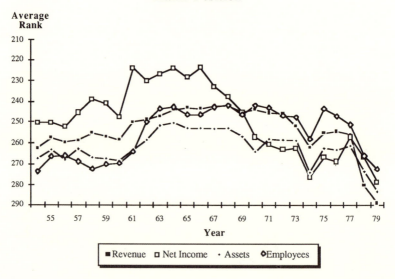

Related-Constrained. The Related-Constrained group behaved in a fashion similar to the Dominant-Linked group. As Figure 6.14 shows, their overall performance improved gradually to better than the *Fortune* 500 average in the early sixties and then gradually worsened until the last two years of the data, when it worsened markedly, due in part to firms leaving the 500 rankings (see Figure 6.1). Net income position for these firms was very good until 1970 when relative productivity on this dimension fell, as did relative performance. Relative employee productivity was good until 1962, but was worse in the post-1973 period. Rank performance on all dimensions tended to move together in the last decade examined.

The volatility of rank shifts for this group showed an overall increase after 1963 with the higher and independent levels of net income volatility common to other groups in the post 1969 period (Figure 6.15).

Figure 6.15. Related-Constrained Strategy—Volatility

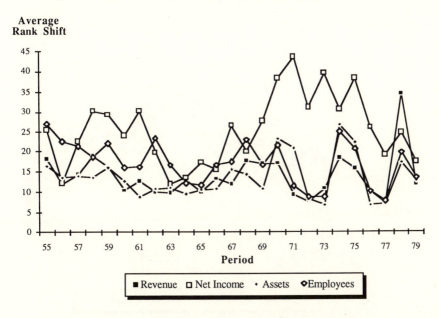

Table 6.2 shows that this group had comparatively high levels of relative uncertainty associated with rank shifts on all dimensions except net income. The uncertainty level associated with ranks shifts for numbers of employees was especially high, indicating this strategy group made more changes in the number of employees than did the other groups. This indicates that staffing was possibly more of a discretionary strategic variable for this group than for the other groups. All statistics are significant at the .001 level.

Related-Linked. The behavior of the Related-Linked strategy firms showed relatively high agreement among ranks of all dimensions, with an accelerating improvement to a better than *Fortune* 500 average position in 1968 (Figure 6.16). Interestingly enough, relatively poor employee productivity was first clearly evidenced in this year. Overall performance declined at a decreasing rate through the end of the study period. The effects of firms entering the 500 rankings contributed to the improvement in earlier years, and to the decline in later years, but most of this behavior was attributable to performance within the 500 rankings.

Figure 6.16. Related-Linked Strategy—Average Rank Position

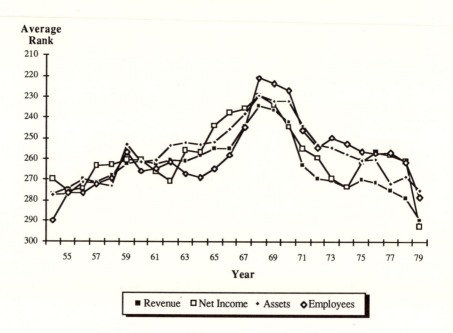

This group had none of the high spikes in volatility associated with the other groups (Figure 6.17), but did show net income moving somewhat independently of the other three dimensions in terms of this measure in the last 10 years. The directional shifts in Figure 6.18 are interesting in that they show that average asset rank movements were greatest in 1959, 1969 and 1977, while employee rank shifts dominated in 1967, 1968, and 1973. Operating revenue showed the greatest average net shift in 1971.

Figure 6.17. Related-Linked Strategy—Volatility

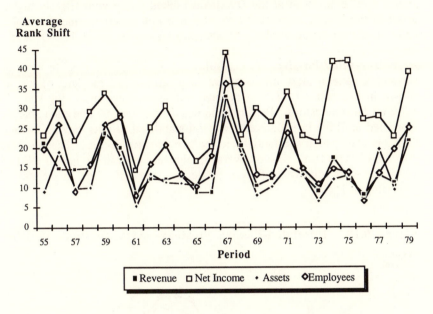

Figure 6.18. Related-Linked Strategy—Direction

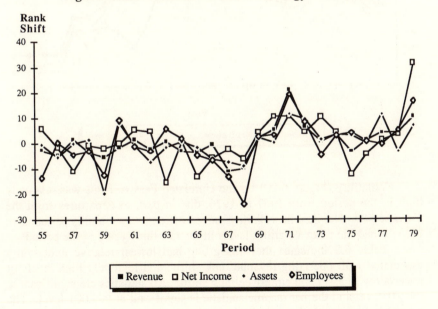

In terms of information statistics, the Related-Linked group had results similar to those of the Dominant-Linked group with slightly higher levels of uncertainty associated with all dimensions except net income, which had a substantially lower level. All statistics are significant at the .001 level.

Unrelated-Passive. Firms following an Unrelated-Passive strategy showed a general slow improvement in position until the late sixties, as shown in Figure 6.19. They exhibited one anomalous improving spurt in 1959 on all dimensions. Performance peaked in 1968-69 and then sharply worsened until the last four years when it stabilized. Firms leaving the 500 rankings contributed substantially to the performance decline. The net asset position of these firms was, on average, relatively poor in the period 1961 to 1975 and poor relative employee productivity was the rule in the period beginning in 1967.

Figure 6.19. Unrelated-Passive Strategy—Average Rank Position

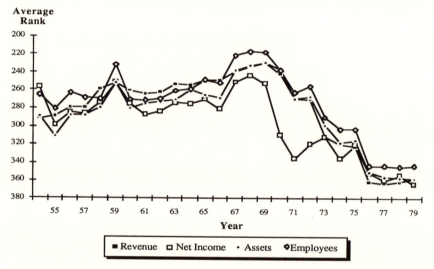

Volatility (Figure 6.20) for the Unrelated-Passive firms was relatively high in the period from 1967 to 1976, due in part, to departures from the *Fortune* 500. Net income volatility moved off on its own in this period also, but rejoined the other volatility levels in the last three years of the period.

Table 6.2 indicates that this group had lowest relative uncertainty associated with operating revenue rank shifts, and relatively high levels of uncertainty in asset and employee rank shifts. All statistics are significant at the .01 level and the net income statistic is significant at the .001 level. The relatively high level of uncertainty associated with asset rank shifts indicates the key role of mergers and acquisitions for this group, the inequality between upper and lower entropies on this dimension implies "lumpy" and uncertain growth patterns.

Figure 6.20. Unrelated-Passive Strategy—Volatility

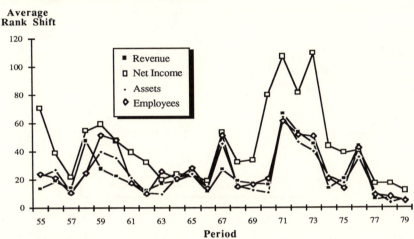

Average Rank Shift

Acquisitive Conglomerates. Figure 6.21 graphs the performance of Acquisitive-Conglomerate firms. All dimensions improved in rank position until 1968, sharply so in the three years leading up to that year, then worsened in position more slowly. The improvement in position was aided by firms entering the 500, but the decline took place largely within those rankings. In almost all periods Acquisitive-Conglomerate firms had unfavorable relative employee productivity and net income positions.

High volatility characterized the Acquisitive-Conglomerate group, especially in the merger and acquisition period, 1966-1969 (Figure 6.22). Also note the strong tie between asset and employee volatilities in the following period.

The information statistics for this group support the key role that mergers and acquisitions played in strategy. Relative uncertainty associated with asset rank shifts was quite high, indicating that, as is common knowledge, this was more of a discretionary strategic variable for Acquisitions-Conglomerates than for any other strategy group. Significance is at the .01 level while significance of net income shifts is at the .001 level. The higher level of upper entropy (compared to lower entropy) associated with asset rank shifts indicates that there were fewer steps in worsening asset rank position than in improving it, that is, for this group, improvements were more uncertain, again in agreement with common knowledge.

Figure 6.21.   Acquisitive-Conglomerate Strategy—Average Rank Position

Figure 6.22.   Acquisitive-Conglomerate Strategy—Volatility

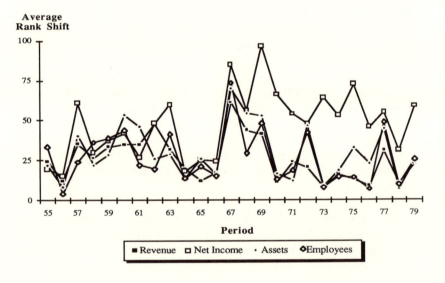

Conclusions. The above analysis clearly shows, in agreement with Rumelt's findings, that firms classified by different strategies had different patterns of performance on both inputs and outputs. To understand the relative position of each strategic group vis a vis the others more clearly, the following section will examine strategic group performance on a dimension-by-dimension basis.

Comparative Analysis by Dimension

Having seen the performance of each strategy group as a whole, we will now break down the analysis on a dimensional basis to permit a comparative analysis. The analysis begins with an overall comparison to establish the context for the dimensional comparisons.

Overall Comparison. The overall performance of firms in the nine strategy groupings on each of the four dimensions of performance is summarized in the table below. These results varied only little when firms not ranked in the *Fortune* 500 in a certain year were dropped from the analysis in that year. The only difference was the relative performance of the Acquisitive-Conglomerate group worsened to the point where it was the eighth best, rather than the sixth best, performer. Note that in Rumelt's construction of his samples, firms were added to the Acquisitive-Conglomerate group to obtain more significance of results, (Rumelt, 1974, p. 89). The results, naturally, varied somewhat on each of the four dimensions; these variations will be explained in the remainder of this section.

Table 6.3. Overall Performance of Groups on All Four Measures

High Performers	Dominant-Vertical
	Dominant-Unrelated
	Dominant-Constrained
Medium performers	Related-Constrained
	Related-Linked
	Dominant-Linked
Low Performers	Unrelated-Passive
	Acquisitive-Conglomerate
	Single-Business

As in the Rumelt study, this set of classifications separates the firms into groups that display significant and consistent differences in economic performance. The striking contrast between the findings of this study and those of Rumelt, however, is in the generally superior rank performance of the firms with dominant business strategies (with the exception of the Dominant-Linked group, which will be examined later) over the firms with related business strategies. The contrast continues in that the performance of the latter group is better than the performance of firms with businesses which were totally unrelated or of firms that had a single business orientation.   Rumelt's finding that Dominant-Constrained and Related-Constrained groups outperformed others led him to conclude that performance was more linked to diversification strategies which limited business scope than to the actual amount of diversification. The findings from this study challenge that conclusion. The data here show that of those firms that diversified, those with higher specialization ratios generally maintained better rank positions than did firms with lower specialization ratios.   This suggests that the *amount* of diversification was a more important factor in determining corporate performance than Rumelt concluded.

Net Income. The average rankings on net income provide the results that are most directly comparable to Rumelt's financial performance variables. The three variables he used that were most strongly related to diversification were price-earnings ratio, return on equity (ROE)—net income less preferred dividends divided by book equity,—and return on capital (ROE)—net income plus interest divided by invested capital. While the average ranking according to net income is not the same variable as ROC or ROE, it is an accepted and useful measure of financial performance. Thus the findings from net income analysis receive the most attention in this chapter.

As can be seen in Figures 6.23 and 6.24, the Dominant-Vertical group maintained the highest net income ranking and did so with the most stability, over the 26-year period. Because the Dominant-Unrelated group had only three firms in it, one of which was Ford Motor Company which went public in 1955 and jumped to a net income rank of 3, no substantial results can be drawn from this group's performance. The Dominant-Constrained group performed well, with average rankings of 225 in 1954 to 303 in 1979, although their performance was surpassed by the Dominant-Vertical group in every year.

The Related-Constrained and Related-Linked groups were clearly medium-level performers, however, they achieved more stability than any of the other groups. The Dominant-Linked group which was also a medium performer on net income, experienced much more volatile shifts in rankings than either the Related-Constrained or Related-Linked groups. Performance of the Dominant-Linked group was better than average from 1963 to 1969 for either of the Related groups, but outside of that period it was worse—even worse in a couple of years than were the performances of the unrelated groups. One observation that helps explain the relatively poor performance of the Dominant-Linked group is the substantial number of firms whose ranking shifted to 501, as mentioned previously.

Figure 6.23.   Net Income Position by Strategy Groups—Rumelt's First Five Groups

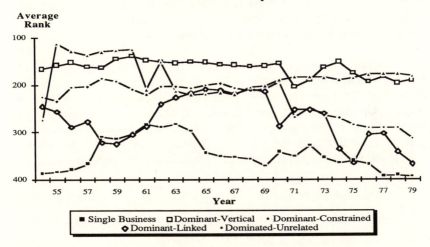

Figure 6.24.   Net Income Position by Strategy Groups—Rumelt's Last Four Groups

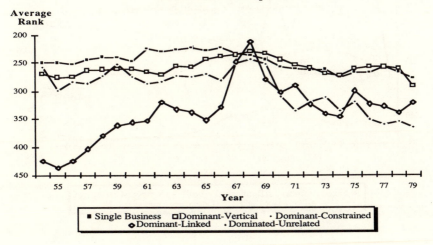

The Unrelated-Passive and Acquisitive-Conglomerate groups showed lower average rankings over the 26-year period than any of the other groups besides Single Business. The heightened merger and acquisition activity of the late 1960s was clearly evident in the sharp peak in the performance of the Acquisitive-Conglomerate in 1969, which quickly tailed off in subsequent years.

The performance of the Single-Business group was rather dismal compared to the other groups, and is dramatically displayed in Figure 6.23. In the case of Single Business firms, the low average rankings are truly reflective of low individual firm rankings rather than being due to a large number of firms having been assigned a rank of 501.

Assets. The average ranks on assets for the nine groups were similar to those obtained on net income in that, again, the Dominant-Vertical group showed the best and most consistent average rank (see Figures 6.25 and 6.26). Up through the late sixties, the Dominant-Constrained group outranked the Related groups while the Dominant-Linked group ranked as well as or better than the Related subgroups. In 1970, however, both Dominant groups began to trail the two Related groups in average asset rank.

Figure 6.25. Asset Position by Strategy Groups—Rumelt's First Five Groups

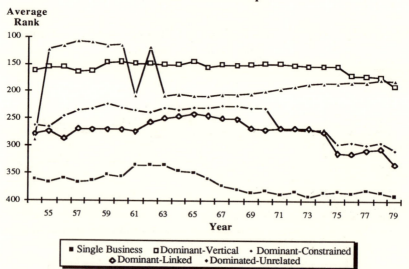

■ Single Business   □ Dominant-Vertical   • Dominant-Constrained
◊ Dominant-Linked   ♦ Dominated-Unrelated

Figure 6.26. Asset Position by Strategy Groups—Rumelt's Last Four Groups

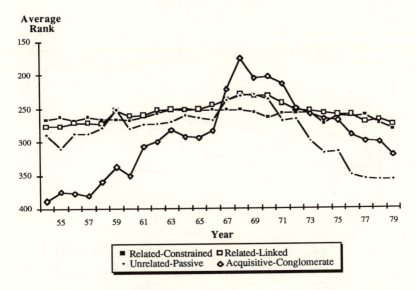

As in the net income analysis, the Related groups generally performed behind the Dominant groups, while the unrelated groups followed behind the related groups. Again, the peak in performance of the Acquisitive-Conglomerate group was in 1969, consistent with the heavy merger and acquisition activity of that time. As in the previous analysis, the Single Business group ranked worse than any of the other groups.

Revenues. Analysis along the revenue dimension indicates quite clearly the same story revealed in the last two analyses: the Dominant-Vertical, Dominant-Constrained, and Dominant-Unrelated groups maintained better average rankings than the other groups (see Figures 6.27 and 6.28). Again, the stability of the Dominant-Vertical groups was impressive.

The Related groups achieved rankings on revenues similar to those on net income and assets; however, the behavior of the Dominant-Linked and Unrelated-Passive groups on this dimension were somewhat different. The Dominant-Linked group generally performed slightly worse than the related group, and the Unrelated-Passive group, while being a low-level performer on assets and net income dimensions, was, at least for a few years, a medium performer on operating revenues. The behavior of the Acquisitive-Conglomerate and the Single Business groups with regard to operating revenues was very similar to the two group's behaviors in the preceding analyses.

Figure 6.27.   Revenue Position by Strategy Groups—Rumelt's First Five Groups

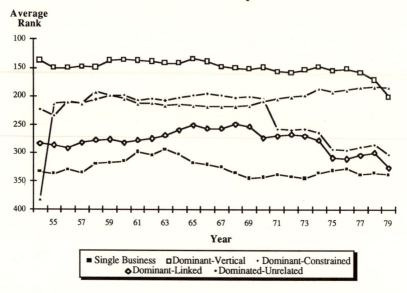

Figure 6.28.   Revenue Position by Strategy Groups—Rumelt's Last Four Groups

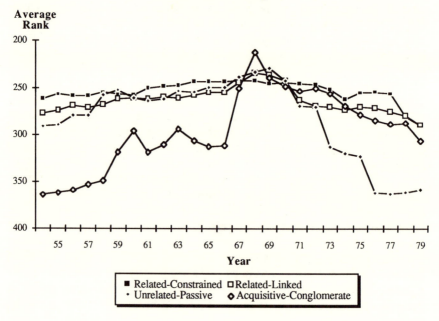

Employees. The analysis of the rankings in terms of number of employees is interesting in that it did not provide the separation of the groups into distinct and consistent behavioral patterns that occurred in the analyses of the financial variables. In some ways the behaviors of the groups appeared quite similar. With the exception of the Dominant-Vertical and Dominant-Constrained groups, many of the groups hovered consistently around a ranking of approximately 250. The peak in the employment rankings of the Acquisitive-Conglomerate group was again noticeable in this analysis, although not as sharp as on other dimensions. The performance of the Single Business group was consistent in that it received the worst average rank, although in this case that was to the good of the group. since it means that the group members were producing output with relatively fewer employees than were the other groups.

A low average rank *number* (better position) for number of employees indicates that the firm or groups of firms retained relatively more employees than did firms with higher rank *numbers* (worse positions). One might hypothesize that a firm ranking favorably on net income might have been further down the list for the number of employees, indicating an efficient use of human resources. This was not the case for the Dominant-Vertical group which had the best ranking on net income. As indicated in Figures 6.29 and 6.30 the Dominant-Vertical group had the highest (best) ranking on employees as well, suggesting a corporate strategy yielding high returns to both capital and labor. Similarly the Single Business group, which ranked lowest on net income, also ranked lowest on number of employees. The analysis of rankings by number of employees warrants further attention in that it raises some interesting questions regarding human resource strategy aside from diversification. The analysis thus far suggests that a labor-intensive strategy seems to follow financial performance, in that improved financial positions were followed in time by a relative increase in number of employees.

Comparison of Strategy Results to Rumelt Study. The findings related to diversification strategy in this study support some of Rumelt's earlier findings but challenge others. Table 6.4 presents a comparison between the results of this analysis and Rumelt's results in terms of the rankings of strategy groups by their economic performance.

Figure 6.29.   Employee Position by Strategy Groups—Rumelt's First Five Groups

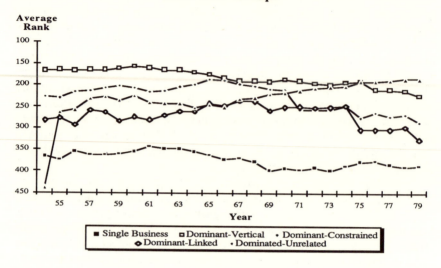

Figure 6.30.   Employee Position by Strategy Groups—Rumelt's Last Four Groups

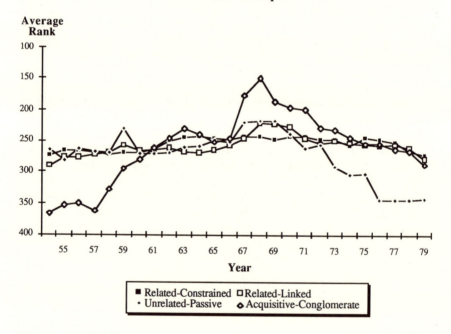

Table 6.4. Comparison of Rankings by Economic Performance

Category	Rumelt	Present Study only in 500	all firms
Single Business	4	9	9
Dominant-Vertical	6	1	1
Dominant-Constrained	1	3	3
Dominant-Linked	-	6	6
Dominant-Unrelated	-	2	2
Related-Constrained	2	4	4
Related-Linked	3	5	5
Unrelated-Passive	7	7	7
Acquisitive-Conglomerate	5	8	8

As the above table shows, there is considerable disagreement between Rumelt's rankings of the strategic groups by performance and the rankings generated by ordinal time series analysis. Specifically, if the agreement between sets of rankings is measured by Spearman's rho, then Rumelt's rankings and the rankings in this study (less the two groups not considered by Rumelt) yield a rho of 0.25, indicating that there is some relationship between Rumelt's results and our results, but not enough to reject the null hypothesis.

Based on the above analysis, a comparison of the major findings is offered in Table 6.5. As a major point of agreement with Rumelt, we find that diversification strategies tend to separate groups of firms into recognizable and consistent patterns of economic performance.

In terms of overall performance positions of particular strategy groups, we support Rumelt's finding that the Dominant-Constrained group was a high performer, and that the unrelated groups were generally low performers. We also support his finding that the Related-Constrained group outperforms the Related-Linked group, and that the Dominant-Constrained group outperforms the Dominant-Linked group. His conclusion that successful firms diversified with a strategy of "sticking close to business at home" is generally supported by this study.

Just as we strongly support the above findings and conclusions, we also have reason to challenge some of Rumelt's other results. Our findings raise serious questions about his overall conclusion, that economic performance was more related to the way in which firms diversified (i.e., constrained versus linked) than to how much a firm diversified. Our findings suggest it is the *amount* of diversification that was critical; those firms that diversified only modestly in amount performed better than or, in one case as well as, those firms that diversified to a greater extent. Secondly, the superior performance of the Dominant-Vertical group in our analysis was strikingly different from Rumelt's characterization of them as the low performer. At a minimum, our findings suggest rethinking the conclusions Rumelt drew about vertically integrated firms, their unique entry and exit barriers, and the overall strength of vertical integration as a corporate strategy.

Table 6.5. Comparison of Major Strategy Findings

Rumelt

1. Dominant-Constrained and Related-Constrained were best performers.
2. Dominant-Vertical and Unrelated-Passive were lowest performers.
3. Among dominant firms, Dominant-Vertical were low performers and Dominant-Constrained were high performers.
4. Among Related firms, Related-Constrained were high and Related-Lined were low.
5. Among Unrelated firms, Unrelated-Passive were lowest performers.
6. Performance differences among strategic categories were linked more to the way a firm diversified than to overall diversity.

Present Study

1. Dominant-Constrained, Dominant-Vertical, and Dominant-Unrelated were best performers.
2. Unrelated-Passive, Acquisitive-Conglomerate, and Single Business were lowest performers.
3. Among Dominant firms, Dominant-Linked were low performers and Dominant-Vertical were high.
4. Among Related firms, Relative-Constrained were high and Related-Linked were low.
5. Among unrelated firms, Acquisitive-Conglomerate were lowest.
6. Performance differences among categories were linked more to overall diversification than to the way a firm diversified.

The third conclusion we draw that differs somewhat from Rumelt, is that neither extreme of the diversification strategy (Single Business versus unrelated diversification) appeared to be associated with high economic performance. This conclusion is based on the relatively low performance of the Single Business group on one hand, and of the Unrelated-Passive and Acquisitive-Conglomerate groups on the other. Thus, from a normative standpoint we suggest that a strategy involving some modest constrained *or* linked diversification appeared to be more successful financially than either a Single Business focus or a completely unrelated broad product orientation.

STRUCTURE FINDINGS

The sample of 239 firms was also analyzed by Rumelt's organization structure categories. Because the firms were examined over the full 26-year period, the problem of firms entering and leaving the *Fortune* 500 was again present. Figure 6.31 charts this behavior for these classifications, and shows that the bulk of the changes are absorbed in the category of miscellaneous structures (which is not analyzed here) and in the Product Structure category. If only firms in the top 500 are considered, the relative performance of this group improved in the early and late part of the period studied but, again, the results of the analysis were not changed.

As with the analysis of the results based on the strategy categories for the structure analysis, we will present first the results analysis by type of structure examined along the four performance dimensions, and then present the analysis on a comparative dimension-by-dimension basis.

Figure 6.31. Cumulative Change in Number of Firms in the 500—Rumelt's Structure Categories

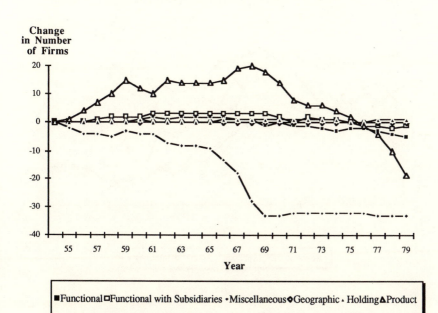

By Structure Type

Functional. Functional structure firms showed poorer than average performance on all dimensions for all but three years on operating revenue (see Figure 6.32). These firms generally showed a worsening trend over the period of analysis; the association among the four dimensions was weak. In the period following 1959, these firms had relatively high average employee productivity.

The information statistics in Table 6.6 indicate that firms with Functional Structures had levels of uncertainty associated with relative rank shifts (see chapter 3) which one would expect. That is, net income shifts had the highest uncertainty, operating revenue came next, followed by assets and employees. The higher levels of uncertainty indicated by the upper entropy measures as compared to the lower entropy measures, indicate the greater number of steps associated with firms in this group that declined in rank.

Figure 6.32. Average Rank Position—Functional Structure

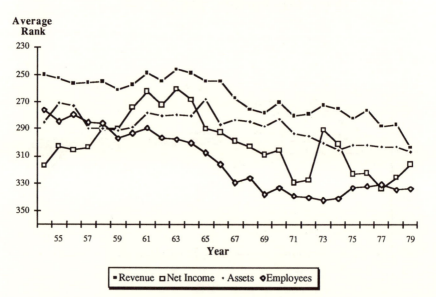

Table 6.6. Information Statistic Comparison: Rumelt's Structure Categories, 1954-1979

	Operating Revenue	NI	Assets	Employees
Product Structure (102)				
Total Entropy	0.479***	0.542***	0.477	0.490***
Lower Entropy	0.213	0.255	0.204	0.207
Diagonal Entropy	0.050	0.034	0.048	0.042
Upper Entropy	0.217	0.253	0.226	0.240
Functional Structure (15)				
Total Entropy	0.465***	0.561***	0.358**	0.351**
Lower Entropy	0.164	0.203	0.115	0.120
Diagonal Entropy	0.116	0.110	0.100	0.095
Upper Entropy	0.184	0.247	0.143	0.135
Functional with Subsidiaries (15)				
Total Entropy	0.277*	0.360**	0.260	0.324**
Lower Entropy	0.100	0.122	0.085	0.112
Diagonal Entropy	0.074	0.095	0.074	0.090
Upper Entropy	0.103	0.143	0.101	0.122
Geographic Structure (4)				
Total Entropy	0.243	0.199	0.000	0.000
Lower Entropy	0.066	0.062	0.000	0.000
Diagonal Entropy	0.111	0.075	0.000	0.000
Upper Entropy	0.066	0.062	0.000	0.000

Holding Company—Not enough firms to generate statistics.
Significance levels (difference from point distribution):   * .05   + .02   ** .01   *** .001

Functional with Subsidiaries. Figure 6.33 shows that except for the last five years of analysis, Functional with Subsidiaries firms performed near to or better than the *Fortune* 500 average. They generally showed a good employee and asset position and a good net income position from 1957 on. Performance dimensions were more tightly associated with each other than was the case for functionally structured organizations.

The information statistics associated with this group showed lower levels of uncertainty than those for the other structure groups, indicating a relative amount of within group stability. Surprisingly, the second highest relative uncertainty level for this group was associated with shifts in numbers of employees, implying there was less stability here than there was for operating revenue or asset positions.

Figure 6.33. Average Rank Position—Functional with Subsidiaries Structure

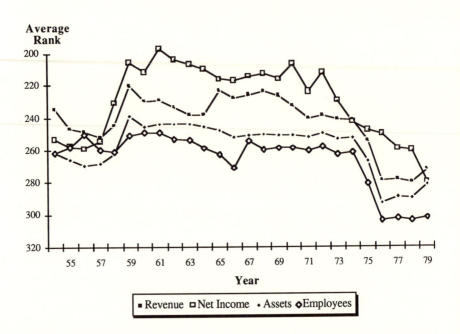

Product Division. Product-Division structured firms showed a highly associated set of dimensions which improved in position until 1968, when a steadily worsening trend set in (see Figure 6.34). This latter trend was preceded by one year by an adverse relative employee productivity position. These firms showed a better than average performance overall for the period 1958 to 1974. From 1971 on, these firms had an adverse net income position.

The information statistics for this group (Table 6.6) show that the largest uncertainty in rank shifts was associated with net income shifts. This is as expected, but as in the Functional with Subsidiary group, the next highest uncertainty level, nearly 50% of maximum possible uncertainty, was associated with shifts in the relative number of employees. From this we can conclude that relative employee levels were quite volatile for this group of firms. The statistics for operating revenue and asset rank shifts were nearly equal and relatively high, suggesting that relative growth within the group of firms with a Product Division structure was substantial on all dimensions.

Figure 6.34.   Average Rank Position—Product/Division Structure

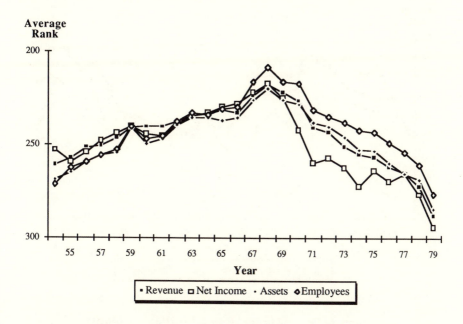

Geographic Division.   There were only three firms in the Geographic Division structure group, so the results shown in Figure 6.35 are hard to generalize. The data do show that those firms performed better than the *Fortune* 500 on all counts. They had a favorable relative asset productivity position for the whole period, but had poor employee relative productivity position from 1962 to 1965 and from 1974 on.   The information statistics for this group indicate that the firms were stable relative to each other on asset and employee dimensions and were most volatile with respect to operating revenue.

Holding Company.   Firms with a Holding Company structure showed poor asset and employee relative productivity position in the period from 1960 to 1974 (Figure 6.36). In all periods, these firms showed output performance poorer than the *Fortune* 500 average. There were not enough firms in each year of the sample to compute information statistics.

Figure 6.35. Average Rank Position—Geographic Structure

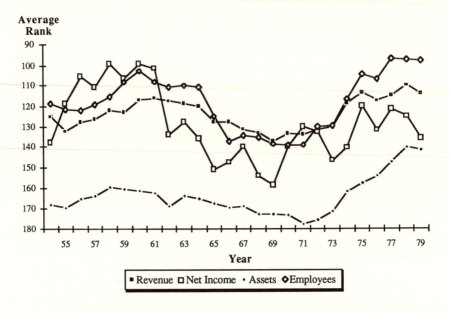

Figure 6.36. Average Rank Position—Holding Company Structure

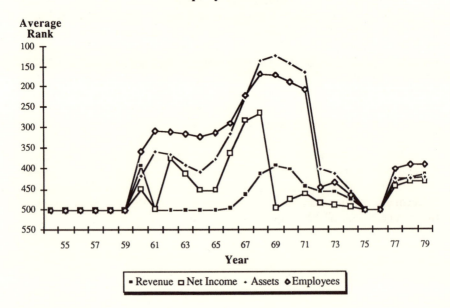

Comparative Analysis by Dimension

We will now turn to an aggregate analysis of the groups of firms classified by organizational structure. The structure groups will be compared on each of the four dimensions.

The striking finding when reviewing the results of the analysis of economic performance for structural types was the relative stability of the average ranking of all the types except the Holding Company. As indicated in Figures 6.37, 6.38, 6.39, and 6.40, average rank patterns for the Functional, Functional with Subsidiaries, Product Division, and Geographic Division groups were almost the same in 1979 as they had been in 1954. It should be noted, however, that the classifications of Geographic Division and Holding Company had so few companies in them that few reliable conclusions can be drawn for these groups. One does see though, in spite of the small subsample size, the volatility of the Holding Company group and the same peak in 1967-1969 for this group as was evidenced by the Acquisitive-Conglomerate strategy group.

Figure 6.37. Net Income Position by Structure Groups— Rumelt's Five Groups

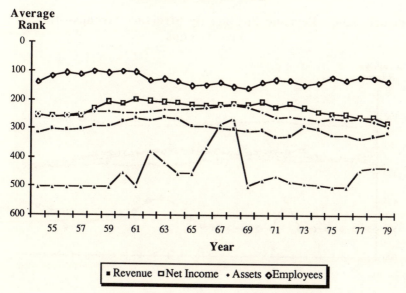

**Figure 6.38. Asset Position by Structure Groups—Rumelts
Five Groups**

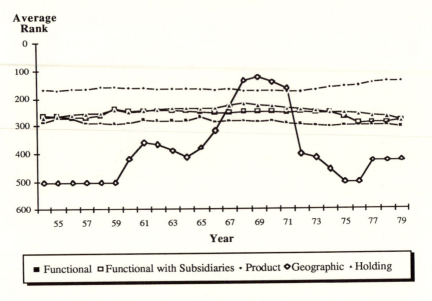

■ Functional □ Functional with Subsidiaries ♦ Product ◇Geographic ▴ Holding

**Figure 6.39. Revenue Position by Structure Groups—Rumelt's
Five Groups**

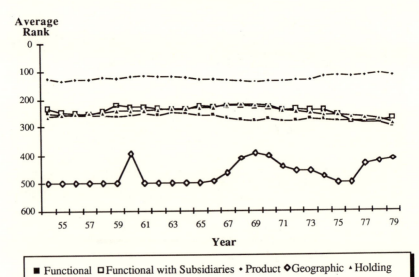

■ Functional □ Functional with Subsidiaries ♦ Product ◇Geographic ▴ Holding

Figure 6.40. Employee Position by Structure Groups—Rumelt's Five Groups

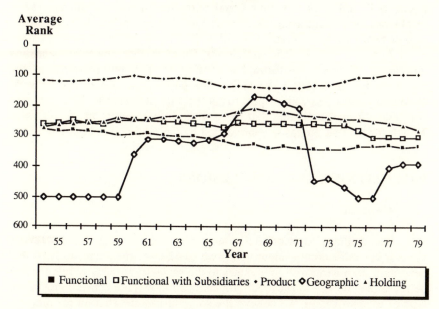

Excluding the Geographic Division and Holding Company groups from the analysis, we observe that the Product Division and Functional with Subsidiaries types of structures generally outperformed the Functional structure group for all financial variables. The Functional structure group trailed behind these other two categories except from 1954 to 1957, which may be a reflection of the last years of the pervasiveness of the U-form organization. It is also interesting to note that the performances of the Product Division and Functional with Subsidiaries groups were very similar, overlapping in some years for all categories except number of employees. In some years the Functional with Subsidiaries group even surpassed the Product Division group, and with respect to number of employees, the analysis indicates that Functional with Subsidiary firms used relatively fewer employees than did Product Division firms. Thus, according to this analysis, little performance difference is evident between these two approaches to structuring the organization. During the years in which a difference was observed, it tended to favor the Functional with Subsidiaries group. This contrasts with Rumelt's finding that Product Division firms were clearly superior.

The somewhat higher average ranking on number of employees for the Product Division compared to the Functional with Subsidiaries and for the Functional with Subsidiaries compared to the Functional group, suggests that there was some relation between a labor-intensive staffing strategy and economic performance. However, this may be true only up to a point since Figure 6.37 indicates that Functional with Subsidiaries group had fewer employees on average than the Product Division group, yet it performed as well or better on net income.

Rumelt's other major structure finding, that the two types of functional structures performed according to different patterns, is not supported by our results. The major rank performance difference between these two groups was with respect to net income, and here the difference was not great. Rumelt's finding that there were differences in the rate of sales growth for the two groups is contradicted by the evidence in Figure 6.39.

IMPLICATIONS AND CONCLUSIONS

General

The findings from ordinal time series analysis suggest the strategic issue of diversification is about which we still know little about, and one that benefits from a variety of approaches to the same set of data. While Rumelt believed that the key to successful diversification was the constraining of the *type* of diversification, we believe the solution is somewhat more complex. Although there appears to be a relationship within the large strategy categories between constrained diversification and economic performance, we see a pattern of higher performance among those firms limiting the amount as well as the type of diversification. To a corporate strategist we can offer the following somewhat ambiguous guideline for consideration: some diversification of any kind is better than none, but a lot of any kind is too much. The key to financial performance seems to be in determining the definition of "some," both in type and amount.

A second major implication from our analysis has to do with the way businesses organize to deliver their products and services. There may be important benefits from the U-form (functional) organization that can be incorporated into a product division structure and will enhance the usefulness of the latter structure. Our finding that the Functional with Subsidiaries group performed as well as or better than the strict Product Division organization makes us reluctant to disregard completely the benefits of organizing by function.

A preliminary assessment of the ordinal time series analysis suggests that our findings differed from Rumelt's for a number of reasons. First, Rumelt's study was biased toward longevity within strategy classifications in that he did not include the entire sample of 246 firms in his financial performance analysis. Only firms that had been in a category for at least 10 years were included in his subsample. Our review of his data indicates that up to 37% of his sample firms were not included in his financial analysis, while all of the 239 firms were included in this analysis. The difference in the data set may explain some of the difference in findings.

Rather than use annual observations for his elementary data points in his financial analysis, Rumelt used decade averages, which were then combined to form a category average. The use of analysis of variance and corrections for time trends produced an estimated mean value of the financial variables for each category. While we do not question the accuracy of Rumelt's statistics, we suggest that his methodology resulted in a set of figures that excluded observation of most long-term trends. The use of one number to represent the activity of a strategy group over 10 years is likely to represent inadequately the year-to-year activity of the group.

Perhaps the primary reason for the differences in findings may have to do with the fact that we used different, and ordinal, financial variables in our study than did Rumelt. The variables we used are accepted indicators of financial performance, and although they are not the same as the ones employed by Rumelt we still believe the results of this study warrant attention. If the selection of differing, but accepted, measures of financial performance suggest alternative strategic approaches to diversification than those recommended by Rumelt and ensuing studies, then the case for the relation of strategy to economic performance has been reopened.

The fact that diversification activity among firms continues to grow, and that strategies of moving into unrelated business areas still have great appeal for numerous corporate strategists, places a premium on empirical knowledge of diversification activity. This continued diversification activity, when viewed in light of Rumelt's finding that related diversification is better than unrelated diversification, and that constrained diversification is the key to economic success, caused us to reconsider Rumelt's study. Through the use of ordinal time series analysis, and using well-accepted data, we have shown that many of Rumelt's findings hold up, but we have also raised serious questions about some of his conclusions. The strategic decision of whether to diversity or not, and how, appears to be more complex than is captured by Rumelt's notion of keeping the businesses similar, or by the notion of specifying a certain amount of diversification.

7

Strategic Product Analysis in Fragmented Industries

Carol Clettenberg
Timothy W. Ruefli

Product strategy is an important part of the overall corporate development decision making process in most industries, but is especially critical in industries that are fragmented in structure—particularly when rapidly changing technologies are involved. Porter (1980) has characterized fragmented industries and has discussed many aspects of competitive strategy in those industries. By his definition, fragmented industries are those in which "no firm has a significant market share and can strongly influence the industry outcome. Usually fragmented industries are populated by a large number of small- and medium-sized companies, many of them privately held" (p. 191). By this definition there are a number of fragmented industries in the U.S. economy (for example, computer software, biotechnology, and industrial robotics)—and many of these are important sources of current and future economic growth. Strategic competitive product evaluation and planning is especially critical in these industries. As Porter indicates. "Although coping with new products is a difficult problem in all industries, it seems especially difficult in fragmented businesses" (p. 212)

Meyer and Roberts (1986), in discussing new product strategy in small high-technology firms, point out that the literature in the area "lacks both conceptual modeling and methods for empirical testing" (p. 806.). A literature review by the authors supports this conclusion. In this chapter we will examine the role that ordinal time series methods can play in strategic product analysis. We will show that ordinal analysis can be used to overcome some of the problems plaguing product analysis in turbulent environments. Our discussion will be framed in the context of fragmented industries, but extending the application of the techniques to other industry contexts is also relevant. After a brief review of existing product analysis techniques, the data requirements and methodological adaptations of the ordinal techniques will be treated. The use of ordinal time series analysis in product evaluation will be demonstrated by an application of the technique to a segment of the domestic computer software industry.

LITERATURE REVIEW

A number of conceptual and analytic techniques for strategic product planning and evaluation within mature industries have appeared in the literature over the past three decades. These include product evaluation matrix methods (Wind and Claycamp, 1976); market share (Wind, 1981); product positioning (Wind and Robinson, 1972); brand-switching matrices, regression analysis (Yoon and Lillien, 1985); Product Beta (Rabino and Wright, 1985); the analytic hierarchy process (Wind and Saaty, 1985); business profiles (Wright, 1978); and risk-return analysis (Wind, 1974). All of these methods require that time series of data be gathered and analyzed to provide information required to make strategic decisions about existing and proposed products.

There is not room here for an exhaustive review of all the techniques for product analysis and evaluation; we will, however, discuss one analytic methodology that relies on time series data for its applicability—the product life cycle (PLC) model. The issues and considerations raised in regard to the product life cycle model will apply, by extension to the other time series-based models.

Originating at Arthur D. Little in the 1950s, the product life cycle as a framework for product strategy has been espoused by a number of researchers, including Levitt (1965), Kotler (1965), and Day (1981). To employ this technique it is necessary for a firm to acquire relatively accurate information about the competing products in terms of their historical sales volume and to track the profit contribution of the firm's own product. The dollar values may need to be adjusted for changes in the value of the dollar over time. "Clean" information is important in the product life cycle model, because identifying the transition from one stage of the PLC to the next is a critical part of this technique. Hayes and Wheelwright (1979a, 1979b) extend the concept of product life cycle to include the process life cycle as a related dimension. Tellis and Crawford (1981) criticize the assumptions underlying the PLC model and propose a product evolutionary cycle instead. Day (1981), following Wind (1981), raises a series of questions regarding the sensitivity of the technique to measurement:

Should one use unit volume, current or constant dollar total revenue, or per capita consumption to measure sales? What adjustments should be made to eliminate the effects of economic conditions?

Further complicating the identification of boundaries is the variety of possible life cycle patterns. This makes it unlikely that a product's position in its life cycle can be established simply by observing changes in the past sales pattern. The implications of the difference between a temporary or even an extended pause in sales growth versus a true topping out of growth are profound. [Thus one cannot avoid forecasting the future sales path of the product if sensible judgments about the present life cycle position are to be made.] (p. 64)

Similar comments can be made about most of the other strategic product evaluation models. Even a cursory examination of the vast majority of product planning and evaluation techniques indicates that effective use of these methodologies requires extensive and relatively clean data. Without exception, the quantitative models employ cardinal or ratio data as their inputs, and thus are subject to many of the problems associated with cardinal data outlined in chapters 1 and 2. In consonance with the theme of this book, the rest of this chapter will discuss the use of ordinal time series analysis in strategic product evaluation and planning. The next section discusses modifications to be made to the ordinal methodology developed for analyzing industries and corporations to make it applicable to products.

DATA AND METHODOLOGY CONSIDERATIONS

In previous chapters, the assumption has been made that the entities to be evaluated by the ordinal methodologies were firms or groups of firms, and that the data were firm-oriented. The first step in applying ordinal time series analysis to product analysis is to recognize that products can be used analogously to firms as elements of analysis. Data for strategic product analysis employing ordinal time series analysis are therefore product-oriented data. These data are usually acquired in cardinal form, although in the example in the latter part of this chapter, consisting of periodic product rankings in a trade publication, the data were already in ordinal form. Cardinal data for product analysis include dollar sales volumes, contribution margins, physical sales volume, and prices. Further information in terms of product type, manufacturer, market segment, and technology is required to classify the products into groups for the analysis. Given that the data are in cardinal form, they must be transformed into rankings as outlined in chapter 2. It is this step that makes ordinal time series analysis particularly appropriate for product analysis in fragmented industries. Data from fragmented industries, especially emerging fragmented industries, are likely to be "dirty," because most of the firms are small, many are private, industry standards are lacking, and third-party data collection activities are not likely to be well-organized.

One key difference between analysis of firms and analysis of products is that product analysis is usually undertaken using shorter time intervals than the standard one-year interval employed in industry analysis. For product analysis, weekly, monthly, or bimonthly intervals should be considered.

When a time series of rankings of products has been developed along one or more dimensions, the statistics developed in chapters 2 and 3 can be generated. The position statistic indicates the relative performance level of a product or group of products *vis a vis* the other product groups at each point in time. The volatility statistic maintains an interpretation analogous to that given in chapter 2 in that it gives a measure of the turbulence in the market in terms of the average number of rank shifts from one period to the next. The direction statistic can be applied to pairs of products or to product groups to develop a measure of association over time indicating the degree of competition, complementarity, or independence of the products.

Further input to the strategic product planning process can be provided by generating information statistics, as described in chapter 3, which provide measures of uncertainty associated with products or product groups. A history of ordinal data on a set of products in a market can be used to generate a rank transition matrix over a period of time. As was the case for industry analysis, the transition matrix for products may yield important information. A block-diagonal structure would indicate a segmentation of the market into product groups, whereas a widely dispersed set of nonzero values in a matrix would indicate a relatively unstable market, as compared to a market represented by a matrix with nonzero entries clustered close to the main diagonal. Statistics that quantify these structures can be computed using the variant of the entropy measure proposed in chapter 3.

The total information statistic for a set of products measures the fraction of total possible uncertainty exhibited by that set of products over a period of time. On an aggregated basis, this statistic is similar to product Beta introduced by Rabino and Wright (1985). The advantage of the information statistic over point statistics such as Beta is that the information statistic can be decomposed into uncertainties associated with increases, maintenance, and decreases in position, because it is log-linear. The ordinal information statistic presented here measures uncertainty for the whole group of products on a relative basis, while product Beta provides a measure for individual products.

The upper, diagonal, and lower information statistics that comprise the total information statistic, as described in chapter 3, show patterns of product introduction, acceptance, and decline. For example, a group of products with the lower entropy considerably larger than the upper entropy will have exhibited behavior in which the average entity gradually improved its rank position through many steps until it experienced a rapid worsening in rank. This type of behavior would be exhibited by products in a market where products with improved technological characteristics were introduced and gradually displaced existing products while the products with the oldest technology were discontinued.

On the other hand, where the subentropies for a group of products are such that the upper entropy is much greater than lower entropy, this indicates that the average product jumped to the top of the rankings and gradually worsened in position. This behavior over time is graphed in figure 3.2 in chapter 3. An example of this type of behavior would be exhibited by products in a market characterized by a fad or fashion element, in which new products quickly captured the attention of consumers and then gradually declined in popularity as newer fad products were introduced. These are extremes of behavior; more frequently encountered situations have upper entropy nearly equal to lower entropy indicating a process that behaves more symmetrically as depicted in Figure 3.3 in chapter 3. The subentropies can be interpreted as an expectation of the average behavior of firms in an industry or industry subgroup in terms of improvement, maintenance, and worsening in rank.

The claimed advantages of the ordinal method in the analysis of firms and industries can be made with even greater force with respect to analysis of products. The relative insensitivity of the methodology to "dirty" data is especially important when dealing with products. Frequently a product analyst must work with data as soon as it is released, without waiting for revisions and corrections. The response cycle for product planning is usually much shorter than for firm level analysis. The ability of ordinal techniques to move from one level of a hierarchy to another means that an analyst can make evaluations at the levels of: (1) individual products, (2) product lines, (3) product groups, and (4) the entire market. Alternatively, the data can be regrouped and analyzed at the levels of local markets, regional markets, national markets, and global markets. Ordinal techniques are generally lower in cost than cardinal techniques—their data requirements are less precise because the need to check assumptions underlying the data treatments are less stringent than in the usual cardinal analysis, (see, e.g., Daniel, 1978, p. 16).

SOFTWARE EXAMPLE

The microcomputer software industry is a dynamic, fast-paced environment. In 1983 and 1984, the growth rate for this industry was impressive. Many small entrepreneurial software companies sprang up, offering exciting new products. Some products, such as Lotus 1-2-3, were able to sustain enormous popularity, others had a brief period of popularity and then slowly faded into obscurity, while still others never emerged from obscurity. Thus this industry provides an excellent example for the use of ordinal time series analysis. This chapter undertakes a strategic analysis of the microcomputer software products from 1983 to 1984.

DATA

The *Softsel Hotlist,* a weekly publication, has been used by many in the last few years to monitor the popularity of microcomputer software products. This list is produced by Softsel Computer Products, Inc., the world's largest distributor of software for personal computers (PC's). They stock over 5,000 products from nearly 300 vendors, servicing over 9,000 dealers worldwide, including retailers, mass-merchandisers, and systems consultants. Softsel was the first to provide information, such as the *Hotlist*, needed by retailers to evaluate and select products from the thousands available in the market.

With the myriad of new products available, it is often difficult to determine trends in this list. By using the ordinal time series analysis methodology, however, one can graphically represent trends in groups of products; by extrapolating these trends, one can arrive at predictions of future problems and opportunities in the software market. Ordinal time series analysis is well-suited as a basis for forecasting, since the trends it generates are relative trends that have had much of the noise removed from them.

Two years of *Softsel Hotlist* data in the business software category were gathered, covering the period from January 3, 1983 through December 17, 1984. Out of these data, 51 weeks were selected for analysis. In most cases, every other week was selected: however, there were a few weeks with missing information which required an adjustment to this approach. A full list of the dates chosen for analysis is included in Appendix A.

During the period of analysis, 147 products produced by 64 companies were ranked in the top 30. (The best rank was 1, the worst rank was 30.) Those not appearing in the top 30 business software products for a given week were given a rank of 31. Appendix B contains a list of products and companies included in this analysis. The entire set of data was first analyzed. The data were then grouped in four ways: by type of product, by company, by the number of machines upon which the product was available, and by whether or not the product ran on the IBM PC. Analyses were performed on each of these sets of categories.

RESULTS

Entire Market

One level on which ordinal statistics can be generated is that of the whole market, defined in terms of those items appearing in the rankings. Statistics at this level measure the behavior of the entire set of products. Since the position statistic is a constant for the entire set, only the volatility and information statistics have nontrivial results.

Figure 7.1. Bimonthly Volatility—Softsel Hotlist 1983-1984

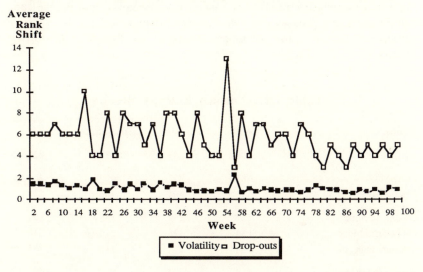

Volatility. In examining the volatility of the entire time series graphed in Figure 7.1, the Softsel list was relatively consistent, and stabilized over time, with a volatility range that averaged about 1.5 rank changes per product in the earliest bimonthly periods and settled down to an average of 1.0 rank changes per product in the last six bimonthly periods. These data indicate that the average product shifted less than two positions in any week but one. However, looking at the graph of the number of products that dropped off the list (which equals the number that were added to the list), one can see that every two weeks a large number of products disappeared. In the initial weeks, an average of six products per period left (and were added) to the list. In later periods, this rate of turnover dropped to an average of 4.5 per period. Coupled with the low volatility statistic, these data mean that entry and exit from the list occurred at the bottom of the list; products did not jump from off the list to the top or middle, and products leaving the list did not drop from the top or middle as a rule. There were periods where there were exceptions to the modest turnover level; in weeks 30 and 80, at least one third of the products dropped from the list.

Information Statistics. The information statistics reveal both the uncertainty of the movement in rankings (total entropy) as well as the tendency for a product to improve (lower entropy), worsen (upper entropy), or remain at the same rank (diagonal entropy). The top line of Table 7.1 shows these statistics for the entire set of products. Notice that the total uncertainty is 63% of the maximum possible—indicating that the volatility of 1.5 to 1.0 rank shifts per product on average was spread over a large number of products, rather than being due to a few highly volatile products. The lower entropy is considerably smaller than the upper entropy, indicating that on average a product rose faster in the rankings than it fell. This is in agreement with an intuitive understanding of the dynamics of software lifecycles.

Table 7.1. Normed Entropy Results

Group	Total	Lower	Diagonal	Upper
All products	.630	.249	.054	.327
On IBM	.631	.232	.095	.304
Not on IBM	.513	.104	.166	.243
On one machine	.624	.140	.183	.301
On two machines	.654	.128	.214	.312
On more than two	.583	.214	.116	.253
Word processing	.618	.207	.142	.269
Database	.546	.165	.160	.222
Integrated	.199	.029	.048	.122
Spreadsheet	.142	.017	.031	.093
Miscellaneous	.365	.039	.114	.212
Ashton-Tate	.204	.033	.049	.122
MicroSoft	.150	.024	.033	.093
Software Publishing	.417	.116	.126	.175
Rest of Companies	.663	.246	.081	.336

Note: Groups not included had less than two products in the rankings for at least one week.

We have previously used the log-linear property of the entropy function to decompose the uncertainty of a process into the uncertainties of improving, holding and worsening position. This same property of linearity can also be used to determine the uncertainty associated with each rank in the process. For each rank we can compute the three associated entropy statistics. In effect we are decomposing formula 3.2 in chapter 3 to read:

$$H(S)_k = \sum_i [(\sum_{j<i} p_{i,j,k} \ln p_{i,j,k})/(q \ln(q)) \qquad \text{(lower)}$$

$$+ (\sum_{j=i} p_{i,j,k} \ln p_{i,j,k})/(q \ln(q)) \qquad \text{(diagonal)} \qquad (7.1)$$

$$+ (\sum_{j>i} p_{i,j,k}) \ln p_{i,j,k})/(q \ln(q))]. \qquad \text{(upper)}$$

Figure 7.2 graphs the various information statistics for each of the actual ranks, 1 through 31. Note that for a product with a rank of 1, it was very likely that the rank movement of the product could have been predicted, because the uncertainty was very low. This is because Lotus 1-2-3 held the first position for the majority of the period studied and made the probability of staying in rank 1 nearly one. For ranks between 10 and 22, the movement of the product was quite random, with uncertainty that was close to the maximum possible. The graph shows that there was a tendency for a product with a rank better than 24 to improve quickly in rank and then slowly worsen. A product ranked from 24 to 30, however, tended to slowly improve in rank but quickly fall. This may have been due to a tendency of new products to require some time to become recognized by new purchasers after breaking into the bottom of the rankings. The average product tended to quickly rise to its best rank, then slowly to worsen in rank as purchaser interest dwindled. Products tended to move quickly out of the rankings after hitting a low rank in the bottom sixth of the rankings. Very few products were able to sustain their high (or low) rank, as indicated by the very small diagonal entropy. The strategic implication here is that if this pattern holds into the future, once a product has initially appeared at the bottom of the charts it should be heavily promoted and monitored for its rate of upward movement. Those products moving slowly upward through the lowest ranks should be considered candidates for early market withdrawal unless their contribution margin at the time is sufficient to justify their continuation.

Figure 7.2. Softsel Hotlist Information Statistics by Rank

By grouping products according to various classifications, the strategic analyst can uncover additional information about the market. For one thing, product subgroups have a position statistic that is meaningful. In the following sections we will examine various product subgroup statistics.

IBM Compatibility

One of the strategic decisions that must be made in producing software products is to determine with what machines the software will be compatible. By grouping the Softsel data into two categories, one for products that can be used on the IBM PC and clones, and one for products to be used on other machines, some definite behavioral differences can be noticed.

Volatility. Figure 7.3 shows that the volatility for both IBM-compatible and non-IBM-compatible products was about equal in the first six months of the study, but the IBM-compatible products maintained an average volatility of about 1.4 rank shifts per period, while non-IBM-compatible products reduced in volatility to about half a rank shift per period. This may be due to the high number of these products that have dropped out of the list, and the lower number that have been added. Both sets of products contributed to the volatility spike in week 56.

Figure 7.3. Compatibility by Type of System—Volatility

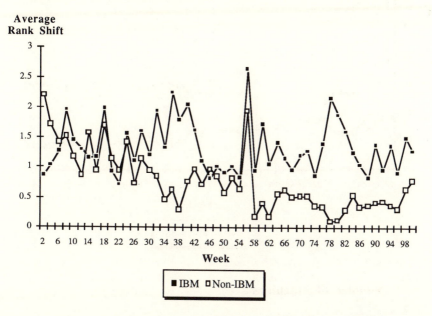

Position. The average rank for IBM-compatible products is consistently better than for products without this capability (see Figure 7.4). This difference increases in later weeks, and a simple trend-line extrapolation predicts the long term strength of IBM compatible products which has been borne out by actual events.

Information Statistics. The second set of figures in Table 7.1 shows that products designed for the IBM and clones had an uncertainty level nearly equal to the total set of software products, while products for other machines were considerably more certain in their rank shift behavior. Further analysis reveals that although both categories had a tendency to worsen in rank through a greater number of steps, the disparity between lower and upper entropy statistics was greater for non-IBM compatible software. This implies that non-IBM compatible products moved up in the rankings in a relatively small number of steps.

Figure 7.4. Compatibility by Type of System—Position

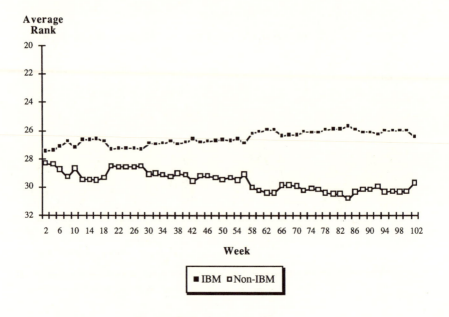

Number of Machines

Another decision that must be made in software product strategy involves determining whether it is beneficial to provide a product which runs on a number of different types of computer equipment. To demonstrate patterns in this phenomenon, the software products were divided into three categories:

(1) products available for only one machine
(2) products available for two machines
(3) products available for more than two machines

These classifications were determined by examining the number of machines listed for the product in the latest week in which the product appeared on the *Hotlist*.

Volatility. The volatility of one-machine products tended to be lower than the other two categories for the period studied (see Figure 7.5). The last half of 1984 showed a converging of volatility levels for all groups until week 90, after which products running on two systems improved at the expense of the other categories. The large jump in volatility at week 56 seen in the previous two analyses can also be seen in this analysis; however, only software packages running on more than one machine were significant contributors to rank shift activity.

Figure 7.5.   Compatibility by Number of Systems—Volatility

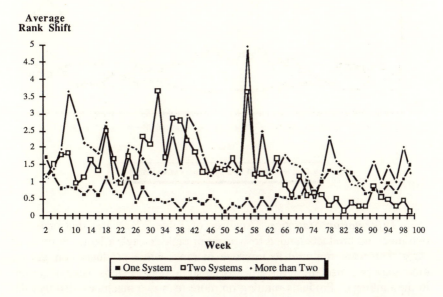

Position. The average rank (Figure 7.6) for products that ran on more than two machines was significantly better than the average rank for the other two categories. In the last half of 1984, however, the rank of products which only ran on one machine began to improve over those which ran on two machines. This was due in part to the emerging dominance of IBM compatible machines. During the period in which one-machine products improved in rank, the products running on more than two machines worsened significantly. While this analysis indicates the comparatively better performance of one-machine products, it does not indicate which brands of machine were involved. It would be necessary for an analyst to make a finer partitioning of the data to determine which brands of machines were used for these one-machine products that improved the group's average rank in the end of 1984.

Figure 7.6. Compatibility by Number of Systems—Position

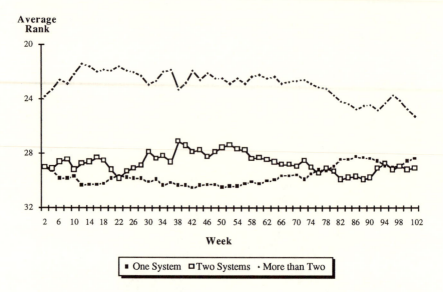

Information Statistics. Analysis of Table 7.1 reveals that one- and two-machine products tended to worsen in rank through a larger number of steps than were required to improve in rank, while products that ran on more than two machines took a nearly equal number of steps rising as falling in the rankings. Products running on more than two machines also had the most stable transition process overall.

Product Type

Yet another strategic decision in regard to software products is to determine just what type of products to produce. To illustrate the information provided by ordinal analysis in this regard, the products on the *Softsel Hotlist* were grouped by application as follows:

- Accounting
- Word Processing
- Financial
- Spreadsheets

- Integrated
- Databases
- Desk Organizer
- Miscellaneous

Graphs for these groups can be found in Figures 7.7 to 7.12.

Volatility. Figures 7.7 to 7.9 graph the volatility within the various application groups. The volatility in the market at week 56, noticed in the last analyses, is not easily recognized in this grouping of software products. Spreadsheet, accounting, and word processing packages experienced large spikes relative to their other weeks at this time, but these spikes were not nearly as large as the spike seen for financial products in week 40 of Figure 7.7, or for integrated software in week 80 (see Figure 7.8). This means that the overall market volatility in week 56 was due largely to rank shifts between individual products, as opposed to shifts within product groups.

Figure 7.7. Selected Software Products—Volatility

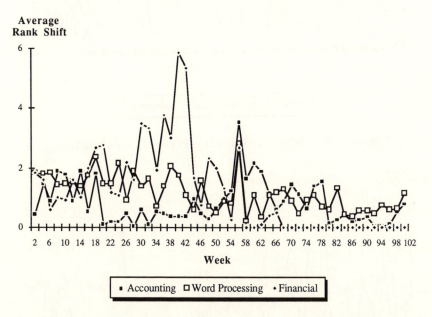

Position. The average rank graphs (Figures 7.10 to 7.12) reveal that desk organizers had just started to become popular at the end of 1984, while financial products, which peaked in popularity in week 38, were losing favor. Databases and word processing products appear to have the most consistent ratings although their averages are quite poor. Spreadsheets peaked in rank around week 64 while integrated packages boomed around week 82 and thus slowly tapered off. The relatively poor aggregate showing of all the product types in the rankings is due to the fact that for each product type there were a large number of products that were not in the top 30 (i.e., had a rank of 31) which worsened the average rank for the application category as a whole.

Figure 7.8. Selected Software Products—Position

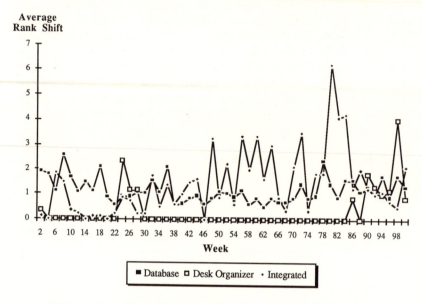

Figure 7.9. Selected Software Products—Volatility

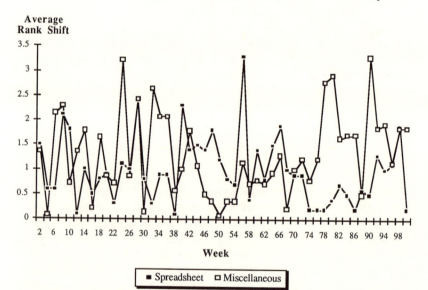

Figure 7.10. Selected Software Products—Position

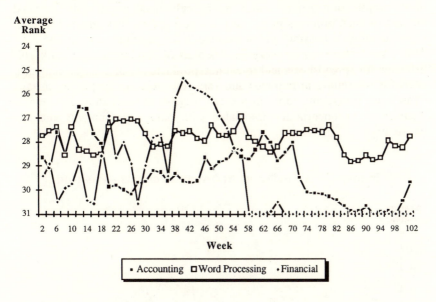

Figure 7.11. Selected Software Products—Volatility

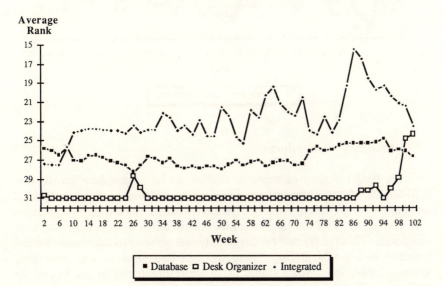

Information Statistics. Although information statistics for some of the application groups could not be calculated because of the small number of such products in the rankings at one time, the groups for which calculations were possible are represented in the fourth data set in Table 7.1. This shows there was a very low degree of randomness in rank shift behavior for spreadsheets and integrated products—with a larger number of steps for worsening in rankings and very few steps for improving in rank. Only word processing (and, in a small way, databases) showed a relative balance in the uncertainty associated with rank improvements and rank worsenings.

Figure 7.12. Selected Software Products—Position

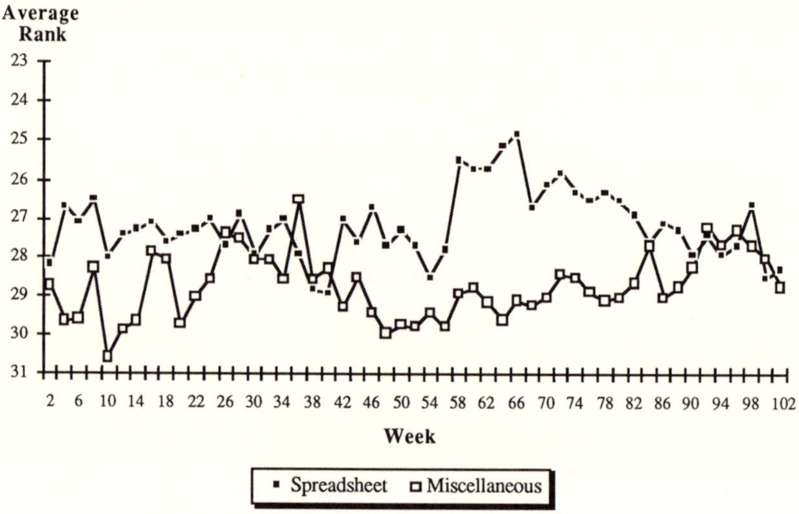

Average Rank vs. Week

Legend: ■ Spreadsheet □ Miscellaneous

Analysis of Producers

A final category of strategic analysis to be treated here involves an assessment of the companies producing the software. This analysis is developed by grouping the products into separate categories by producer. The companies with the largest number of products were put into separate categories. Companies that produced only one or two products were lumped together in a single group. There was one exception to this procedure: Lotus Corporation. Since Lotus 1-2-3 was consistently in the top of the ratings each week, this company was singled out for a category by itself. The resulting categories were:

—Ashton-Tate   —Software Publishing
—Atari   —VisiCorp
—Commodore   —Lotus
—Continental   —Other companies
—Microsoft

The graphs for these groups appear in Figures 7.13 to 7.18.

Figure 7.13.   Selected Software Companies—Volatility

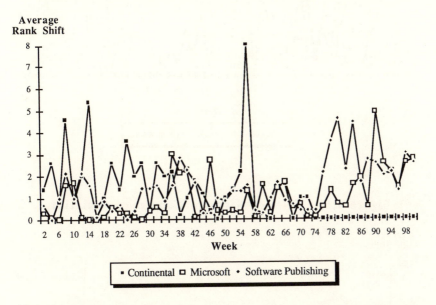

Volatility. The most volatile company throughout the period was Ashton-Tate (Figure 7.14), although VisiCorp's volatility (Figure 7.15) rivaled Ashton-Tate's in 1983. Continental showed a large spike in volatility in week 58 before completely dying off (see Figure 7.13). The position graph (Figure 7.17) shows that this spike was the result of a severe drop in average rating. Lotus showed its largest volatility in week 82, when Symphony entered the picture, resulting in an improvement of 10 spots in the rating (Figure 7.15). Commodore's stability (Figure 7.14) through week 52 and then after week 82 was due to its being out of the rankings, except for the period from week 54 through week 80. Ashton-Tate, on the other hand, showed a cyclic pattern of volatility (Figure 7.14).

Figure 7.14. Selected Software Companies—Volatility

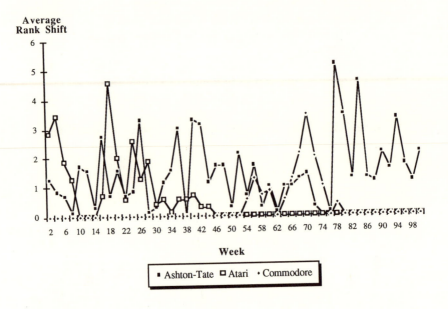

Figure 7.15. Selected Software Companies—Volatility

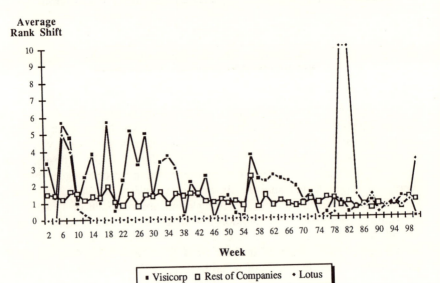

Figure 7.16. Selected Software Companies—Position

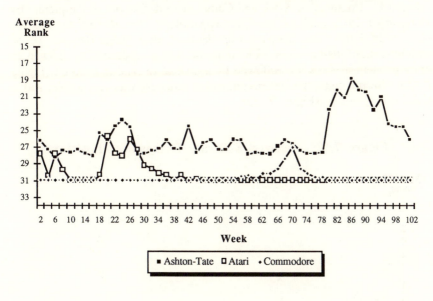

Figure 7.17. Selected Software Companies—Position

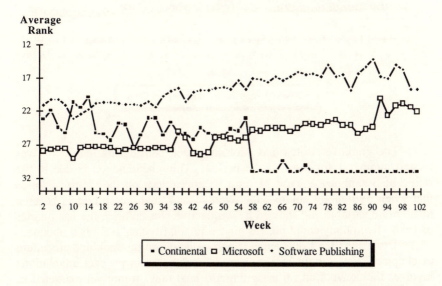

Position. Average rank showed an improving trend throughout the two years for both Software Publishing and Microsoft (Figure 7.17).

Software Publishing showed the steadiest pattern of gain of all of those examined. Continental, Atari, and Commodore drifted out of the picture by the end of 1984, with no products appearing in the *Hotlist* for the last quarter of 1984. VisiCorp's rating declined throughout the two years, although it still had a slight showing in the listing. Ashton-Tate showed an improvement in week 74, followed by a gradual decline in position (Figure 7.16). Surprisingly, the "other companies" category was very stable, with a solid average of 29 (Figure 7.18).

Figure 7.18. Selected Software Companies—Position

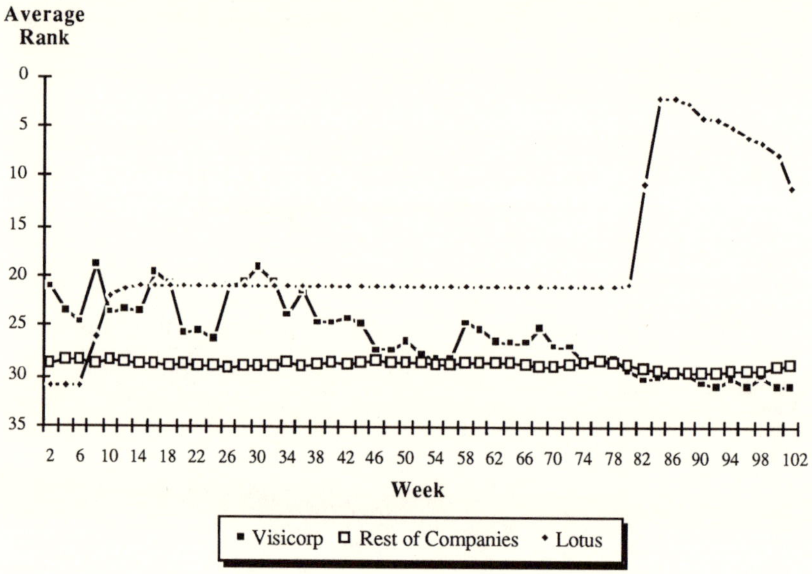

The graph for Lotus may look incorrect, considering that 1-2-3 was ranked number 1 for most of the period. This phenomenon is due to the rating of Symphony at rank 31 until its appearance on the charts. Notice that when Symphony entered, the average rank of Lotus products became much more variable and showed a considerable worsening in the last quarter of 1984. Symphony could not sustain the popularity that 1-2-3 had obtained.

The results for Lotus suggest one variation on the rankings procedure of chapter 2 that should be considered for revision in product adaptations involves the convention for assigning artificial ranks to not yet marketed or to discontinued products. The variation suggested here is to use a varying number of ranked entities in each time period, ranking only those products that are actually in the market in the time period under consideration. This convention would avoid biasing the rankings of producers who marketed five products over time, but who had only one product in the market at any one time. If, say, the n+1 convention was used in that case, each of the five products could have been the market leader, but the producer's average ranking would be very poor.

When this convention was applied to products produced by Lotus during the period studied, the result was as depicted in Figure 7.19. Here it can be seen that Lotus improved rapidly to the first rank within weeks of the introduction of 1-2-3. The product and the company held this position until the fortieth period studied, when the introduction of Symphony worsened Lotus's position to between fifteenth and sixteenth. The popularity of Symphony improved the position of the firm in ensuing weeks to an average rank of two, but in the last periods of the study Lotus began losing position. To discover what caused this loss in position, rankings of the individual products must be examined.

Figure 7.19.   Lotus Development Corporation—Position Using Only Products in the Top 30

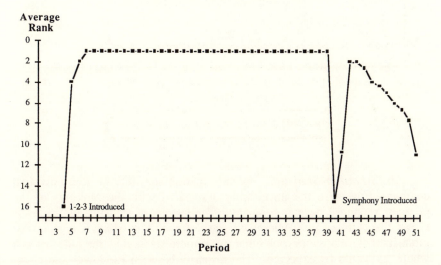

Figure 7.20 breaks the performance of Lotus down into the three products it produced during the course of the study. Until the thirty-ninth data point, the company position was identical to its only product, 1-2-3. The introduction of Symphony, and of 1-2-3 to Symphony (a bridge program) resulted in the loss of company position as mentioned above; but Figure 7.20 shows that in the forty-second period, 1-2-3 to Symphony and Symphony actually displaced 1-2-3 to third rank. As an intermediate

product, 1-2-3 to Symphony faded from the rankings very quickly. Symphony itself dropped to third position, which it held for five periods; it then gradually worsened in rank. Lotus 1-2-3 regained its premier position in the forty-third period and remained there throughout the rest of the study period.

Figure 7.20. Lotus Development Corporation—Position by Product Using Only Products in the Top 30

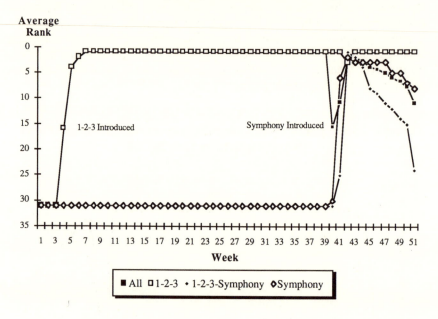

Information Statistics. The information statistics for the individual companies measure the uncertainty associated with the rankings of the products produced by that company. The last set of statistics in Table 7.1 shows that Ashton-Tate, Microsoft, and Software Publishing had groups of products that, relative to each other, were more stable than the industry as a whole, as would be expected. The disparity between the lower and upper entropy statistics indicates that new products improved in the rankings in a few steps and then worsened in a gradual fashion.

CONCLUSIONS

Software Products

The *Softsel Hotlist* for business software underwent a number of changes in listed entities in 1983-1984, but this phenomenon was not uniform across the group as a whole. Products designed to run on IBM and compatible PCs were, in general, more popular than software for other microcomputers, such as the Macintosh. Greater success was experienced for products that were available for more than two types of operating systems. Desk organizer software looked promising at the end of 1984, while interest in financial software was dwindling. Lotus, although still a very strong competitor, appeared to be most successful in only one product: 1-2-3. Software Publishing, on the other hand, showed a steady increase in popularity, impressive considering the volatility in the industry.

Surprisingly, there were no cyclic effects in this list during 1983 and 1984, at least as evidenced by these groupings. Also, differences between 1983-1984 trends and trends generated in subsequent years should be examined.

General

This chapter has presented an application of ordinal time series methodology to strategic product analysis. The methodology was shown to have the ability to utilize data that were not particularly precise to reveal strategic information about product behavior. The patterns of behavior revealed by ordinal time series analysis are relative in nature and are largely devoid of themarket effects that affect all products nearly equally. This characteristic means that ordinal statistics provide a good, stable base for forecasting, but it also means that such forecasts will be relative in nature. To discern absolute effects on products, cardinal data must be employed.

Thus, ordinal analysis should be regarded as one of the methodologies that can be employed by a strategy analyst. The ability of ordinal analysis to produce results even with poor data suggests that it should be regarded as an overview or first-cut technique. Patterns revealed by the application of ordinal analysis could then, perhaps by investment in better data, be subjected to more traditional cardinal analysis techniques.

APPENDIX A
Dates for Data Collection

1983			1984		
Week	Month	Day	Week	Month	Day
1	January	3	52	January	2
2	January	17	54	January	16
4	January	31	57	February	6
6	February	14	59	February	20
8	February	28	61	March	5
10	March	14	63	March	19
12	March	28	65	April	2
14	April	11	67	April	16
15	April	18	69	April	30
19	May	16	71	May	14
20	May	23	73	May	28
22	June	6	75	June	11
24	June	20	77	June	25
26	July	4	79	July	9
28	July	18	81	July	23
30	August	1	83	August	6
32	August	15	85	August	20
34	August	29	87	September	3
37	September	19	89	September	17
38	September	26	91	October	1
40	October	10	93	October	15
42	October	24	95	October	29
44	November	7	97	November	12
46	November	21	100	December	3
48	December	5	102	December	17
50	December	19			

APPENDIX B

List of Products—Sorted by ID

Software	Company	ID
1-2-3	Lotus	1
1-2-3 to Symphony	Lotus	2
1st Base	Desktop Software	3
1st Class Mail	Continental software	4
Accounts Receivable	Commodore	5
Accts Rec. Mgmt and invoicing	Timeworks	6
Accounts Payable	Commodore	7
Atari Writer	Atari	8
Back to Basics General Ledger	Peachtree	9
Bank Street Writer	Broderbund	10
Bottom Line Strategist	Ashton-Tate	11
Bookends	Sensible Software	12
Bookkeeper	Atari	13
Bookkeeper Kit	Atari	14
Cash Plan	Microsoft	15
Chart	Microsoft	16
Check Ease	T&F	17
Data Base Manager II	Alpha	18
DB MASTER	Stoneware	19
DB Master Utility Pak #1	Stoneware	20
DB Master Utility Pak #2	Stoneware	21
Data Manager	Timeworks	22
Data Management System	Atari	23
Data Perfect	LJK Enterprises	24
Desk Organizer	Warner Software	25
Dictionary	Sierra On-line	26
Dollars & Sense	Monogram	27
Easy Calc 64	Commodore	28
Easyfiler	IUS	29
Easy Script 64	Commodore	30
Easy Spell 64	Commodore	31
Easywriter II	IUS	32
Extended Report Writer	Microrim	33
Family Cash Flow	APX	34
Family Finance	Atari	35
FCM	Continental	36
Filevision	Telos Software	37
File Manager	Synapse	38
File Manager +	Synapse	39
Financial Planning Lang.	Ashton-Tate	40
Flashcalc	VisiCorp	41
Format II	Kensington	42
Frame Up	Beagle Bros	43
Framework	Ashton-Tate	44
Friday	Ashton-Tate	45

Software	Company	ID
General Accounting	BPI	46
General Ledger	BPI	47
General Ledger	Commodore	48
General Ledger	Peachtree	49
General Ledger	Timeworks	50
General Manager II	Sierra On-line	51
Harvard Project Manager	Harvard Software	52
Hayden Speller	Hayden Software	53
Heswriter	HesWare	54
Home Accountant	Continental	55
Home Filing Manager	Atari	56
Home Financial Management	Thom EMI	57
Homeword	Sierra On-line	58
Household Finance	Creative	59
InfoStar	MicroPro	60
Inventory Management	Commodore	61
K-Paint	Micro Data Base Sys.	62
K-Text	Micro Data Base Sys.	63
Knowledge Manager	Micro Data Base Sys.	64
Letter Perfect	LJK Enterprises	65
List Handler	Silicon Valley	66
Macalender	Videx	67
Magicalc	Artsci	68
Magic Window II	Artsci	69
MailMerge	MicroPro	70
Main Street Filer	Main Street Software	71
Management Edge	Human Edge	72
Megafiler	Megahaus	73
Megamerge	Megahaus	74
Megaspell	Megahaus	75
Megawriter/Apple	Magahaus	76
MS Project	Microsoft	77
Microsoft Word	Microsoft	78
Multimate	Softword	79
Multiplan	Microsoft	80
Multiplan	HesWare	81
Multi-Tool Budget	Microsoft	82
Multi-Tool Fin. Statement	Microsoft	83
Omnicalc	HesWare	84
Open Access	SPI	85
PFS:File	Software Publishing	86
PFS:File & Report	Software Publishing	87
PFS:Graph	Software Publishing	88
PFS:Proof	Software Publishing	89
PFS:Report	Software Publishing	90
PFS:Write	Software Publishing	91
Paper Clip Word Processing	Batteries Inc	92
Payroll	BPI	93
Peachtext 5000	Peachtree	94
Peach Pak	Peachtree	95
Personal Investor	PBL Corp.	96

Software	Company	ID
Pie writer	Hayden	97
Power-Base	Power-Base Systems	98
Practicalc 20	Micro Software	99
Property Mgmt	Continental	100
Quick Code	Fox&Geller	101
R:Base 4000	Microrim	102
R:Base Clout	Microrim	103
R:Base Report Writer	Microrim	104
Real Estate Analyzer II	Howard	105
Screenwriter II	Sierra On-line	106
Select Write	Select	107
Sensible Speller	Sensible Software	108
Sidekick	Borland Int'l	109
Spell Perfect	LJK Enterprises	110
SpellStar	MicroPro	111
Spell Wizard	DataSoft	112
Solutions General Ledger	Software Publishing	113
Solutions Mailing	Software Publishing	114
SuperCalc	Sorcim	115
SuperCalc 2	Sorcim	116
SuperCalc 3	Sorcim	117
SuperText Prof	Muse	118
Supertext II	Muse	119
Symphony	Lotus	120
Tax Advantage	Continental	121
Tax Break Planner	Proforma	122
Tax Manager	Micro Lab	123
Tax Preparer	Howard	124
Tax Preparer 1985	Howardsoft	125
Text Wizard	Datasoft	126
Thinktank	Living Videotext	127
Time Wise	Atari	128
TKI Solver	Software Arts	129
Versa Form	Applied Software	130
Vicalc	UMI	131
Vicheck	UMI	132
VisiCalc	VisiCorp	133
VisiFile	VisiCorp	134
VisiSchedule	VisiCorp	135
VisiTrend/Plot	VisiCorp	136
VisiWord	VisiCorp	137
Volkswriter	Lifetree	138
Volkswriter Deluxe	Lifetree	139
Word Handler	Silicon Va.Software	140
Word Perfect	Satellite Software	141
Word Processor Prof.	Mirage Concepts	142
WordStar	MicroPro	143
WordStar 2000	MicroPro	144
dBase II	Ashton-Tate	145
dBaseIII	Ashton-Tate	146
dBase Upgrade	Ashton-Tate	147

8

World Export Activity

Michelle Binzel
Timothy W. Ruefli

This chapter presents an application of ordinal time series methodology to an analysis of selected aspects of the world export economy. The ordinal time series statistics provide insight into the long-term behavior of a population that includes most of the countries of the world, and subgroups of countries within that population. Data on gross export earnings for 159 countries over a 20-year period are utilized in this analysis in order to demonstrate the applicability of the methodology to the international economic system. More specifically, the interest here is to examine the relative performance of various economic and geographic groups of countries. Further, intragroup behavior for selected groups is examined in terms of measures of relative stability of a group. In each case the intent is to examine whether ordinal time series statistics are consistent with more generally accepted broad economic trends relating to world exports.

The rest of this chapter is divided into six parts. The next section presents a review of the literature,the section following, an overview of methodological considerations. The chapter's fourth section gives a description of the data employed in this application of ordinal time series methodology. The fifth section discusses rank statistics with respect to world export activity, and the sixth section covers the informaiton statistics. The final section summarizes the study and presents conclusions.

LITERATURE REVIEW

In spite of the high levels of concern expressed by representatives of business, government, and academia concerning the world trade economy, an extensive literature search by the authors revealed only one study (Kindleberger, 1983) of long-term trends in international trade on a worldwide basis. However, this study does not utilize any method of data analysis being purely descriptive in nature. Several sources provide information on one year trends in international trade on an annual or sporadic basis; see for example, *International Trade* (1950-1986), *Review of International Trade and Development* (1969, 1975, 1977), Hall (1984). Other sources provide information on annual trends in a given country or group of countries, or analysis of long-term economic patterns of trade in one country; see, for example, the *White Paper on International Trade, 1955-1984*, *Ministry of International Trade and Industry*, 1985, Gorman (1980), or Fischer (1984).

Reasons for the dearth of empirical studies on the global economy can be traced to: (1) the problems of data acquisition and manipulation, and (2) the lack of a model that is complex enough to capture key factors of the world trade economy, yet simple enough to make calculations feasible. Data problems are particularly severe in the international arena. Cardinal data are often of poor quality, there are a multiplicity of trends to be accounted for in the cardinal data, and the sheer number of different elements in the export bundle for most countries argues for a myriad of indices to translate various currency measures into a constant measure. The material in this chapter will address the ways in which ordinal time series analysis can resolve these data problems and add to the understanding of the world trade economy.

Previous studies that have used data on international trade have generally used cardinal data to make predictions about future trade performance, and have used models (see, e.g., Adams, et al., 1969; Samuelson, 1973) that are considerably more complex than the one described in this chapter. Because of the complexity of the models involved, these studies focus on individual countries, rather than on the trade relationships between and among countries. However, there is a theoretical basis for the analysis of these interrelationships and long-term patterns of trade—the literature on long waves of economic activity.

The idea that economic activity follows long-term cycles or waves was first proposed by the Russian economist Kondratieff in the 1920s (Kondratieff, 1926). His analysis was later taken up by Schumpeter (1939) and extended to include three types of cycles -- Kondratieff, lasting about 50 years; Juglar, lasting around 10 years; and Kitchens, lasting around 40 months. Several recent authors, including Shuman and Rosenqu (1972), Rostow (1975), and Forrester (1975) have extended this work.

METHODOLOGICAL CONSIDERATIONS

Ordinal time series analysis of the global trade economy uses input data in the form of rankings of each country's international economic activity over time for each of the selected performance dimensions.

Dimensions of performance that can be analyzed using relative rank methodology include exports, imports and trade balances. These data can be aggregated on a country-by-country basis, or they can be broken down by product classifications. If the data on country performance are in cardinal form (i.e., absolute numerical levels of performance), they must be transformed to yield ordinal rankings, that is, the countries must be ordered for each year along each dimension, and assigned ranks based on their performance.

The use of ordinal time series data to analyze global economic behavior has some advantages and disadvantages associated with it. First, in deriving ordinal rankings from cardinal data some information is obviously lost, obscuring some of the details of each country behavior. However, the advantages of ordinal time series analysis stem, in large part, from the transformation of cardinal to ordinal data, and the concomitant information "loss." While it is true that some information which may be of interest is lost in this transformation, it is also true that much of the short-term and midterm noise is also lost by the same process. Ordinal time series analysis reveals significant longer-term trends in global economic behavior as well as behaviors that are the result of a group of countries having been affected in a differential fashion. For example, ordinal time series analysis will not reveal the effects of a raw material price increase or a global recession that equally affects all countries being analyzed; but it will make evident the effects of such a price increase or, say, a change in public policy, or a spate of inflation that has negative impacts on some countries and not on others.

One of the most pernicious problems in this type of analysis, that of the proper discount rate to use in making intertemporal comparisons of international trade performance, is also eliminated by ordinal time series analysis through the use of ordinal data. Furthermore, ordinal data require that well-known parametric statistical techniques be abandoned for lesser known nonparametric techniques. However, the use of ordinal data avoids unrealistic parametric assumptions, and nonparametric techniques have the advantage of ease of computation. Given the obviousness and virtues of the use of ordinal rankings, it might be supposed that they have heretofore had wide application to studies of the world economy, but an extensive literature review by the authors revealed no remotely similar use of ordinal time series analysis.

Data and Groupings

A data set was developed specifically for the following analysis. The set included export data on all exporters, with the exception of those listed in Table 8.1. The majority of the latter were excluded because they had exports under $1 million. The notable exception to this is Albania, for which data were unavailable from any source after 1964. In several cases, countries were combined because separate data were unavailable for the entire relevant period. For example, Pakistan and Bangladesh are grouped together, and North Korea has been included with China.

Table 8.1. Countries Excluded from Study

Albania, American Samoa, Antigua and Barbda, Bhutan, Botswana, British Virgin Islands, Comoro Island, Dominica, French Guina, Grenada, Monserrat, North Korea, St. Kitts-Nevis, St. Lucia, Sikkim, and St. Vincent and the Grenadines

Data were collected for the period 1961-1980. The data for this study were available in cardinal form and had to be transformed by ranking the countries in each year studied. Actual figures for the gross dollar value of exports were obtained and countries assigned ranks by this measure; the country with the largest dollar value of exports was ranked number one, the next largest was ranked number two, and so on, in each year.

The primary data source was the United Nations (U. N.) *Statistical Yearbook*. A two-year lag between the year of the exports and the date of publication was utilized. For example, figures for gross exports in 1971 were obtained from the *Statistical Yearbook* published in 1973. When data were unavailable after a two year lag, numbers were obtained from the first subsequent edition in which they were presented. Despite this procedure, data were missing for approximately 10% of the entries. These missing data were obtained from a variety of other sources; in order of frequency of use these were: the UN's *Yearbook of International Trade Statistics*, and *Handbook of International Trade and Development Statistics*; *Europa Year Book, World Almanac and Book of Facts*; and *Information Please Almanac*. For purposes of analysis, the countries were grouped in several ways. The initial trivial partition is to consider all exporting countries as a group. A second set of groupings can be formed as in Table 8.2 by considering countries as either developed countries, less developed countries (LDCs), or planned economies. The above designations were obtained from the 1982 U.N. *Statistical Yearbook*. The countries included in each group are shown in Tables 8.2 and 8.3. Based on these categories, the developing countries were divided into four groups for the second analysis: (1) Major petroleum exporters—countries with petroleum exports comprising at least 50%of their total exports in 1974; (2) Major exporters of manufactured goods—countries for which manufactured goods totaled more than $50 million, and accounted for at least one-third of their total exports in 1974; (3) High per capita income developing countries—countries not included in either of the previous groups that had per capita incomes of $250 or more in 1974; 4)

Low per capita income countries—countries that had per capita incomes less than $250 in 1974. Table 8.3 presents lists of the countries in each group. For these classifications, 1974 was selected as the base year because U.N. trade statistics are indexed to 1974. In addition, the world oil market underwent substantial changes in 1974, making it interesting to separate the major oil exporters in that year to monitor their performance.

Table 8.2. Country Groups: Economic Characteristics I

Developed Countries

Australia, Austria, Belguim-Luxembourg, Canada, Denmark, Finland, France, Germany, Gibraltar, Greece, Iceland, Ireland, Israel, Italy, Japan, Malta, Netherlands, New Zealand, Norway, Paeroe Islands, Portugal, South Africa, Spain, Sweden, Switzerland, United Kingdom, United States, and Yogoslavia

Less Developed Countries

Afghanistan , Algeria, Angola, Argentina , Bahamas, Bahrein, Barbados, Belize, Benin, Bermuda, Bolivia, Brazil, Brunei, Burma, Cameroon, U.R., Cape Verde, Central African Republic, Chad, Chili, Colombia, Congo, Costa Rica, Cuba , Democratic Yemen, Democratic Kampuchea, Djibouti, Dominican Republic, Ecuador, Egypt, El Salvador, Ethiopia, Falkland Islands, Fiji, French Polynesia, Gabon, Gambia, Ghana, Greenland, Guadeloupe, Guam, Guatemala, Guinea-Bissau, Guyana, Haiti, Honduras, Hong Kong, India, Indonesia, Iran, Iraq, Ivory Coast, Jamaica, Jordan, Kenya, Kiribati, Republic of Korea, Kuwait, Lao P. Democratic Republic, Lebanon, Liberia, Libyan Ahab Jamah, Macau, Madagascar, Malawi, Malaysia, Mali, Martinique, Mauritania, Mauritius, Mexico, Morocco, Mozambique, Nepal, Netherlands Antilles, New Caledonia, Nicaragua, Niger, Nigeria, Oman, Panama, Pakistan and Bangladesh, Papoa New Guinea, Paraguay, Peru, Philippines, Qatar, Reunion, Ruanda-Urundi, Sao Tome and Principe, Saudi Arabia, Senegal, Seychelles, Sierra Leone, Singapore, Solomon Islands, Somalia, Somoa, Sri Lanka, Sudan, Suriname, Syrian Arab Republic, Taiwan, Thailand, Togo, Tonga, Trinidad and Tobago, Tunisia, Turkey, U. R. of Tanzania, U. S. Virgin Islands, Uganda, United Arab Emirates, Upper Volta, Uruguay, Vanutu, Venezuela, Yemen, Zaire, Zambia, and Zimbabwe

Planned Economies

Bulgaria, China, Czechoslovakia, German D. R., Hungary, Mongolia, Poland, Romania, U.S.S.R., and Viet Nam

Table 8.3. Country Groups:
Economic Characteristics II

Oil Exporters
Algeria, Angola, Bahrein, Brunei, Ecuador, Gabon, Indonesia, Iran, Iraq, Kuwait, Libyan Ahab Jamah, Nigeria, Oman, Qatar, Saudi Arabia, Trinidad and Tobago, United Arab Emirates, and Venezuela

Low Income Countries
Afghanistan, Benin, Chad, Central African Republic, Democratic Yemen, Ethiopia, Gambia, Guinea-Bissau, Haiti, Lao P. Democratic Republic, Malawi, Mali, Nepal, Niger, Pakistan and Bangladesh, Ruanda-Urundi, Somalia, Somoa, Sudan, U.R. of Tanzania, Uganda, Upper Volta, and Yemen

Manufactured Goods Exporters
Hong Kong, Republic of Korea, Lebanon, Mexico, and Singapore

High Income Countries
Argentina, Bahamas, Barbados, Belize, Bermuda, Bolivia, Brazil, Burma, Cameroon, U.R., Cape Verde, Chili, Colombia, Congo, Costa Rica, Cuba, Cyprus, Democratic Kampuchea, Djibouti, Dominican Republic, Egypt, El Salvador, Falkland Islands, Fiji, French Polynesia, Ghana, Greenland, Guadeloupe, Guam, Guatemala, Guyana, Honduras, India, Ivory Coast, Jamaica, Jordan, Kenya, Kiribati, Liberia, Macau, Madagascar, Malaysia, Martinique, Mauritania, Mauritius, Morocco, Mozambique, Netherlands Antilles, New Caledonia, Nicaragua, Panama, Papoa New Guinea, Paraguay, Peru, Philippines, Reunion, Senegal, Seychelles, Sao Tome and Principe, Sierra Leone, Solomon Islands, Sri Lanka, Suriname, Syrian Arab Republic, Taiwan, Thailand, Togo, Tonga, Tunisia, Turkey, U.S. Virgin Islands, Uruguay, Vanutu, Zaire, Zambia, and Zimbabwe

Yet another analysis divided the countries into nine regional groups. Table 8.4 lists the countries by region for all exporters. A final partitioning separated countries according to their affiliation with well-known custom unions, trade associations, and cartels. These groupings are listed in Table 8.5.

The final grouping was by type of commodities exported. Using the first two digits of the standard industrial classification (SIC) code, exports were divided into seven types—food, raw materials, fuel, chemicals, machinery, defense goods and other manufactured goods. Using these export categories, countries with over 40% of their exports in a particular category, as well as countries with 25% to 40% of their exports of each type were identified. It should be noted that many countries appear in two groups, and that a few have such diverse exports that they are not members of any of these commodity groups. The commodity groupings are shown in Table 8.6.

Table 8.4. Geographic Regions

Africa
Algeria, Angola, Benin, Cameroon, U.R., Cape Verde, Chad, Central African Republic, Congo, Djibouti, Egypt, Ethiopia, Gabon, Gambia, Ghana, Guinea-Bissau, Ivory Coast, Kenya, Liberia, Libyan Ahab Jamah, Madagascar, Malawi, Mali, Mauritania, Mauritius, Morocco, Mozambique, Niger, Nigeria, Reunion, Ruanda-Urundi, Sao Tome and Principa, Senegal, Seychelles, Sierra Leone, Somalia, South Africa, Sudan, Togo, Tunisia, U.R. of Tanzania, Uganda, Upper Volta, Zaire, Zambia, and Zimbabwe

North and Central America
Bahamas, Barbados, Bermuda, Belize (British Honduras), Canada, Costa Rica, Cuba, Dominican Republic, El Salvador, Greenland, Guadeloupe, Guatemala, Haiti, Honduras, Jamaica, Martinique, Mexico, Netherlands Antilles, Nicaragua, Panama, Trinidad and Tobago, U.S. Virgin Islands, and United States

Western Europe
Austria, Belgium-Luxembourg, Denmark, Finland, France, Gibraltar, Greece, Iceland, Italy, Malta, Netherlands, Norway, Faeroe Islands, Portugal, Spain, Sweden, Switzerland, United Kingdom, and W. Germany

South East Asia
Afghanistan, Brunei, Burma, Democratic Kampuchea (Cambodia), E. and W. Pakistan, India, Indonesia, Malaysia, Lao P. Democratic Republic, Nepal, Philippines, Singapore, Sri Lanka, Thailand, and Viet Nam

Middle East
Bahrein, Cyprus, Democratic Yemen, Iran, Iraq, Israel, Jordan, Kuwait, Lebanon, Oman (Muscat and Oman), Qatar, Saudi Arabia, Syrian Arab Republic, Turkey, United Arab Emirates, and Yemen

South America
Argentina, Bolivia, Brazil, Chili, Colombia, Ecuador, Falkland Islands, Guyana, Paraguay, Peru, Suriname, Uraguay, and Venezuela

Eastern Europe
Bulgaria, Czechoslovakia, E. Germany, Hungary, Poland, Romania, U.S.S.R., and Yugoslavia

Middle East
Bahrein, Cyprus, Democratic Yemen, Iran, Iraq, Israel, Jordan, Kuwait, Lebanon, Oman (Muscat and Oman), Qatar, Saudi Arabia, Syrian Arab Republic, Turkey, United Arab Emirates, and Yemen

East Asia
China, Hong Kong, Japan, Republic of Korea, Macau, Mongolia, and Taiwan

Oceania
Australia, Fiji, French Polynesia, Guam, Kiribati, New Caledonia, New Zealand, Papoa New Guinea, Solomon Islands, Somoa, Tonga, and Vanutu

Table 8.5.   Trade Relationship Groups

Arab League
Algeria, Bahrein,Democratic Yemen, Djibouti, Egypt, Iraq, Jordan, Kuwait, Lebanon, Libyan Ahab Jamah, Mauritania, Morocco, Oman, Qatar, Saudi Arabia, Somalia, Sudan, Syrian Arab Republic, Tunisia, United Arab Emirates, Yemen.

Central America
Bahamas, Barbados, Costa Rica, Dominican Republic, El Salvador, Guadeloupe, Guatemala, Haiti, Honduras, Jamaica, Mexico, Nicaragua, Panama, Trinidad and Tobago, U.S. Virgin Islands.

Asociacion Latino-Americana
Argentina Bolivia, Brazil, Chile Colombia, Ecuador, Mexico, Paraguay, Peru, Uruguay,Venezuela

Union of Central Africa
Cameroon, U.R., Central African Republic, Congo, Gabon.

OPEC
Algeria, Ecuador, Gabon, Indonesia, Iraq, Kuwait, Libyan Ahab Jamah, Nigeria, Qatar, Saudi Arabia, United Arab Emirates, Venezuela.

Bangkok Agreement
India, Republic of Korea, Sri Lanka

Communist Governments
Afghanistan, Angola, Bulgaria, China, Cuba, Czechoslovakia, Democratic Kampuchea, Democratic Yemen, Ethiopia, German D.R., Hungary, Lao P. Democratic Republic, Mongolia, Poland, Romania, U.S.S.R., Viet Nam, Yugoslavia.

EEC
Belgium-Luxembourg, Denmark, France, Germany, F.R., Greece, Ireland, Italy, Netherlands, United Kingdom.

EFTA
Austria, Faeroe Islands, Finland, Iceland, Norway, Portugal, Sweden, Switzerland.

Economic Community of W. Africa
Benin, Cape Verde, Gambia, Ghana, Guinea-Bissau, Liberia, Nigeria, Sierra Leone.

British Commonwealth
Australia, Bermuda, Falkland Islands, Hong Kong, New Zealand, United Kingdom.

Eastern Europe
Bulgaria, Czechoslovakia, German D.R., Hungary, Poland, Romania, U.S.S.R..

W. African Economic Community
Ivory Coast, Mali, Mauritania, Niger, Senegal, Upper Volta

Carribean Community
Barbados, Belize, Guyana, Jamaica, Trinidad and Tobago

ASEAN
Indonesia, Malaysia, Philippines, Singapore, Thailand.

North America
Bahamas, Cuba, Dominican Republic, Haiti, Jamaica, Mexico, United States.

Central American Common Market
Costa Rica, El Salvador, Guatemala, Honduras, Nicaragua.

Table 8.6. Commodity Groups

Over 40% Food
Argentina, Barbados, Belize, Burma, Cameroon, U.R., Cape Verde, Chad, Colombia,
Costa Rica, Cuba, Djibouti, Dominican Republic, El Salvador, Ethiopia, Faeroe Islands,
Fiji, Ghana, Greenland, Guadaloupe, Guam, Guatemala, Guyana, Haiti, Honduras, Iceland,
Ivory Coast, Kenya, Madagascar, Malawi, Mali, Mauritius, Mozambique, New Zealand,
Nicaragua, Panama, Reunion, Ruanda-Urundi, Sao Tome and Principe, Solomon Islands,
Somalia, Sri Lanka, U.R. of Tanzania, Uganda, Vanutu

20-40% Chemicals
Bermuda

Over 40% Fuel
Afghanistan, Algeria, Angola, Bahamas, Bahrein, Bermuda, Brunei, Congo, Democratic
Yemen, Ecuador, Egypt, Gabon, Gibraltar, Indonesia, Iran, Iraq, Kuwait, Libyan Ahab
Jamah, Martinique, Mexico, Netherland Antilles, Nigeria, Norway, Oman, Qatar, Saudi
Arabia, Syrian Arab Republic, Trinidad and Tobago, Tunisia, U.S.S.R., U.S. Virgin
Islands, United Arab Emirates, Venezuela.

20-40% Machinery
Czechoslovakia, France, Germany, F.R., Hungary, Poland, Singapore, Sweden,
Switzerland, United Kingdom, United States.

Over 40% Materials
Benin, Bolivia, Central African Republic, Democratic Kampuchea, Falkland Islands,
Gambia, Guinea-Bissau, Guyana, Kiribati, Lao P. Democratic Republic, Liberia, Malaysia,
Mali, Mauritania, Nepal Niger, Papoa New Guinea, Paraguay, Seychelles, Solomon Islands,
Somoa, Sudan, Togo, Tonga, Upper Volta.

20-40% Materials
China, French Polynesia, Jordan, Mongolia, Morocco, Philippines, Senegal, Vanutu

20-40% Manufactured Goods
Cyprus, Finland, India, Lebanon, Peru, Portugal, Zimbabwe

20-40% Food
Australia, Benin, Brazil, Central African Republic, Cyprus, Ireland, Japan, Martinique,
Mongolia, Papoa New Guinea, Senegal, Thailand, Tonga, Turkey, Upper Volta, Uruguay,
Viet Nam, Yemen, Zimbabwe

Over 40% Manufactured Goods
Chile, E. and W. Pakistan, Hong Kong, Israel, Korea, Republic of, Macau, Malta, New
Caledonia, Sierra Leone, Taiwan, Zaire, Zambia

20-40% Fuel
Cameroon, U.R. of Tanzania, Kenya, Singapore

20-40% Defense
French Polynesia, South Africa, Yugoslavia

No Export Over 20%
Austria, Belgium-Luxembourg, Canada, Denmark, Greece, Italy Netherlands, Romania,
Spain

Over 40% Chemicals
Jamaica, Suriname

Over 40% Machinery
Bulgaria, German D.R.

RANK STATISTICS AND ANALYSIS

For the analysis presented in this chapter, data were collected on 159 countries, ranked over 20 years along the dimension of exports. Application of rank statistics giving the position, direction, and volatility of any group of countries, and information statistics measuring the uncertainty associated with rank shifts as developed in chapters 2 and 3 is straightforward. The set of countries in this analysis is closed, so there is no need for the assignment of artificial ranks for countries that have not entered or that have left the rankings.

Volatility

As described in chapter 2 the volatility statistic provides an analyst with a measure of the total movement of countries both up and down in rank. This statistic thus provides a measure of the change in trade activity, or the volatility associated with a given group or subgroup of countries. Figure 8.1 plots the volatility for all exporters for the period 1961-1980. The graph shows that volatility for the world group was fairly steady, with large shifts above the value of three in only five years—1971, 1972, 1974, 1979, and 1980. The spike in 1974 was due to the quadrupling of world oil prices during 1974 (United Nations Conference on Trade and Development, 1977, p. 4); the graph shows that this event had differential effects on various countries. The increase in volatility in the 1978-1980 period can also be linked to oil price increases (U. N. Conference, 1981, p. 10). Most of the spike for world exporters in 1971 and 1972 can be explained by the 80% rise in oil prices in this period (U. N. Conference, 1975, p. 3). The rest of that spike in world volatility was due to a 108% increase of the real prices of principal commodity exports between mid-1972 and 1974 (U. N. Conference, 1977, p. 23). This large price increase resulted, in part, from exceptionally unfavorable climatic conditions in many parts of the world, which led to diminished agricultural production. Increased demand for raw materials by the industrialized countries also contributed to the commodity price rise (Secretariat of the Contracting Parties to the General Agreement on Tariffs and Trade, 1973, pp. 28-29).

In order to further confirm the factors discussed in the preceding paragraphs as causes for the spikes in volatility, it is useful to examine graphs that break down the countries of the world into various groupings. Figures 8.2 and 8.3 plot volatility for the economic subgroups defined in Tables 8.2 and 8.3, while Figures 8.4 and 8.5 plot volatility for regional subgroups listed in Table 8.4. Figure 8.6 shows the average absolute rank shift for selected trade groups.

Figure 8.1.   World Export Volatility

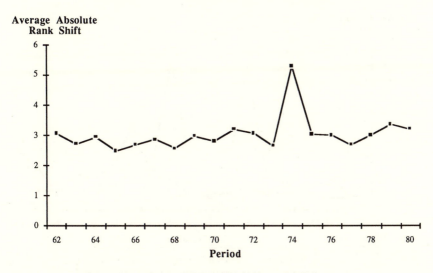

Figure 8.2 shows the volatility of three economic subgroups: developed countries, less developed countries, and planned economies. Among these groups, only less developed countries show all three spikes corresponding to the volatility increases shown in Figure 8.1 for the years 1972, 1974, and 1979-1980. In addition, the less developed countries show an increase in volatility in 1968. The first two of these spikes reflect changes in exports that affected the positions of only the less developed countries, thus providing an example of a change that had a differential effect. The developed countries and the planned economies also had spikes in 1974, showing the universal effect of the oil price increase.

The spike in the less developed country average absolute rank shift in 1968 had several explanations. First, 1968 was a very good year for trade. There was a growth of 11% in export volume being traded, while prices were fairly stable (Secretariat, 1969, pp. 1-2). Secondly, there was a large increase in demand for commodities by developed countries recovering from an economic downturn in 1967. In addition, several special factors contributed to the increase in world trade. These factors included liberalization of world trade, mainly tariff reductions and completion of the European Economic Community (EEC) Customs Union, as well as timing factors such as dock strikes (U. N. Conference on Trade and Development, 1969, p. 6).

Figure 8.2. Volatility by Export Subgroups

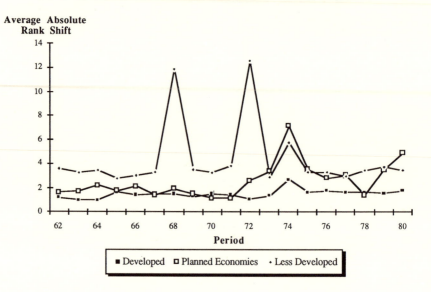

Figure 8.3. Volatility by Developing Country Subgroups

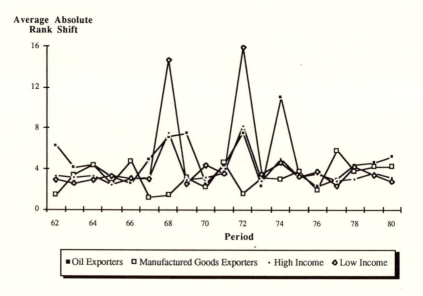

Figure 8.3 further breaks down the less developed countries grouping into four groups: oil exporters, manufactured goods exporters, and high and low income groups. Examining first the rank shift behavior of the oil exporting countries, it can be seen that volatility increased markedly in 1972 and reached another peak in 1974. This is consistent with the large relative increases in oil prices that occurred in the period 1971-1974. The smaller peak in volatility in 1968-1969 was also consistent with the general climate for commodities during that period. Large spikes in export rank volatility for the low income countries in 1968 and 1972 were caused by high demand for primary commodities in those years. It is logical that the low income countries would experience volatility from this source, since they acquired a large percentage of their export earnings from this source (Secretariat of the Contracting Parties to the General Agreement on Tariffs and Trade, 1969, pp. 114-115).

Figures 8.4 and 8.5 show volatility for six of the nine regional subgroups. It is interesting to note that Figure 8.4 shows the Middle East attained high volatility in 1971, a point early in the oil price rise trend, and remained high in 1972 before dropping in 1973 and spiking again in 1974. Southeast Asia followed a similar trend, but at a lower level. This shows the effects of costly imported oil on the nascent manufacturers in this region (Secretariat, 1975, p. 159)

Figure 8.4. Volatility by Geographic Subgroups

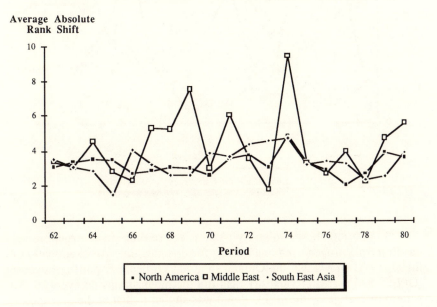

Figure 8.5 shows the most changeable volatility for East Asia. This was caused by the steadily improving average rank experienced by the East Asian exporters. These declines were caused by expanding demand for manufactured goods (1975, pp. 82-83).

All six of the regional groups shown in Figures 8.4 and 8.5 reached their highest levels of volatility in 1974, again showing the pervasive effect of the Arab oil embargo and the concomitant increases in oil prices. The three groups composed primarily of developed countries, North America, Eastern Europe, and Western Europe, were much less volatile on average than the other three groups which are composed primarily of developing countries. However, Eastern Europe had a very large increase in volatility in 1974, due to the large improvement in rank experienced by the USSR following the oil price increases and the simultaneous worsening in ranks experienced by their oil-importing Eastern Bloc trading partners.

Figure 8.5. Volatility by Geographic Subgroups

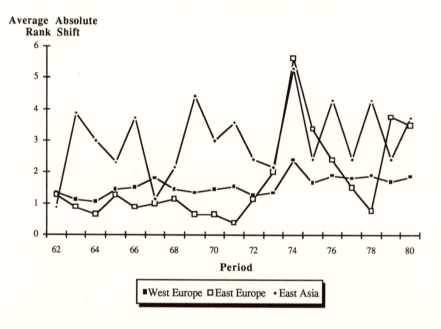

Figure 8.6 shows volatility patterns for selected trade groupings and the Eastern European regional group for comparison. An examination of these graphs shows that the Organization of Petroleum Exporting Countries (OPEC) had a greater volatility than did the other groups on average. The pattern of change by the OPEC group was similar to that of the oil exporting

DCs in Figure 8.3, with high levels of activity in 1968, 1969, and 1971-1975. However, the two patterns are not identical. This is because OPEC is a subset of all LDC oil exporters. Interestingly, a comparison of these two groups reveals that the peaks in OPEC rank shift volatility lagged behind the peaks in the LDC oil exporters by one period. For example, oil exporting LDCs showed peaks in 1968, 1971, and 1974, while OPEC peaked in 1969, 1972, and 1975. This behavior may be due to OPEC having limited their supply in 1968, 1971, and 1974, and having taken their profit in 1969, 1972, and 1975.

Another interesting feature of Figure 8.6 is the remarkable stability of the three European groups—the European Economy Community (EEC), the European Free Trade Association (EFTA), and Eastern Europe—until 1973. Two of the groups reacted to the 1974 oil price increases, but the EEC did not, and maintained its stable behavior throughout the remainder of the period. Although the EEC was dependent on imported oil, these countries were able to maintain their positions in the international export market during this period of extreme turbulence.

Figure 8.6. Volatility by Regions and Trade Groups

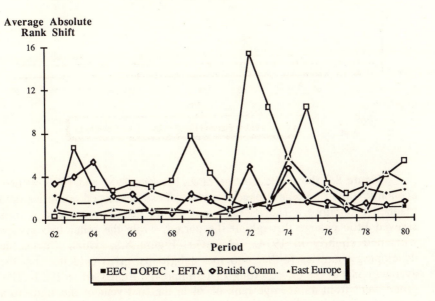

Average Absolute
Rank Shift

Position

The position statistic, average rank, as described in chapter 2, provides a measure of the relative positions of subgroups of exporting countries in each year by export rank. The pattern of this statistic over time shows whether the export earnings of countries in a given subgroup have improved (decreased in average rank) or worsened (increased in average rank) with respect to other subgroups.

Figure 8.7.   Position by Economic Subgroups

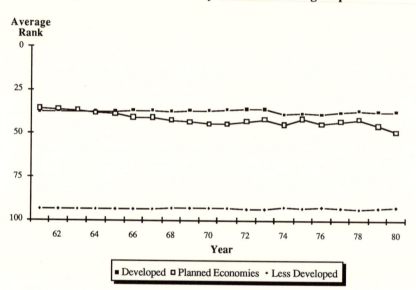

Figure 8.7 shows the average ranks between 1951 and 1980 of three economic subgroups: developed countries, Less developed countries, and planned economies. The average rank of the less developed countries showed little change throughout the period, while the other two groups worsened slightly in 1974. However, Figure 8.8, which breaks the developing countries further into four subgroups, gives evidence that the average ranks of the oil-exporting LDCs improved from 1961 to 1980. This group went from an average rank of 74 in the first year of the study to a rank of 40 in the last year, an improvement of 34 positions. The manufacturing exporters followed a similar pattern of rank improvement until 1974, when the oil price increases reversed their fortunes. Another interesting feature in Figure 8.8 is the substantial improvement in the position of the low income group of countries between 1968 and 1971.

Because of the makeup of this group, this improvement can be related to the Viet Nam war, as well as to the other factors previously discussed. From a policy viewpoint, perhaps the most significant feature of graph is that, despite the massive flows of foreign aid into both the high and low income developing countries, both groups showed worsened rank positions.

Figure 8.8. Position by Developing Country Subgroups

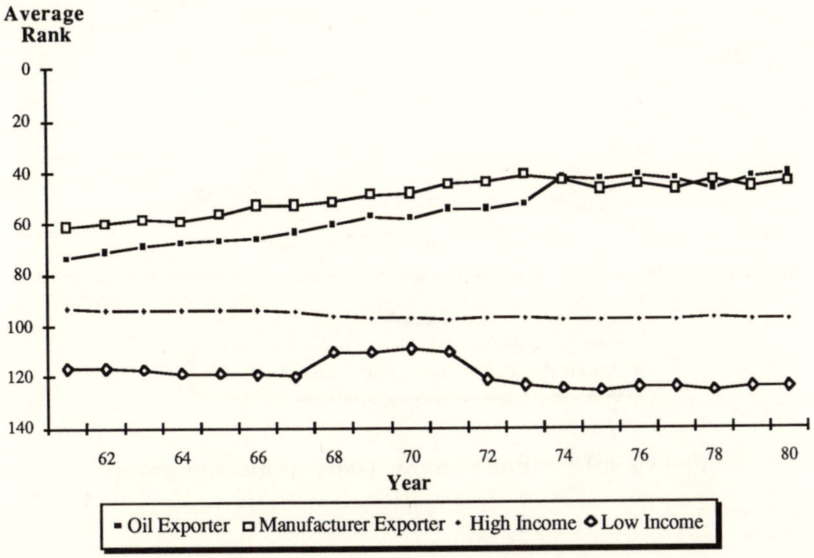

Figures 8.9 and 8.10 show the positions of six of the nine regional subgroups. Basic trends in these figures show the average ranks of the Middle East and East Asia groups improved, while those of the South American and Southeast Asian groups worsened. North America and Western Europe maintained their rank positions at a relatively constant level. These patterns are consistent with the economic trends discussed in the section on volatility statistics.

The positions of several of the trade groups are graphed in Figure 8.11. The only group to show an average rank improvement of over 20 rank positions during the period was OPEC. The OPEC group showed small but steady average rank improvements between 1961 and 1971. OPEC had steeper improvement in position in the period 1971 to 1976, but this trend was reversed in 1977 and 1978, when its position worsened. EFTA and EEC countries on average had the same aggregate rank at the end of the period studied as they had at the beginning. The Eastern European group lost an average of 15 rank positions, while the British Commonwealth gained 5 positions due to the coupling of their developed status and substantially increased oil production.

Figure 8.9.   Position by Geographic Subgroups

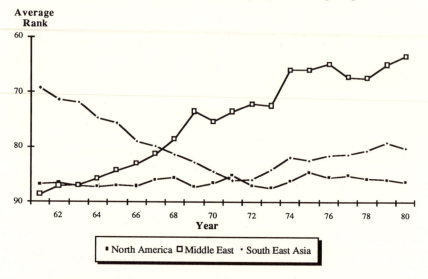

Figure 8.10.   Position by Geographic Subgroups

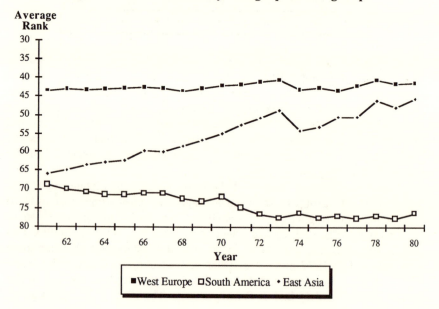

Figure 8.11. Position by Regions and Trade Groups

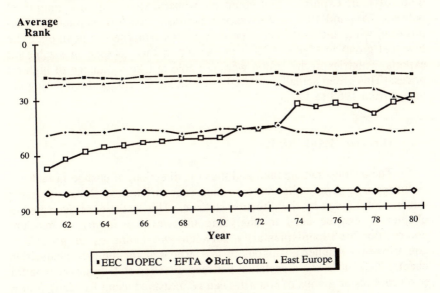

Figure 8.12. Position by Type of Exports

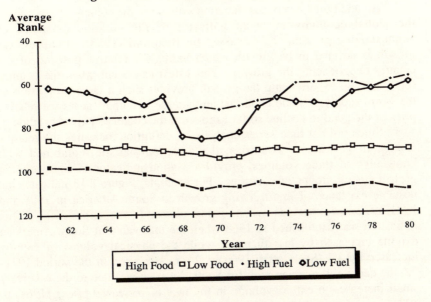

The position of four of the commodity groups is shown in Figure 8.12. The only group that improved in rank position overall was the one composed of countries whose exports of fuel (high fuel) comprised 40% or more of their exports. The countries whose exports of fuel comprised between 25% and 40% of their export earnings (low fuel) maintained their position, while the two food exporting groups worsened in position. The low fuel group in Figure 8.12 is interesting in that, in spite of sizable oil exports, countries in this group were not able to take advantage of high oil prices. This group actually suffered a worsening in rank position during the period from 1969 to 1972.

Directed Rank Shifts

The average net amount, and thus the direction, of change in rank for countries in a given subgroup from one year to the next along a selected dimension is given by the direction statistic. This statistic, as described in chapter 2, can be used in analyzing the world economy to measure competition or complementarity between two countries or groups of countries in a manner analogous to that proposed for industry analysis in chapter 2. That is, the association between direction statistics over time for two countries or groups of countries can be measured using Kendall's Tau B to see if changes in their economic activity were positively, negatively, or not correlated.

An additional use of the direction statistic in the context of analysis of the global economy is as an indicator of the possible existence of "immiserizing growth," as discussed by Bhagwati (1958). Immiserizing growth is defined to be growth which harms the relative position of the country experiencing the growth. This effect can occur when the country (or countries) experiencing the growth provides such a large proportion of the world supply of some good that an increase in output causes the relative prics of the good to decline so far as to harm the country's export position.

Since ordinal time series analysis by definition measures the relative change in position of countries, the direction statistic, combined with knowledge of trade volumes, provides a good indicator of immiserizing growth among groups of countries. For example, Figure 8.13 indicates the possible existence of immiserizing growth in South America in 1968 and 1971-1972, two periods when export demand was expanding. This indication was established in 1968 when the unit value of South American exports increased by less than 2% while the physical volume of exports increased by 3% (Secretariat, 1969, p. 243). However, in the period 1971-72, the decline in average rank for South America was due to the relatively small increases in export volume in the face of increased prices (1969, p. 122).

Ordinal analysis suggests that in addition to the simple one-way cause and effect reason given for the existence of immiserizing growth by

Bhagwati (1958), there may be a reason why a country can expand its volume of output through not so far as to reduce prices sufficiently to harm its rank position, and yet still lose rank position. Bhagwati's explanation for immiserizing growth was basically one of market saturation and declining marginal values; ordinal analysis shows that an inferior export mix could also lead to the same result. That is, a country could increase its export volume without causing price drops sufficient to cause loss of position, but still lose position. This could be because other countries had restricted supply of another commodity, increasing the price of the restricted product so much that their export position was improved relative to the country that increased its physical volume of exports. Thus the latter country could experience immiserizing growth as a result of having a worse product mix. In the case of South America cited above, the improving position of the OPEC countries was, in part, responsible for the worsening position of the South American group in the period 1971-1972.

Figure 8.13. Direction by Export Subgroups

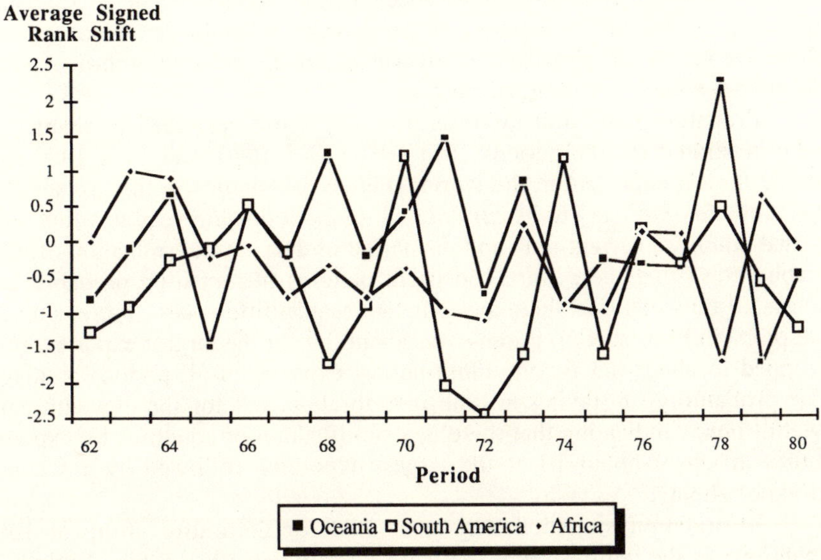

Average Signed Rank Shift — Period — ■ Oceania □ South America • Africa

Forecasting

Ordinal time series analysis uses historical data, but the trends it reveals can be used as the basis for forecasts of global economy environments. Because the data have essentially been transformed to eliminate nondifferential effects of business cycles, ordinal time series data make a good basis for generating forecasts. For example, the average rank behavior of the Eastern Asian group (Figure 8.10), if projected, implies that performance of that subgroup, may continue to improve, and that their position may well surpass in this decade by the Western European group.

INFORMATION STATISTICS

In addition to the measures presented above, which are measures of country group behavior at a point in time, or from one point in time to the next, ordinal time series analysis provides a measure of the relative uncertainty involved in rank shift activity of groups of countries over a number of years. Comparison of the three sets of statistics into which the total entropy measure can be decomposed gives the analyst an indication of the relative uncertainty associated with increasing, maintaining, or decreasing rank within the group. For example, a group of countries with the upper entropy considerably larger than the lower entropy will exhibit behavior in which the average country gradually improves its rank position through many steps until it experiences a rapid worsening in rank. This gives the analyst an expectation of the average behavior of countries in a global economy or global economy subgroup in terms of improvement, maintenance, and worsening of rank.

Probability and transition matrices like those described in chapter 3 were generated for the periods 1961-1980, 1961-1970, and 1971-1980 for the 50 largest exporters in the world. Figure 8.14 indicates the probability that a country will stay in its current rank in the following year as a function of that country's current rank and the period of data. An examination of this graph shows that there were consistent patterns in transition probabilities across all three periods, there are some noticeable differences. For example, the probability of staying in rank was about 0.9 for the largest exporter, and dropped to about 0.3 for the ninth-largest exporter in all periods studied. The probability of staying in rank rose to about 0.7 for the eleventh and twelfth ranks, indicating that there is a stratification of countries by exports into a group of about 10 of the largest exporters, followed by a second group of about 10.

Information statistics were generated for the entire group of 159 countries for the periods 1961-1980, 1961-1970, and 1971-1980. Table 8.7 displays the entropies for the entire world export economy for these periods. The 10-year subperiods exhibited lower levels of uncertainty in their rank transitions than did the 20-year period. Based on the type of analysis outlined in chapter 3, this implies that there was a change in the fundamental process underlying the generation of transitions at some point in the period from 1961 to 1980.

Figure 8.14. Diagonal Probabilities for the 50 Largest Exporting Countries

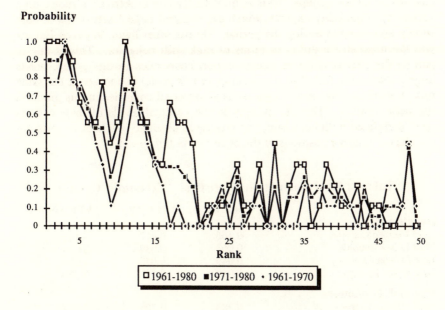

Table 8.7. Information Statistics: World

World	1961-1980	1961-1970	1971-1980
Total Normed Entropy	0.411	0.324	0.347
Total Lower Entropy	0.178	0.133	0.153
Total Diagonal Entropy	0.046	0.042	0.036
Total Upper Entropy	0.187	0.149	0.157

Information statistics for the economic and regional subgroups are tabulated in Tables 8.8 and 8.9. As expected, Table 8.8 shows that the oil-exporting country group exhibited relatively high uncertainty in all cases. The only group with higher uncertainty was the low income LDC group. All groups except LDCs that export manufactured goods had a higher level of uncertainty associated with rank shifts in the second decade studied than they did in the first decade, indicating the increasing turbulence in the world trade economy.

Table 8.9 reports information statistics for the nine regional subgroups. Comparisons across the rows indicate that, as was the case for the world export economy, 1971-1980 was a more uncertain period for all of the regional subgroups except the Middle East. The first column of information statistics indicates that in the period from 1961 to 1980, countries in Africa had the highest level of uncertainty associated with rank changes of all the groups. This is most likely due to Africa's reliance on a variety of commodity exports, which experienced large fluctuations in both supply and demand during the period. On the other hand, Western Europe was the most stable group in terms of rank shift behavior. This is due in part to the stratification in size of export economies in this group, but is largely due to the fact that all countries in this group export about the same mix of items, so that any change tends to affect all countries in this group in the same fashion. That is, changes in the cardinal levels of their exports were correlated with each other, so change in absolute levels of exports did not change relative positions of the countries in this group.

Table 8.8. Information Statistics: Economic Groups

	1961-80	1961-70	1971-80
Developed			
Total Normed Entropy	0.166	0.117	0.163
Total Lower Entropy	0.059	0.039	0.054
Total Diagonal Entropy	0.049	0.040	0.054
Total Upper Entropy	0.058	0.037	0.056
Planned Economies			
Total Normed Entropy	0.283	0.205	0.332
Total Lower Entropy	0.096	0.069	0.110
Total Diagonal Entropy	0.092	0.067	0.112
Total Upper Entropy	0.096	0.069	0.110
Developing			
Oil Exporters			
Total Normed Entropy	0.437	0.366	0.394
Total Lower Entropy	0.163	0.129	0.150
Total Diagonal Entropy	0.112	0.109	0.100
Total Upper Entropy	0.161	0.128	0.145
Manufactured Goods Exporters			
Total Normed Entropy	0.356	0.343	0.338
Total Lower Entropy	0.120	0.113	0.113
Total Diagonal Entropy	0.106	0.108	0.111
Total Upper Entropy	0.130	0.122	0.113
High Income			
Total Normed Entropy	0.436	0.354	0.383
Total Lower Entropy	0.184	0.143	0.164
Total Diagonal Entropy	0.067	0.064	0.057
Total Upper Entropy	0.185	0.147	0.162
Low Income			
Total Normed Entropy	0.442	0.343	0.389
Total Lower Entropy	0.171	0.129	0.146
Total Diagonal Entropy	0.095	0.073	0.095
Total Upper Entropy	0.175	0.141	0.149

Table 8.9. Information Statistics: Regional Groups

	1961-80	1961-70	1971-80
Africa			
Total Normed Entropy	0.428	0.349	0.369
Total Lower Entropy	0.168	0.129	0.148
Total Diagonal Entropy	0.086	0.076	0.078
Total Upper Entropy	0.174	0.144	0.143
North America			
Total Normed Entropy	0.360	0.299	0.311
Total Lower Entropy	0.138	0.111	0.119
Total Diagonal Entropy	0.079	0.071	0.072
Total Upper Entropy	0.142	0.117	0.120
Western Europe			
Total Normed Entropy	0.114	0.068	0.123
Total Lower Entropy	0.040	0.022	0.040
Total Diagonal Entropy	0.034	0.023	0.041
Total Upper Entropy	0.040	0.022	0.042
Southeast Asia			
Total Normed Entropy	0.316	0.243	0.284
Total Lower Entropy	0.114	0.088	0.093
Total Diagonal Entropy	0.090	0.071	0.093
Total Upper Entropy	0.111	0.085	0.098
South America			
Total Normed Entropy	0.294	0.234	0.240
Total Lower Entropy	0.096	0.074	0.070
Total Diagonal Entropy	0.102	0.087	0.100
Total Upper Entropy	0.098	0.074	0.071
Eastern Europe			
Total Normed Entropy	0.226	0.146	0.264
Total Lower Entropy	0.081	0.049	0.086
Total Diagonal Entropy	0.071	0.047	0.093
Total Upper Entropy	0.075	0.049	0.086
Middle East			
Total Normed Entropy	0.374	0.315	0.294
Total Lower Entropy	0.133	0.109	0.097
Total Diagonal Entropy	0.105	0.095	0.090
Total Upper Entropy	0.136	0.112	0.106
East Asia			
Total Normed Entropy	0.341	0.102	0.375
Total Lower Entropy	0.118	0.036	0.127
Total Diagonal Entropy	0.105	0.031	0.116
Total Upper Entropy	0.118	0.036	0.132
Oceania			
Total Normed Entropy	0.359	0.274	0.334
Total Lower Entropy	0.134	0.098	0.133
Total Diagonal Entropy	0.091	0.087	0.078
Total Upper Entropy	0.134	0.089	0.123

CONCLUSIONS

This chapter showed how ordinal time series analysis can provide a methodology to assist in analyzing the global economic system, and groups of countries along multiple dimensions. The analysis was longitudinal, and revealed underlying trends in group performance. Problems of developing appropriate multi-period deflators and confounding effects from short term economic cycle noise were approached by mapping country performance onto ordinal scales. In addition, it was shown that ordinal time series analysis can aid a researcher or analyst by developing information statistics which measure the relative uncertainty of rank shifts along each of the dimensions considered. The use of the methodology in international economic analysis was illustrated by an application to the global export economy; extension to other measures of global economic activity, for example imports and trade balances, is immediate. Nor are the applications of the methodology limited only to countries; applications exist in public policy where states or other governmental entities can be analyzed; analyses of groups of exporters to, or importers from, an individual country are also possible.

Although the methodology is robust and comparatively easy to apply, and has been shown to reveal strategic insights into the behavior of groups of countries, it should also be noted that the methodology is not proposed as a panacea for the problem of analyzing the international economy. So complex a problem requires multiple approaches to reveal each facet of the situation; ordinal time series analysis is presented as one of the methodologies that can be employed by the analyst. Its appropriate use is in developing categories of behavior and identifying broad global economic trends, the details of which can be filled in by more conventional analytic and ad hoc techniques.

One purpose of this chapter was to evaluate whether the results of ordinal time series analysis were consistent with major economic trends during the period studied. Examination of the statistics shows that ordinal time series analysis was very useful in screening out trends such as inflationary price increases which affected all countries equally while preserving information indicating trends that affected countries unequally.

The best example of this is the effect of oil price increases. At the country-specific level, changes in rank can be seen that are attributable to wars, the rise and fall in specific commodity prices, and meteorological occurrences. However, a problem concerning the use of this methodology for groups of countries is the absolute size of the difference in the dollar value of exports of the largest and smallest countries. This leads to several difficulties. First, the dollar value of U. S. exports can rise or fall by a large percentage relative to those of other countries, but the United States would remain number one in rank due to its large volume of exports. This is also true of other leading exporters. The second problem is related to the first. Since the smaller countries have gross export earnings that are very close in dollar value to earnings of countries in neighboring ranks, trends in commodity prices, and so on will produce changes in rank. However, export earnings of the largest exporters are further apart. This reduces the occurrence of interesting rank shifts as a result of small trends. In addition, subgroups with diverse dollar values of exports will not show high levels of information statistics, because there is no movement within the subgroup. For the reasons outlined above, it might be interesting to look at the percentage changes in dollar values of exports. These changes could also be ranked and analyzed by subgroups.

A line of analysis that was not followed here, but should be, is to assess the effects of trends in U.S. import policy and economic performance on the exports of the other countries of the world. Given that the United States imports one-eighth of the world's exports, such an analysis might reveal some interesting behavior.

9

International Competition in the Microelectronics Industry: Identification of Industry Strategies

Timothy W. Ruefli
George Kozmetsky
Piyu Yue

INTRODUCTION

Problem Statement

In the past quarter-century U.S. manufacturing firms have experienced increasing competition from firms in foreign countries. Foreign-based firms have captured substantial shares of overseas and domestic markets from U.S. firms. Industries that have been subject to intense and effective foreign competition include steel, automobiles, shipbuilding, precision machinery, optical equipment, and consumer electronics, among others.

While competition has come from firms in a number of foreign countries, Japanese firms have been notable for their success in penetrating our foreign and domestic markets. As one observer concludes, "Japan appears to be a special case. . . . The United States does not seem to have a serious competitive problem with its traditional European rivals" (Scott, 1985, p. 69). Of particular interest in this chapter is the fact that Japanese firms have become a major force in the global market for microelectronics. While microelectronics is a wide and substantial market in and of itself, numerous observers have pointed out that the importance of some segments of the microelectronics market, especially semiconductors or chips, extends beyond the limits of that market: "Chips . . . are key to computers, telephones, and other electronic gear that accounted for $2500 billion of U.S. industrial output last year" (*Fortune*, April 13, 1987, p. 89). Sumney and Berger state; "Indeed, leadership in semiconductors—in terms of both technical achievement and market share—is necessary for success in the emerging information age," (1987, p. 33).

In the past two decades, Japanese firms have increased their share of the microelectronics market from a token amount to near dominance in some submarkets. Accounts in the popular and business presses have documented this phenomenon: "In the past decade the Japanese have made devastating inroads into the world's semiconductor markets, once America's private domain" (*Wall Street Journal*, 1987c). "In 1986, Japan's share of the world market in integrated circuits, the most important category of semiconductors, exceeded the United States' share for the first time, according to a study by a Pentagon advisory group called the Defense Science Board" (*Washington Post National Weekly Edition*, 1987, p. 10). Table 9.1 shows the trend in declining U.S. share of the semiconductor market between 1975-1985.

Table 9.1. U. S. -Japan Trade Balance in Semiconductor Devices

Year	U. S.-Japan Semiconductor Trade Balance ($ millions)	U. S. Share of Semiconductor Market (percent
75	251	64
76	293	61
77	151	60
78	156	58
79	180	60
80	143	60
81	10	55
82	-359	55
83	-691	53
84	-2,300	51
85	-2,000	38 (estimate)

Source: Guenther, 1985, p. 15.

U.S. firms have charged that Japanese firms acquired this additional market share through uncompetitive practices, primarily by dumping products on the world market at an unfair price, while at the same time restricting penetration of the Japanese domestic market (United States International Trade Commission, 1985a, 1985b, 1986). They point to the lower average returns on both assets and sales that the Japanese firms have made in the market in almost every year of the last two decades. Japanese firms have claimed that was not the case; the increase in market share, they say, was due to superior technology, superior service, favorable exchange rates, and so forth. They claim the lower returns were simply a result of their lower market share, the smaller size of their firms, and their strategy of emphasizing the long-term aspects of the market. They suggest that U.S. firms voluntarily gave up high volume/low margin markets in order to concentrate on the low volume/high margin custom semiconductor markets (Saba, 1986).

As one Japanese business writer concludes: "Finally it should be pointed out that the Japanese semiconductor market is very likely the most competitive national market in the world. Within this context it is clearly a misconception to think that Japanese companies are somehow acting in unison to put the U.S. electronics industry at a disadvantage and to disrupt the U.S. market." (Saba, 1986, p. 57). Other observers (Christopher, 1986) support the position that problems in the U.S. industry, and not unfair practices by the Japanese, are the root causes of U. S. trade problems.

Noyce and Wolff summarize an opposing view of the Japanese national industrial strategy:

> One of the basic outgrowths of Japan's strategy has been the creation of overcapacity in the targeted industries as many companies simultaneously follow the guidance of the government and invest in those industries accordingly. To compensate for the resulting excess capacity, the Japanese government and industry have commonly acted to limit imports while selling the remaining production in the global market at prices below the cost of production.
>
> Not only do the low-price exports dispose of excess production, they carve out market share in the export markets and in many cases drive competing foreign firms out of business. At that point it becomes possible to raise prices and begin to earn a profit on the overseas sales. The profits from those sales, in turn, make it possible for individual Japanese companies in the targeted industry—most of which (by government design) are vertically integrated conglomerates—to cross-subsidize the next generation of loss-producing targeted product lines. (Noyce and Wolff, 1986, p. 62).

The controversy summarized above has been going on for two decades and for many observers has crystalized into a question of whether or not Japanese firms are competing unfairly. While answering the question of the existence of fair competition is important, there is, however, a prior and strategically more important problem of determining how the Japanese firms *as a group* are competing with U.S. firms. The historic emphasis on the question of fairness has led to approaches that are based on a price-cost approach. That is, as required by antidumping laws, accounting data at the individual product level are collected monthly and analyzed to determine if Japanese firms are pricing in the U.S. market at a level that is below cost. Because of the nature of the cost structures of firms, determination of the cost of an individual product can be a problematic undertaking. Further, because such an approach must be carried out firm by firm and product by product, it does not reveal broader patterns unless it is exhaustive in nature or based on an unbiased statistical sample. No study addressing the question of how a nation's semiconductor companies as a group compete with the semiconductor firms in another country has appeared in the literature to date.

Overview

The crux of the problem of sorting out the claims and counterclaims with regard to U.S. and Japanese trade is that there is a lack of generally accepted methodologies and measures for identifying different industry strategies and for ascertaining when the strategies have been employed. The focus in strategic management research has traditionally been at the level of business, market, or corporate strategy. It is important to note that the emphasis in this research is on identifying industry strategy in general, and the strategy employed by Japanese microelectronics firms in particular.

In this chapter an empirical investigation of the competition between U.S. and Japanese firms in the microelectronics industry will be undertaken. Using firm level data, a methodology will be devised that will permit the identification of certain types of industry-level strategies in a bilateral global market. Because of the unavailability of the appropriate data at the level of product lines, the results reported will necessarily be based on aggregate data. However, the data employed will be sufficient to motivate the application of the ordinal methodology, and to illustrate the types of results that would be forthcoming if the product-line data were made available.

LITERATURE REVIEW

Nature of the Dispute

Since the focus in this research is on the nature of industry strategies, and while strategies may be implemented in short periods of time, their effects occur over long periods of time, thus a longitudinal approach was deemed to be most appropriate. Therefore, before introducing the methodological considerations, it is pertinent to briefly review some of the history of key aspects of competition between the U.S. and Japan in microelectronics.

The controversy over U.S. - Japanese competition in microelectronics began in the early 1970s. As Reich and Mankin (1986, p. 78) observe; "Some of the most famous examples of the 'Japanese invasion' come from the memory chip wars of 1973-75 and 1981-83, when U.S. chip makers ceded a large part of the 16K and then the 64K dynamic memory market to Japanese manufacturers producing at lower cost." Note that Reich and Mankin in the foregoing passage, state that it was the U. S. firms that gave up the market while at the same time they maintain that the Japanese firms had lower manufacturing costs and excess capacity. Noyce and Wolff provide further insight into some of the barriers faced by U.S. firms:

> The Japanese semiconductor market was officially protected until 1975. Imports were restricted and in all but one case (Texas Instruments) direct investment by U.S. companies was barred. As a result of U.S. government pressure, these restrictions were phased out by 1975, but in the years before this so-called liberalization, the U.S. share of the Japanese market was frozen in the 9 to 14 percent range. (Noyce and Wolff, 1986, pp. 64-65).

While Reich and Mankin placed the trade conflicts in semiconductors in the periods 1973-1975 and 1981-1983, others have placed the origin of the conflict specifically in the market for dynamic random access memory (DRAM) in the intervening period: "The Japanese assault on the DRAM market in the late 1970s added several new dimensions to the prevailing competitive calculus" (Finan and LaMond, 1985, p. 166). These authors go on to state that some resolution was achieved in this period by concerted action on the part of U.S. firms:

> The Semiconductor Industry Association (SIA), which includes all but one major U.S. semiconductor producer, has responded to the Japanese with its own signals. The first occasion came in 1979, when Japanese firms were pricing 16K DRAMs in the U.S. market below their home market price. After the SIA indicated its willingness to file a dumping complaint, Japanese firms altered their pricing behavior. (Finan and LaMond, 1985, p. 169)

In the early 1980s U.S. manufacturers persuaded the government to investigate charges of dumping on the part of the Japanese manufacturers. The investigation proceeded on a product-line basis. The conclusion in the case of 256K DRAM chips: "Based on our overall assessment of the condition of the industry, we conclude that there is a reasonable indication that the domestic industry is experiencing material injury" (United States International Trade Commission, 1985a, p. 11). The report went on to relate that the evidence was based on price-cost studies: "For most quarters, these data (weighted average net selling prices) show overselling [*sic*] by the Japanese, sometimes by very wide margins." (p. 13). "The alleged dumping margin is approximately ninety-four percent of U.S. price" (p. 23).

A similar finding was reached in the case of erasable programmable read only memories: "We determine that there is a reasonable indication that an industry in the United States is materially injured or threatened with material injury by reason of imports of erasable programmable read only memories (EPROM's) from Japan which are allegedly being sold at less than fair value (LTFV)." (United States International Trade Commission, 1985b, p. 3.) A subsequent report confirmed the original finding for 256K DRAMs and extended it to larger chips: (United States International Trade Commission, 1986).

The findings of the International Trade Commission were not, however, the end of the conflict—it has continued: "The current trade feud dates to a 1983-84 boom in chips, the result of soaring sales world-wide of videocassette recorders, personal computers, and other appliances that use them" (*Washington Post National Weekly Edition*, April 13, 1987, p. 10.) The issue was temporarily resolved by an agreement negotiated between the two countries: "The semiconductor accord called for Japanese chip makers to stop dumping—selling their products below the cost of production or fair market value in Japan—both in the U.S. and in third-country markets" (*Wall Street Journal*, April 6, 1987, LXXIX, No. 66, p. 25). Further, the Japanese Ministry of International Trade and Industry was to devise a method for monitoring that would assure compliance with the agreement.

As was mentioned above, the U.S.- Japan trade conflict, while recognized as taking place in the context of international competitiveness, was narrowed to the issue of unfair pricing: "The issue here is predatory pricing—pricing that is held below the cost of production to buy a dominant share of the market" (*Washington Post National Weekly Edition*, April 13, 1987, Vol 4, No 24, p. 16). Predatory pricing, while easy to define in the abstract, is difficult to measure in practice, and surrogate measures were often employed. International Trade Commission Vice Chairman Susan W. Liebler stated the categories for those measures: "The stronger the evidence of the following. . . .the more likely that an affirmative determination [of injury] will be made: (1) large and increasing market share, (2) high dumping margins, (3) homogeneous products, (4) declining prices, and barriers to entry to other foreign producers (low elasticity of supply of other imports)" (United States International Trade Commission, 1985b, p. 26).

Evidence compiled on an item by item basis in market transactions proved conclusive enough to lead the International Trade Commission to act. There were, however, a number of doubts raised by the commission itself: "It is difficult to ascertain whether U.S. producers or the Japanese led the downward price spiral, or whether the price spiral was forced by the market" (United States International Trade Commission, 1985a, p. 14). Such doubts are not unreasonable, given the inductive nature of the evidence used in the process. What would be required to alleviate those doubts, is a methodology that would identify patterns of strategic behavior at the industry level and would show when a particular group of manufacturers was pricing at unreasonable levels relative to cost, given their position in the market. Researchers have been searching for an approach to deal with such problems, and have done so under the rubric of "international competitiveness." The next section of this chapter will examine some of the dimensions of that concept.

Concept of International Competitiveness

By using the term international competitiveness researchers, imply that there is something about competition in the global arena that differentiates it from competition in the domestic market setting. The implication is that the models of competition that have been developed for the U.S. economy are not directly applicable to international trade situations. While the reasons for this inapplicability are not always stated explicitly, they seem to involve the recognition that foreign governments are often more active participants in domestic and international trade than is the U.S. government, and that foreign firms are able to engage in activities that would be considered collusion if performed by U. S. firms. Further, there is an understanding that there may be cultural differences that influence business conduct: "The U.S. corporate culture stresses maximizing quarterly profits; Japan's is more concerned with stability, market share and the long view" (*Washington Post National Weekly Edition,* 1987, p. 22).

There is a general recognition that competitiveness of an industry is a multifaceted concept: "The international competitiveness of an industry refers to its ability to sell its output in domestic and key export markets at a positive rate of return on investment and in competition with foreign rivals. There are many measures of trends in international competitiveness, none of which can stand alone" (Guenther, 1985, p. 10). Such gross definitions are not particularly useful in identifying industry level strategies—except at the level of survival versus nonsurvival of an industry. What is required is a methodology that will recognize finer distinctions among the behavior of the firms that constitute a national industry and will provide a means for the researcher to achieve a characterization of the strategy employed by that group of firms.

Scott and Lodge (1985, p. 5) are more to the point in terms of this research, although they are focussing on the issue at a national level:

> Evaluation of national competitiveness poses two basic questions: how and in what dimensions do we measure the competitiveness of a national economy, and what standards do we use in determining adequacy? For example, most analyses of competitiveness focus on the trade balance as the key indicator of performance. Is it, however, more important than other factors like market share, real incomes, profitability, and relative changes in productivity? We

believe it is the performance pattern measured in several dimensions that is the key, not performance in a single dimension.

Scott and Lodge go on to state that "the significant measures [of national competitiveness] are relative, not absolute." (Scott and Lodge, 1985, p. 6). In the spirit of their observation, the next section of this chapter will demonstrate an approach employing relative measures to determine patterns of industry strategies used in international competition.

MEASURES

The material discussed to this point clearly implies that an adequate system for measuring international competitiveness will require the use of multiple dimensions of conduct or performance. We will suggest an approach based on identifying patterns of positions over time that will be illustrated for a case involving two variables. The extension to multiple variables will be seen to be immediate.

As justification for the selection of the two variables used in this study, it can be noted that the arguments regarding international competition between the United States and Japan at the industry level revolve around two factors: market share and profitability. The basic charge against the Japanese firms, stated in simplified form, is that they acted in concert to give up returns in order to acquire market share. Thus, for the purposes of the rest of this analysis, we will focus on market share and profitability as the two key measures of competitive behavior. To provide a context for the ordinal methodology, the next section will discuss the general relationship between the two measures as related in the literature.

Market Share and Profitability

The relationship between market share and profitability has been widely discussed; the literature on the subject is too voluminous to review completely here. Instead, selected contributions that convey the gist of the state of knowledge will be mentioned. The positive association between profitability and market share, which studies based on the PIMS (Profit Impact of Market Share) database (Schoeffer and Heany, 1973) and studies of other researchers (Boston Consulting Group, 1972; Henderson, 1979; Shepherd, 1972; Buzzell, Gale, and Sultan, 1975; Rumelt and Wensley, 1981) have discovered, is claimed to be persistent and strong. Other studies have shown, to the contrary, that even within a single industry, statistically significant differences in the relationship between market share and profitability can be found between groups of firms (Hatten, Schendel, and Cooper, 1978; Hatten and Schendel, 1977). There is other strong statistical evidence that the market share—profitability relationship differs for particular industries (Bass, Cattin and Wittink, 1978; Gale, 1972; Bass, 1974). In addition, some research papers report that the relationship between market share and profitability is context-specific (Prescott, Kohli, and Venkatraman, 1986; Bettis and Mahajan, 1985).

The evidence generally supports a positive relationship between market share and profitability in situations where the experience curve operates, as is the case for the industry under consideration in this study. The semiconductor industry is often cited as an example of a situation where the experience curve is significant: "the potential for cost reduction is of the utmost importance in industries characterized by strong experience effects and highly growing markets, such as the semi-conductor and the computer industries in recent years" (Hax and Majluf, 1984, p. 110). Other studies have supported this finding (Boston Consulting Group, 1972; Henderson, 1979), thus leading to the conclusion that in this industry segment, market share conveys the power to obtain returns.

The problem of determining the nature of competitive behavior in a two-variable case will first be approached from a traditional perspective using cardinal data. This approach will be seen to yield inconclusive results because of the lack of benchmarks either in the data, or in other sources. A second analysis will be performed using ordinal data, and the relative framework inherent in that data will be shown to provide a frame of reference for assessing competitive behavior on an international basis. The next section will review the specific measures used in the study.

Cardinal Approach

Market Share. Market share is a commonly used measure of market power in the strategy literature. The body of literature cited earlier testifies to the significant role market share plays in the strategy literature. In this study, market share for a group of firms S in any year is measured by the fraction operating revenues from the operations of the group S is of the total operating revenues of all the firms in the bilateral global market.

Profitability Measure. The concept of the experience curve, which underlies an assumption of a market share-profitability relationship, relates volume of output (expressed as market share) to average net margin (cumulated as net income). The use of net income in cardinal terms as a measure of profits raises the problems of traditional time series analysis cited in the first few chapters of this book. One way to avoid these problems is to employ a ratio measure of profitability. While a variety of profitability ratios were candidates for use in this study, the one selected was average return on assets (ROA), defined as net income before taxes and extraordinary items, divided by total assets. Although ROA is subject to variances and biases produced by accounting practices, as would be the case if return on equity were used, ROA does not suffer from the problem of differing amounts of financial leverage. As an alternative, the analysis was replicated with similar results using return on sales (ROS) in place of return on assets.

Ordinal Measures

Given the above definitions in cardinal terms, we can easily define the corresponding ordinal measures. Because problems of inflation and trends do not affect ordinal statistics, the ordinal analysis could employ net income as the appropriate measure of profits. Thus the ordinal measure of a firm's profitability in any year was its rank by net income (before taxes and extraordinary items) in that year; the ordinal profitability of a group of firms S was the value of its net income position statistic in that year. Because of the effects of the ordinal transformation, ordinal profitability is necessarily a more gross measure in absolute terms than is cardinal profitability.

Ordinal market share data can be developed in two ways. One way is to compute cardinal market share and then rank the firms on that dimension for each year. A simpler approach is to use just the rankings of the firms on the dimension of operating revenues. Ordinal operating revenue and cardinal market share are obviously directly correlated.

DATA

Sample

An examination of the semiconductor industry reveals different classes of firms, as identified by Sumney and Berger (1987, p. 34): "The U.S. semiconductor industry consists of two types of firms. So-called captive manufacturers, such as IBM and AT&T, produce integrated circuits to satisfy internal needs. The remaining semiconductor firms are merchant suppliers, selling to outsiders." The data desired for this study were semiconductor product line data for U.S. and Japanese merchant suppliers over the last 20 years. These data have been collected monthly for at least the last 5 years by a national accounting firm as a result of a joint agreement between the Semiconductor Industry Association in the U.S. and a corresponding Japanese industry association. Access to these data was requested by the authors, but, because of the proprietary nature of the data, access was denied. Therefore, alternative, more accessible, data sources were used.

Three data bases were used as sources for this research. The Nikkei Industrial database produced by the *Nihon Keizai Shimbun* and the Datext CD-ROM International, High Tech, and Technology databases produced by Lotus Corporation provided data on Japanese firms. The Datext databases and Standard & Poor's Industrial Compustat database were the sources for U.S. firms. Because data specific to the semiconductor industry were not available for either country, the next higher level of industry aggregation was employed; thus the data presented here are for the Japanese and U.S. portions of the global microelectronics industry.

For the U.S. industry, Leibowitz (1987) lists 21 public and 18 private microelectronics manufacturers. No data were available for the 18 private firms, while 13 of the 21 public firms had data available. These 13 companies comprise the sample of U.S. firms in this study (Table 9.2). For the Japanese semiconductor industry, the Nikkei data base includes semiconductor manufacturers in the category of microelectronics components manufacturers and lists 33 companies in this industry. These 33 firms comprise the sample of Japanese firms for this analysis (Table 9.2).

For the Japanese firms, data at the level of corporate divisions were available, while for the U.S. firms only corporate level data were available. Thus the entities analyzed are not necessarily homogeneous in terms of their product. For some, semiconductors are the primary product, while for others, such as TDK in Japan and Motorola and Texas Instruments in the U.S., produce a wide variety of electronics products and services. Although this mixed sample limits the applicability of the results, it was the best available, and does serve to illustrate the applicability of the methodologies employed. Firms with large captive semiconductor production such as IBM and AT&T in the U.S. and Fujitsu, NEC, and Sony in Japan were intentionally omitted from this study.

Dimensions

The specific data items selected for analysis from the three databases were chosen so that the resulting performance dimensions would be as comparable as possible. These dimensions were: operating revenue, defined as sales of finished goods and services net of returns and discounts; net income, defined as gross profit net of selling, general, and administrative expenses, plus nonoperating income; total assets, defined as current plus fixed assets. These data were available for the two-decade period 1967-1986.

Table 9.2.   U.S. and Japanese Microelectronics Firms in Sample

U. S. Firms	Japanese Firms
Advanced Micro Devices	Alps Electric
Analog Devices	CMK
General Instrument	Iaiwa Shinku
Intel	Elna
LSI LOgic	Fuji Electrochemical
Motorola	Futaba
National Semiconductor	Hitachi Condenser
Seeq Technology	Hokuriki Electric Industry
Silicon General	Hosiken Electronics
Silicon Systems	Japan Resistor Mfg.
Siliconix	Kinseki
Standard Microsystems	KOA
Texas Instruments	Kyocera
	Matsuo Electric
	Mictsum Electric
	Murata Manufacturing
	Nichicon Capacitor
	Nippon Chemi-con
	Nippon Ferrite
	Nippon Tungsten
	Okaya Electric Industries
	Rohm
	Shinko Electric Industries
	Shizuki Electric
	Sumitomo Special Metals
	Sunx
	Tabuchi Electric
	Taiyo Yuden
	TDK
	Teikoku Tsushin Kogyo
	Toko
	Towa Electron
	Yagishita Electric

The net income data were before taxes, to minimize incompatibilities caused by difference in the U.S. and Japanese tax structures. The data were, however, still subject to problems of compatibility caused by differences in accounting systems in the two countries. The use of ratio and ordinal data in this study was intended to ameliorate those differences. From these basic dimensions, the two-country global market share and the ratio of return on assets were generated for the period from 1967 to 1986. The data for the Japanese sample in the Nikkei data base were stated in current yen and the data for the U.S. sample were stated in current dollars, but since only ratio analysis and ordinal analysis were employed in this research, currency devaluation and translation into current dollars were not required.

ANALYSIS

Ratio Analysis

To examine the microelectronics industry from a bilateral market share perspective, the shares for the U.S. and Japanese firms in the sample were computed for each year from 1967 to 1986. The total sample market was defined as the sum of the operating revenues of all of the firms in the sample. Table 9.3 shows that the share of the U.S. sample firms of the two-country global microelectronics market has, in the last 20 years, dropped from 87% to 69%. This is a less precipitous drop than was shown in Table 9.1 for all semiconductor companies, but reveals a similar pattern.

At the same time as the sample of Japanese firms as a group were gaining share, they generally experienced lower returns than the sample of their U.S. counterparts. As shown in Table 9.3 in the period 1967-1980, sample U.S. firms' average return on assets fluctuated from 18% to 27%, while the sample of Japanese firms' returns ranged from 19% to 6%. In that period, Japan's share of the market more than doubled, going from 12.6% to 26.4%. In the period 1981-1983, the sample of U.S. firms experienced lower returns (15-16%) and Japan's share of the market was stabilized. However, in 1984, U.S. returns jumped to 22% and in the ensuing year (1985) the sample of Japanese firms added almost 7% to its market share while their ROA was stable. Lower U.S. sample ROA in the last two years of the study (11-12%) was accompanied by a rollback of nearly 5% (from 35% to 30%) in Japan's sample's market share. Overall, Japanese sample firms' market share doubled between 1967 and 1974, and nearly trebled by 1985. Japan's ROA was equal to or greater than U.S. returns only in 1967, 1970, and 1985. In 1975 the ROA for the sample of Japanese firms dropped sharply to less than half of their level for the previous year. From 1980 to 1986 returns for Japanese firm were relatively steady.

The two right-hand columns of Table 9.3 report the Student's t statistic and its associated significance level for the difference in ROA between the sample of U.S. firms and the sample of Japanese firms. As can be seen, the differences in ROA were not statistically significant in the period 1967-1974. From 1975 to 1980 and again from 1982 to 1984, however, the differences in ROA were significant. These are two periods in which the literature reports managers of U.S. firms accusing the Japanese of unfair competition. The differences in ROA are not incompatible with the charge of unfair pricing, but they do not prove it. As the Japanese point out, their firms have much smaller market shares and therefore should be expected to earn much lower returns. To verify this claim average market share statistics were calculated.

Table 9.3. Share and Return on Assets in Bilateral Microelectronics Markets Japanese Versus U. S. Firms

Year	Market Share		ROA		ROA Difference	
	U. S.	Japan	U. S.	Japan	t-Statistic	PR<
67	87.40%	12.60%	0.18	0.18	1.760	.085
68	86.53%	13.47%	0.24	0.16	.106	.916
69	82.79%	17.21%	0.21	0.19	.839	.406
70	76.91%	23.09%	0.18	0.18	1.892	.065
71	77.91%	22.09%	0.24	0.17	.127	.899
72	76.76%	23.24%	0.18	0.11	.997	.324
73	74.73%	25.27%	0.23	0.14	1.328	.191
74	74.60%	25.40%	0.21	0.14	1.481	.146
+75	78.88%	21.12%	0.21	0.06	4.673**	.000
+76	76.25%	23.75%	0.26	0.10	3.697**	.001
+77	71.66%	28.34%	0.24	0.16	2.116*	.040
+78	71.87%	28.13%	0.27	0.10	4.007**	.000
+79	75.38%	24.62%	0.26	0.10	4.502**	.000
80	73.92%	26.08%	0.22	0.13	3.084**	.004
81	70.11%	29.89%	0.16	0.13	1.226	.227
82	70.50%	29.50%	0.16	0.14	2.155*	.037
+83	71.49%	28.51%	0.15	0.12	2.386*	.021
+84	71.12%	28.88%	0.22	0.13	4.755**	.000
85	64.65%	35.35%	0.11	0.14	.505	.616
86	69.58%	30.42%	0.12	0.10	1.237	.222

* significant at the .05 level
** significant at the .01 level

As Table 9.4 shows, the number of firms in the sample for each country and for the total fluctuated from year to year. Table 9.4 also shows that the sample of Japanese firms had a significantly smaller share of the two-country global microelectronics market on average than did the sample of U.S. firms. The two right-hand columns of this table report the *t* statistics (two-tailed) and the associated significance levels of the differences in the average market shares. The difference is statistically significant at the .025 level or better in all years examined. Note that in 1970 and after, the average share of the Japanese firms was very near 1%. In addition to being influenced by low share, low returns may also be a function of domestic competition in Japan. Because of size differences between Japanese and U.S. firms and the possibility of differences in return being a function of size or share, it is not possible to make conclusive statements about the significance of Japanese firms' lower returns and growing total share based on this data. Further complicating the issue is that the distribution of returns, share, and size among the competing firms varies from year to year.

Table 9.4. Number of Firms, Average Share and Significance of Differences: Japanese versus U. S. Firms in Bi-lateral Microelectronics Market

	Number of Firms			Average Share		Share Difference	
Year	U. S.	Japan	Total	U. S.	Japan	*t*-stat	PR<
67	4	22	26	21.85%	0.57%	2.523*	.015
68	6	23	29	14.42%	0.59%	2.510*	.016
69	6	23	29	13.80%	0.75%	2.443*	.019
70	6	25	31	12.82%	0.92%	2.351*	.023
71	7	23	30	11.13%	0.88%	2.399*	.021
72	8	25	32	9.59%	0.93%	2.402*	.021
73	9	25	34	8.30%	1.01%	2.486*	.017
74	10	25	35	7.46%	1.02%	2.521*	.015
+75	10	26	36	7.89%	0.81%	2.736**	.009
+76	10	26	36	7.63%	0.91%	2.740**	.009
+77	10	26	36	7.17%	1.09%	2.601*	.013
+78	10	27	37	7.19%	1.04%	2.653*	.011
+79	10	29	39	7.54%	0.85%	2.898**	.006
80	11	30	41	6.72%	0.87%	2.844**	.007
81	11	32	43	6.37%	0.93%	2.701**	.010
82	13	31	44	5.44%	0.95%	2.752**	.009
+83	13	31	44	5.50%	0.92%	2.891**	.006
+84	13	31	44	5.47%	0.93%	2.937**	.005
85	13	31	44	4.97%	1.14%	2.597*	.013
86	11	29	40	6.33%	1.05%	2.498*	.016

* significant at the .05 level
** significant at the .01 level

The data in Table 9.3 indicate that while the sample of Japanese firms had lower returns than the sample of U.S. firms in almost all years, the difference was statistically significant in only 9 out of 20 years. Since, in the industry in which these firms compete, market share and return are assumed to be positively correlated, the data in Tables 9.3 and 9.4 do not provide evidence that the Japanese firms were trading profits for market share. To support that we would have to show that the Japanese firms were accepting an unusually low level of returns given their market share. The problem here is to determine just what constitutes an unusually low level of returns in the absence of a benchmark for returns.

An attempt to establish such a benchmark by hypothesizing a linear relation between market share and profitability, and then comparing the regression lines for U.S. and Japanese firms, respectively, to that hypothesized relationship, proved inconclusive. The failure of this approach was most likely due to the small sample size in each year and the noise in the data from the impact of business cycles and other economic fluctuations. While there are ways of using cardinal data to compensate for such problems, they require more extensive data than are available for this study, and further require the use of sophisticated statistical techniques to justify the adjustment that might be employed.

Not only does ordinal analysis not require more sophisticated mathematical techniques, there is an attribute inherent in multidimensional ordinal analysis that permits the desired computations to be carried out on the available data. Further, the translation from cardinal to ordinal data would tend to mitigate problems in the data caused by differences in the accounting systems of the two countries. This approach will be described in the next section.

Ordinal Analysis

Introduction. The general concern in this study is whether Japanese firms acted in concert to buy market share by giving up returns in an unusual fashion—that is, whether they adopted an industry strategy of giving up short-term profits in favor of market share gains. Further, it is important to determine whether attenuation of returns, if it did exist, was a result of the isolated actions of a few firms, or whether the Japanese firms took concerted action in this regard. Yet a further problem is to differentiate between a situation where Japanese firms gave up returns to acquire share and one in which U.S. firms gave up share to reap higher returns.

Rank Difference. One possible way to measure competition between two groups of firms would be to use the direction statistic, as illustrated in chapter 3 for the railroads, airlines, and trucking companies. This approach is viable when there are more than two subgroups of firms involved. However, when only two groups of firms make up the population being examined, correlations between time series of their respective direction statistics are always going to be negative and significant. This is because the net positive (negative) rank shifts of one group must be exactly matched by net negative (positive) rank shifts of the other group. To make this approach meaningful, data on a wider world market would be required.

An alternative approach that relies on the closed nature of the sets of rankings (that is, only the first n integers are used) can be employed to determine the presence of unusually high levels of returns for levels of market share among subsets of a sample of firms. Given two dimensions of performance rankings, the difference in rank position on dimension j and rank position on another other dimension, k, can be calculated for each firm in each year. Call this statistic the rank difference statistic, then for any firm i, in a given year, t, it is defined as follows:

$$RD_{i,t,j,k} = (r_{i,t,j} - r_{i,t,k}) \qquad (9.1)$$

If all of the firms in a population have proportional performance on both dimensions, then $RD_{i,t,j,k} = 0$ for dimensions j and k for all firms i in period t. Case A in Table 9.5 illustrates this situation. In the table, each firm has the same rank for net income as it does for market share. The basic assumption here is that performance on dimension j is monotonic increasing with performance on dimension k in cardinal terms. Brockett and Kemperman (1980) have shown that this is the simplest assumption that can be made in these circumstances. In ordinal terms, the equivalent assumption is that the rank of a firm on dimension j is equal to its rank on dimension k. In particular, the assumption in this research is that this applies to net income as a function of market share. The evidence in the literature that this is the case for integrated circuits in particular and microelectronics in general was cited above. The relationship may, of course, be weakened when markets are combined across product lines.

If some firm has $RD_{i,t,j,k} > 0$, then its rank performance on dimension k in year t is relatively higher than its rank performance on dimension j. This is so because for relation 9.1 to be positive, the rank number on dimension k must be smaller (indicating better performance) than the rank number on dimension j (indicating worse performance). If relation 9.1 is positive for some firm i, it must be negative for at least one other firm.

Table 9.5. Illustrations of Rank Positions

Market Share Position	Country/ Firm	Net Income Position	Case A Country/ Firm	Case B Country/ Firm	Case C Country Firm
1	U. S.$_1$	1	U. S.$_1$	U. S.$_2$	U. S.$_1$
2	U. S.$_2$	2	U. S.$_2$	U. S.$_1$	U. S.$_2$
3	Japan$_1$	3	Japan$_1$	Japan$_2$	U. S.$_3$
4	Japan$_2$	4	Japan$_2$	Japan$_1$	Japan$_1$
5	U. S.$_3$	5	U. S.$_3$	U. S.$_4$	U. S.$_5$
6	Japan$_3$	6	Japan$_3$	U. S.$_3$	U. S.$_4$
7	U. S.$_4$	7	U. S.$_4$	Japan$_3$	Japan$_3$
8	U. S.$_5$	8	U. S.$_5$	Japan$_5$	Japan$_2$
9	Japan$_4$	9	Japan$_4$	U. S.$_5$	Japan$_5$
10	Japan$_5$	10	Japan$_5$	Japan$_4$	Japan$_4$

Average Rank Difference.   Rank difference is a statistic that applies to individual firms; to derive an analogous statistic for a group of firms, the individual statistics can be averaged. Thus, the average rank difference, (ARD), of a set S of entities in any year t between dimensions j and k is given by:

$$ARD(S)_{t,j,k} = \frac{\sum_i (r_{i,t,j} - r_{i,t,k})}{n} \quad i \, \varepsilon \, S, |S| = n.$$

(9.2)

Note that: $ARD(S)_{t,j,k} = P(S)_{t,j} - P(S)_{t,k}$

For the entire population of firms, ARD is equal to zero, since positive and negative differences for individual firms must cancel out. Systematic differences between two subsets of firms A and B with respect to two dimensions of performance can be investigated by computing ARD(A) and ARD(B) and testing to see if there is a statistically significant difference between the two average rank differences.

Assume that $ARD(A)_{t,j,k} > 0$. This means that group A has, on average, a better rank position on dimension k than on dimension j. If A and B partition the set, and if $ARD(A)_{t,j,k}$ and $ARD(B)_{t,j,k}$ are significantly different, then the interpretation is that either group A traded off position on dimension j for position on dimension k or group B did the reverse. Case C in Table 9.5 illustrates this situation. In the table there are U. S. firms that have a lower rank by market share than Japanese firms, have higher net income ranks.

The statistics cannot ascertain which group was the initiator in the trade-off. Causation, if it can be determined, must be inferred from the relation between the performance dimensions. If j and k are independent dimensions, then external evidence of intent must be sought. If there is evidence that in general higher performance on j leads to higher performance on k, then, in the case here, B was the activist in making the trade-off.

For this analysis the operating revenue (= market share) rank and the net income (NI) rank of the firms in the sample were used. In the case of the U.S. and Japanese microelectronics industries, firms that gave up profits for market share would have net income positions that were worse than their corresponding sales positions, (NI rank - Sales rank) > 0. Firms that lost market share but gained profits would have net income positions that were better than their sales positions, (NI rank - Sales rank) < 0. The average of these differences is computed for all of the U.S. firms and then for all of the Japanese firms. The significance of the differences between the two means in each year is tested by computing Student's t. Statistical significance in this case would indicate that in the year in question the group of firms with positive ARD(NI, Share), in concert, gave up profits to acquire share.

The average rank difference statistics for net income and sales for the years 1967-1986 for all U.S. and Japanese firms in this study are shown in Table 9.6. In this example, the average rank difference for the U.S. is a constant multiple (-2.54) of the average rank difference for Japan since there are 2.54 times as many Japanese as U.S. firms in the sample and since the average rank differences for the group of Japanese firms are of opposite sign to those for the group of U.S. firms. A positive rank difference for a country indicates that the firms in that country are, on average, holding a better share position than they are a profit position, while a negative number indicates that the profit position is better than the share position.

Note that in 1971 the average rank difference for both U.S. and Japanese firms was zero, indicating that in that year, on average, each subset had the same average rank by net income as it did by market share. That is, in that year, on average, net income was a proportion of sales that was constant up to the rank transformation. Case B in Table 9.5 illustrates this situation. In the table, firms do not have identical ranks on both dimensions, but the average of the ranks of each group by market share is equal to the average of its ranks by net income. This is the situation that would be predicted from the underlying economics of the microelectronics industry. That is, market share conveys market power; firms earn profits that are proportional to their market share position. The theory underlying the operations of the experience curve predicts that this is precisely what will occur, and is further evidence that the experience curve operated in this industry before the trade wars began. This case, where market share is proportional to profits, will serve as the benchmark in this study for determining whether a nation's firms are abandoning profits for market share.

As Table 9.6 indicates, there were several years in which Japanese and U.S. firms differed significantly in their relative profit/share positions. Since ranks are assigned on a closed set, the t-test here measures the difference from a mean of zero; that is, if one country's firms have a non-zero difference between profit and share positions, so does the other country. In other words the difference between actual performance and the benchmark case of ARD = 0 is being tested for significance. For the selected dimensions, 1975-1979 and 1983-1984 were the two periods in which actual performance differed significantly from the benchmark. These periods of significant difference in average rank difference are in general agreement with the periods of significant difference in cardinal ROA (see Table 9.3).

Interpretation. The ordinal evidence is much stronger than the cardinal evidence in indicating that the Japanese firms were, as a group, accepting lower returns to gain market share. The reason is that the ordinal approach carries with it an implicit benchmark (ARD = 0), which allows the identification of abnormal performance on one dimension, given performance on another dimension. In this case we can identify when firms settled for lower returns given their market share position. Since, in this industry, higher share usually means higher returns because of the strong effect of the experience curve, there should be a monotonic relation between market share and profitability. That is, on average, market share rank and profitability rank should be equal. This was in fact the case for the electronics industry in 1971, as indicated by the zero levels of average rank difference for both the U.S. and Japanese firms.

The objective of this analysis was to determine whether the Japanese microelectronics firms, as a group, had an identifiable industry strategy of sacrificing returns for share. The empirical results indicate that in those years where there was a significant difference in ARD between U.S. and Japanese firms, not only did the Japanese firms have smaller returns than the U.S. firms, but also, *given their market share, their returns were inordinately smaller than those of the U.S. firms.* That is, there were U.S. firms that had market share smaller than some Japanese firms, but the U.S. firms were earning better returns than were the Japanese—given the latter's higher market shares and the unfettered operation of the experience curve. The same evidence indicates that the profitability of the U.S. firms was inordinately greater than it should have been, given their market share.

Table 9.6. Market Share and Net Income Positions

Year	ARD (U. S.)	ARD (Japan)	t-Statistic	Prob.
67	-0.077	0.030	.075	.940
68	-0.308	0.121	.682	.499
69	-0.154	0.062	.241	.811
70	0.153	-0.062	.252	.802
71	0.0	0.0	.000	1.000
72	-1.615	0.636	2.003	.051
73	-0.846	0.333	1.113	.272
74	-0.308	0.121	.400	.691
+75	-2.923	1.152	3.322**	.002
+76	-2.846	1.121	2.659*	.011
+77	-1.846	0.727	2.724**	.009
+78	-1.000	1.182	2.680**	.010
+79	-3.230	1.273	2.287*	.027
80	-1.923	0.758	1.699	.096
81	-1.00	0.394	.684	.498
82	-1.846	0.727	1.891	.065
+83	-4.615	1.818	3.087**	.003
+84	-5.385	2.121	3.571**	.001
85	-1.692	0.667	1.624	.112
86	-2.385	0.939	1.981	.054

+ year in which differences were significant
* significant at the .05 level
** significant at the .01 level

Note: Positive ARD indicates a nation's firms are trading profits for share; negative ARD indicates a nation's firms have higher profits than share would warrant.

    The Japanese firms had levels of market share that should have enabled them to earn, on average, returns commensurate with that share. That they did not is evidence that as a group they chose not to. That is, they chose a strategy of sacrificing returns to gain share—a market share strategy on an industry basis. The initiative lay with the Japanese manufacturers, since they had the mechanism to earn higher returns for their share position, while the U.S. firms had no such mechanism that would grant them inordinate returns for their share, *ceteris paribus*. That is, if the Japanese firms had chosen to acquire profits commensurate with their share, in theory the U.S. manufacturers should not have been able to stop them.

Based on the theoretical and observed effects of the experience curve, it is more likely that firms would settle for proportionately lower returns in order to gain future sales than be able to leverage higher returns out of a declining share. It is possible that U.S. firms were abandoning high volume markets where they once were cost leaders (e.g., DRAMs) for niche markets where they had lower volumes but higher returns (e.g., custom microprocessors). But if they chose to contest a market, U.S. firms, with their higher share should have been able to do so—unless Japanese firms were willing to cut returns below the point where the market was no longer viable for the U.S. firms. The Japanese executives claim that their low returns were caused by their low market share. The ordinal analysis has shown that the profits of the Japanese firms were lower than their market share would indicate. Further, the analysis has shown that the returns were inordinately low in a fashion that was, on average, consistent across the sample of Japanese firms.

Comparison

The analysis using cardinal data, based on market share and return data, was not able to provide reasonable evidence that the Japanese firms were following a market share strategy by settling for inordinately low returns. Statistics indicated that the Japanese firms were achieving significantly lower returns than were the U.S. firms during two periods 1975-1980 and 1982-1984. This evidence provided by the cardinal analysis was open to several alternative explanations. For one thing, the lower level of returns could merely have been due to the smaller market share of the Japanese firms. For lack of a benchmark or point of reference, selection among these competing explanations could not be made.

The ordinal evidence was more conclusive. Because of the known relation between market share and returns, there was a relative benchmark established between the market share positions and the profitability positions of the U.S. and Japanese firms. The benchmark was established in terms of the proposition that, given the effects of the experience curve, on average, market share position and profitability position should be equal that is, ARD(U.S.) = ARD(Japan) for market share and net income in each year. The ordinal transformation suppressed most of the noise in the cardinal data in the manner discussed in chapters 1 and 2, allowing meaningful results to be achieved on an annual basis. Thus the question that could not be answered with the results of the cardinal analysis was answered with the results of the ordinal analysis.

It is worth noting, however, that the cardinal and ordinal results do not conflict with each other, but rather are mutually reinforcing. The cardinal analysis using ROA is in agreement with the ordinal analyses using net income position and market share rank concerning Japanese pursuit of a market share strategy in the periods 1975-1979 and 1983-1984. This can be seen by comparing the years with statistically significant levels of ARD in Table 9.6 with years showing statistically significant differences in cardinal ROA in Table 9.3. All years with significant ordinal statistics also had significant cardinal statistics. One problem with the cardinal results was that there was no reliable evidence to distinguish between Japanese firms adopting a market share strategy and U.S. firms adopting a strategy that abandoned market share.

There still remains the question of whether the behavior attributed to the Japanese firms is strategic behavior attributable to the group as a whole, or whether it is due to the actions of a small number of firms or the tactical behavior of a larger group of firms. The next section of the chapter will examine these questions.

INDIVIDUAL FIRM ANALYSIS

Approach

One of the benefits of the ordinal methodology is that it makes analysis at various hierarchical levels relatively easy. The analysis up to this point has focussed on the levels of the entire sample and the national samples. In this section the level of the analysis will be brought to the micro level and the relative performance of selected individual firms will be examined. As was the case with the analysis of firms in the transportation industry, the context for the analysis of an individual firm can be either the national sample or the entire sample. In this case, since the comparison is being made between Japanese and U.S. firms, analysis will take place in the context of the entire sample.

The aggregate statistics reported above could have resulted from three types of behavior on the part of the Japanese firms. First, these statistics could have resulted from a substantial number of firms all adopting a market share strategy and maintaining it over a long period of time. Second, the statistics could have resulted from the behavior of a small number of Japanese firms behaving as outliers. Third, the statistics could have resulted from tactical, rather than strategic, bases, where firms varied their emphasis on market share from period to period.

One way to resolve the question of the nature of these behaviors is to examine the ordinal behavior of individual firms in the sample. If only a few of the individual Japanese firms show evidence of a market share emphasis, then the outlier hypothesis probably explains the behavior of the national group. If individual Japanese firms periodically have net income rank superior to sales rank, then the tactical behavior hypothesis holds. If neither of these behaviors obtains, then the first hypothesis is supported.

The firms that will be examined were selected as representative of the pattern of behavior of the firms of their country. To provide contrast, two U.S. firms will first be examined. The dimensions employed in this analysis, in addition to net income and sales, were return on assets, return on sales and assets.

U.S. Examples

Advanced Micro Devices. Advanced Micro Devices (AMD) differs from the other U.S. firms to be treated here in that it was not large enough to be in the sample in the first few years studied. Figure 9.1 indicates this by showing AMD at the forty-fifth rank on all dimensions from 1967 to 1971. Commencing in 1972, the sales and asset ranks of AMD improved fairly rapidly, and then levelled out at about the tenth position. In contrast to the relatively smooth improvement in assets, and sales, net income, return on assets and return on sales exhibited a cyclic behavior with a period of about three or four years. In only three years was market share position better than net income position: 1974, 1985, and 1986. The first year, 1974, was before the Japanese market was "opened" in 1975, and the last two were after the trade agreement.

General Instrument Corporation. The rank performance of General Instrument Corporation (GIC) is shown in Figure 9.2. Here it can be seen that GIC held third position in the rankings on assets, sale, and net income for about the first eleven years studied. During that time, returns did not rank as well, but they gradually improved until the early 1980s. The last nine years saw the first three dimensions worsen slightly in position, while returns suffered greatly in 1984 and 1985. There were only five years in which net income position was inferior to market share position, and those were 1975, 1979, and 1983-1985.

Japanese Examples

Alps Electric. Alps Electric exhibited a pattern of rank behavior common to many Japanese firms. As Figure 9.3 shows, for Alps, net income, assets, and sales ranks were very steady and fairly close for the entire period. There was a slight worsening in position on these three dimensions in the latter two-thirds of the study period. In every year from 1971 to 1984, market share position was superior to net income position.

Return on assets and return on sales followed a cyclic pattern, and gradually worsened in position over the two decades.

Figure 9.1. Advanced Micro Devices Position on Multiple Dimensions

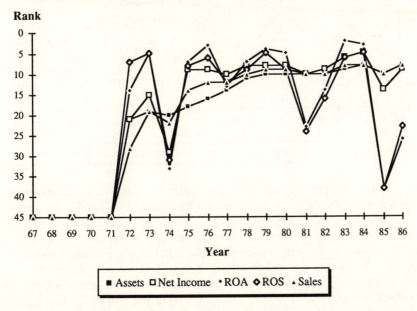

Figure 9.2. General Instrument Position on Multiple Dimensions

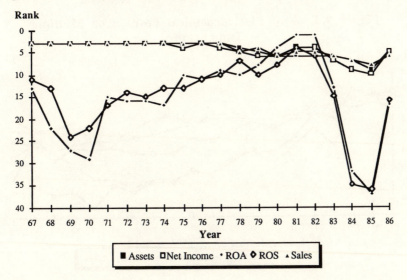

Figure 9.3. Alps Electric Position on Multiple Dimensions

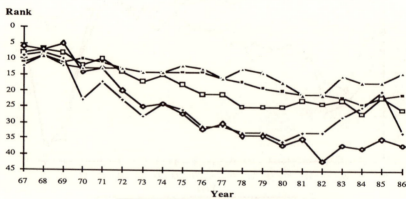

Fuji Electrochemical. Fuji Electrochemical shows a variant on the pattern exhibited by Alps, as Figure 9.4 illustrates. Net income rank, asset rank, and sales rank were fairly close together and quite high in the early part of the study, but worsened in rank over the two decades. The return ranks started in the neighborhood of the other three, but worsened more rapidly. In the last five years, return on sales levelled out, while return on assets improved until 1986. In the first five years of the study, net income position was superior to market share position, but from 1972 on, market share position was superior, indicating that a switch in relative emphasis had taken place.

Figure 9.4. Fuji Electrochemical Position on Multiple Dimensions

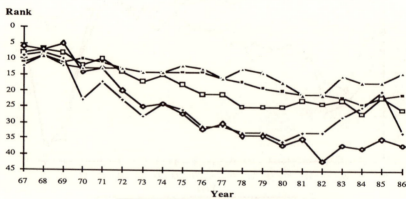

Conclusion

The examples presented above were representative of the behavior of the other firms in the two samples. There were, as would be expected, differences in the details of individual firm behavior, as the examples clearly indicated; but there were no substantial deviations in the overall *pattern* of behavior that would indicate that the statistical results were due to a few outliers, or to tactical behavior.

The data on individual firms give a richer picture of the contrast in behavior of the U.S. and Japanese microelectronics industries. In the early 1970s, when their domestic market was protected, the Japanese firms' behavior in ordinal terms was, on average, similar to that of the U.S. firms. Rank positions were nearly identical across all dimensions, except when an individual firm had an especially bad or good year. In the early to mid-1970s a substantial number of individual Japanese firms changed their strategy, so that market share was emphasized. Thus sales rank was better than net income rank in most years, and ROA and ROS positions were markedly worse than ranks on other positions. The individual firm data revealed that the aggregate statistics were not produced by one or two outliers, nor by a succession of tactical behaviors on the part of a series of individual firms, but by the behavior of a large number of Japanese firms adopting the same ordinal profile at the same time. There were individual Japanese firms that did not adopt a market share strategy at all (Hokuriku Electric and Kocera, for example), but those that did tended to stick with that approach and did not change from year to year.

CONCLUSIONS

Summary

This chapter has examined the U.S.–Japan trade controversy in microelectronics from two methodological perspectives, one cardinal and one ordinal. The history of the trade controversy was briefly reviewed to establish the time line of events and to provide a context for the disagreements. Because of problems of data availability at the product line level, analysis was performed on data at the level of the microelectronics industry. Cardinal analysis was first performed on the U.S. and Japan data to determine if there was evidence to support the proposition made by U.S. manufacturers that the Japanese manufacturers were following a market share strategy by forgoing profits in an inordinate manner. The results of this effort proved inconclusive because data limitations allowed the viability of alternate explanations of the results.

Ordinal times series analysis was then employed on the same data after it had been ranked. A new rank statistic, average rank difference, was defined and then employed to test the assertion of the U.S. manufacturers. The results of the ordinal analysis provided evidence that the Japanese manufacturers, as a group, were settling for inordinately low levels of profitability, given their market share position, in the periods 1975-1980 and 1983-1984. These results were seen to be in agreement with the inconclusive cardinal results.

Limitations

There are a number of limitations of the study reported in this chapter that should be made clear. For the most part, these limitations have to do with the data employed. Because of problems associated with obtaining access to product line data that would have been relatively comparable across firms, this study had no choice but to rely on data on a mixed group of firms. These firms have varied levels of diversification, so the analysis was weakened by product heterogeneity. This mix of products has particular implications for the strength of the market share-profitability relationship used to establish the benchmark for the ordinal analysis. While the relationship in question has been established for many products in the microelectronics industry, it has not been established for mixes of products.

The data used were further limited in that they were not drawn from all of the major producers in the international semiconductor market. European manufacturers were not represented, nor were Korean or other Southeast Asian manufacturers. Further, two significant U.S. chip-makers, IBM and AT&T, and the Japanese firms, Fujitsu, Sony and NEC were excluded from the study, as were a number of private firms. While the exclusion of the other foreign manufacturers may be justified on the grounds that the focus was on the bilateral trade problems of the U.S. and Japan, and the exclusion of the two large U.S. companies could be justified on the grounds that they are not merchant producers, these excluded firms all have an effect on the market that is ignored in the present study.

10

Conclusion: Strategic Position

Timothy W. Ruefli

SUMMARY, CONCLUSION and OVERVIEW

Methodological Motivation

Corporate strategists and researchers in almost all industry settings face problems associated with the quality and availability of industry data for strategic analyses. The federal government has largely removed itself from industry data collection in a number of settings, relying on private data collection firms to step in and ensure the availability and integrity of industry data. The alternatives for an analyst needing data are: (1) to blindly purchase what is thought to be the needed data; (2) to rely on incomplete and error-prone, but easily available data, or (3) to apply a robust technique to the "dirty" data and use the results to determine where more refined (and usually more expensive) data are needed. Ordinal analysis is, as has been mentioned, more robust for dirty data than is cardinal analysis, and therefore has advantages in data-poor environments. In almost any industry, preliminary analyses using ordinal techniques on less reliable, but cheap, data are a prudent step toward determining where more reliable but more expensive data would be cost-effective.

This book has developed a case for the use of ordinal analysis in corporate strategy. The apparent weaknesses in ordinal approaches to measurement of corporate performance were shown to have compensating advantages when it comes to strategic analysis, especially in situations where the data may be either "dirty" or expensive to obtain (or both). The use of nonparametric statistics was also seen to have advantages, in that nonparametric statistics require fewer assumptions about the characteristics of the data distributions and involve less onerous computations than do parametric statistics (Daniel, 1978; Hollander and Wolfe, 1973). Perhaps most important, the underlying conceptual framework of ordinal analysis was seen to be in agreement with the characteristics held to be desirable in corporate strategy.

Summary

Methodology. The first three chapters of the book developed the basic methodology of ordinal time series analysis. The motivation for, and the steps involved in developing, ordinal longitudinal data from cardinal longitudinal data were presented in chapter 1. The three basic rank statistics—Position, Volatility and Direction—were developed and interpreted in chapter 2. A fourth rank statistic, aAverage Rank Difference, was presented in chapter 9, although the material at the end of chapter 2 on comparative rank positions presaged the development of that statistic. Chapter 3 presented the development of transition matrices and information statistics and explained their meaning, both in abstract terms and in terms of an application to the largest U.S. transportation firms.

Applications. Chapters 4 through 9 presented a set of applications of ordinal time series analysis in a variety of contexts. These applications were chosen for a number of reasons. First, they were selected to show the range of possible applications that could be undertaken with generally available data from a variety of data sources. Second, the examples showed that ordinal time series analysis could be successfully undertaken at a variety of levels of industrial enterprise: products, firms, strategic groups, industries, and global economies. Third, the applications were intended to address a range of strategic issues commonly encountered in research and practice, from product strategy in chapter 7, through industry analysis in chapter 4, to global analysis in chapter 8, and strategy identification in chapter 9.

Additional Applications

Since the selection of material for this first book on ordinal time series analysis, applications of the original methodology have proceeded further, as have research developments aimed at extending and strengthening that methodology. A number of the applications have been made by graduate. students in the course of a seminar on corporate strategy research. Presented in the opening sessions of the seminar, over the past five years ordinal analysis has resulted in some remarkable student projects. Several of the applications chapters in this book started as papers for that seminar. The low demand placed by the methodology on both the quality of data and mathematical sophistication of the students has allowed seminar participants to collect time series of data and analyze it from the ordinal perspective in the course of one semester. The positional aspect of ordinal analysis allows the students to see an industry from a new perspective that lends itself to a strategic interpretation. Students are able to experience a gamut of industry analysis activities, from industry definition, through data collection and analysis, to strategic interpretation; they are able to formulate new or replicate existing studies that test hypotheses or illustrate theories.

Student projects have had a wide range of applications from assessments of the impact of league expansions on the performance of sports teams in baseball and basketball, to an examination of the performance of funding sources for not for profit organizations on a longitudinal basis. Other projects have been concerned with the identification of patterns in international trade, with a specific application to the global oil industry; or with various topics in policy analysis including the impact of state and federal government funding of social services on the well-being of residents, and a comparison of military recruiting differences between the Army, Navy, Air Force and Marines.

Analyses have been run on a variety of industries, including: tobacco, banking, brewing, steel, automobiles, hotels and resorts, telecommunications, airlines, magazine publishing, motion picture production, petroleum refining, insurance, public utilities, biotechnology, semiconductors, and aerospace. In each case, students were able to collect data that, while not sufficient for a cardinal time series analysis, was adequate for an ordinal analysis.

Strategic Position

The explicit motivation for employing ordinal time series analysis in strategy research has been methodological. That is, ordinal data were shown to have certain operational advantages over cardinal data in analyzing the performance of firms and groups of firms over time. There is also another, implicit, motivation for employing ordinal time series analysis—one that originated from the studies upon which this book is based, as well as from the numerous other studies listed in the previous section. This more philosophical motivation for using ordinal time series analysis is that conceptually it is particularly appropriate for strategic analyses.

Evidence for the conceptual appropriateness of ordinal time series analysis can be found in a number of places. The results of the applications in this volume have lent themselves quite naturally to interpretations from a variety of strategic perspectives. More broadly, contextual support for an ordinal approach can be found in the observation that the use of rank concepts is common in the language and experience of practicing corporate strategists and senior executives. Executives speak of their firm's position *vis a vis* other firms in their industry. Each year's new rankings in *Fortune*, *Forbes* or *Inc.* are eagerly anticipated. Corporate managers know their rank within their industry on several dimensions, and while progress in absolute terms is significant, more important is the progress that is measured in the number of positions gained in the rankings.

Within corporations, divisions, plants, products, and even groups of employees are often ranked on various measures of performance. From perspectives outside of the corporation, consumer groups develop rankings of products and companies in terms of safety, quality, and performance. Various government agencies rank corporations on the basis of their contribution to tax receipts, or on the number of jobs they supply at local, state, or national levels, or on the level of the amount of pollution they produce or have eliminated. Corporations are also ranked by nonprofit organizations on their amounts of support for charitable, educational, or artistic causes. These are just some of the examples of common uses of rankings. Because no framework for easily analyzing multiple period rankings has been developed thus far, these are all single-period uses of ordinal concepts.

Other evidence for the conceptual appropriateness of ordinal time series analysis arises from observing that many of the normative techniques for strategy analysis recognize, at least implicitly, that relative position should be a prime concern of strategy. Industrial organization theory maintains that industry structure and position within that structure are the prime determinants of the profitability of a firm (Bain, 1968; Scherer, 1980). The lifecycle curve (Hayes and Wheelwright, 1979), the BCG matrix and market share approaches (Buzzell, Gale, and Sultan, 1975; Rumelt and Wensley, 1981; Schoeffler, Buzzell, and Heaney, 1974; Prescott, Kohli, and Venkatraman, 1986; Gale, 1972), share-momentum matrices, and industry attractiveness-business strength matrices (Hax and Majluf, 1984, Ch. 8), and strategy maps (Day, 1987) all involve the concept of relative position as a strategic factor. For the most part, however, these techniques represent position in cardinal or ratio terms within the context of a market or industry, and rely on the graphical presentation they employ to convey the concept of position. Further, these approaches, with few exceptions, are static in nature and lack the dynamic attributes embodied in ordinal time series analysis.

Although this common usage of ordinal concepts in practice is hard to ignore, and although a wide number of strategy tools embody the concept of position in their formulations, as was noted in the first chapter, little effort has been devoted by management researchers toward incorporating ordinal concepts in longitudinal analyses or toward developing a methodology based on ordinal measurement into formal analytic methods for corporate strategy.

The notion of strategic position is relevant to situations where the competitive position of a firm in relation to a reference set of firms, rather than the level of a firm's performance relative to its past performance, should be emphasized. Ordinal analyses orient managers toward a more "strategic" way of thinking in a variety of ways. Even before data is collected for an ordinal analysis, a strategy analyst must define reference groups of competitor firms. The reference set of firms could be the target firm's strategic group, an industry segment, or the whole industry, but a particular reference group must be selected before analysis can proceed. Table 10.1 illustrates the possible levels of the hierarchy that can be used to provide a context for analysis above the level of the firm. In an ordinal analysis, given the rankings of firms at one level of the hierarchy, rankings at lower levels can easily be obtained by reranking the firms with respect to the selected subset. The presentation of data in the context of competitive position further orients managers toward strategic modes of thought. Even the obvious difficulty of making forecasts through linear extrapolations in an ordinal context forces an analyst to consider the future in a more theoretic fashion than is engendered by most cardinal approaches.

Table 10.1. Hierarchy for Analysis

International Economy
International Trade Group
National Economy
Economic Segment
Industry
Strategic Group
Firm

The ordinal approach to industry analysis thus reduces the likelihood of an exclusive focus on the internal problems of the firm and the dependence on cardinal comparisons of current to past performance. In addition, analysis in ordinal space carries with it an inherent context for performance measures. An improvement of 2% in return on assets for a firm by itself cannot be evaluated competitively except in a very trivial sense. An improvement of two positions in terms of ROA rank, however, is a direct competitive evaluation. Further in an ordinal context that can be many bases for performance and comparison. They can vary by dimension of performance, by hierarchical level, and by time period without engendering the need for complex calculations to adjust to the change.

The ordinal transformation screens out factors internal or external to a group of firms that affect all of them to the same extent that the effects of the factors do not cause rank changes. These factors would include not only the "background of constancies" (parameters regarded as fixed over the planning horizon) identified by Kuhn in his systems theoretic study of the airline industry (Kuhn, 1987), yet would also include system conditions that vary, but produce correlated change or change only within the cardinal interval that determines the rank of a firm.

Cardinal analysis allows approaches that treat the firm as unique in its environment; it permits the conclusion that absolute growth or change represents progress; and it leads to conclusions that it is the change over time by itself that is important. Cardinal analysis encourages (or at least does not discourage) the kind of absolutist thinking that leads managers to terminate strategic analyses after the company's strategic moves have been determined, but before competitive responses and the firm's counter-responses have been analyzed. One of the key contributions made by Porter in his first book (1980) was to emphasize the necessity for managers to go beyond the mere formulation of their own strategic moves to consider the reaction of other firms in the strategic group to those possible actions. In this respect, Porter was proposing the use of analysis that, in essence, has the very characteristics inherent in ordinal analysis.

The concept of competitive response is implicit in ordinal analysis, and becomes explicit whenever the next step in the process of generating the rankings is considered. To demonstrate this, consider the problems of forecasting with cardinal and ordinal data, respectively. To generate a simple forecast based on the cardinal data would involve a linear extrapolation of the trend established over the period for which data are available. On the other hand, consider the problem of forecasting the position for a firm based on historical data in ordinal form. In this case it is clear that the position the firm takes next will depend not only on the history of the firm and its performance in the ensuing period, but also on the history of the other firms in the reference group and their performance in the next period. A firm may well continue along its current cardinal trend line, but its strategic position in ordinal terms will also depend on the actions of the other firms and whether or not they follow their historical patterns. Of particular significance in determining the future position of a firm would be the performances of the firms immediately above and immediately below it in rank.

Thus, in planning for changes in the strategic position of a firm, the analyst not only needs to take into account the historical position of the firm and its current capabilities, the analyst also needs to consider the same information about the competition. What an analyst does not have to take into account are those external factors that will affect all firms in the reference group in some proportional manner. While such external forces cannot always be identified *a priori*, historical analysis of ordinal data for the strategic group should give an indication of the nature of those forces.

Ordinal analysis implies the notion of a strategic position for a firm in its competitive environments. In the most general analytic terms, the strategic position of a firm is given by a series of points in a space structured by n orthogonal ordinal performance dimensions, and a time dimension. The strategic position of firm i in that space for the period $T-m$ to T is given by the set of points:

$$SP_{iT} = (r_{i1t}, r_{i2t}, ..., r_{int}), \quad t = T-m, T-m+1,..., T \tag{10.1}$$

By the same logic, the strategic position for a group of firms S can be defined:

$$SP(S)_T = (P_{s1t}, P_{1s2t}, ..., P_{2snt}), \quad t = T-m, T-m+1,..., T \tag{10.2}$$

where P_{Sjt} is the position statistic for group S on performance dimension j at time t.

In the terms described above, the strategic position of an entity would be hard to depict for n larger than 2. Fortunately, because of the generic nature of the ordinal metric, the $(n+1)$-dimensional space described above can be easily mapped into a two-dimensional space. Consider a longitudinal ordinal performance space structured by an x-axis and a y-axis. The x-axis measures time, indicating the longitudinal nature of the performance assessment, while the y-axis in ordinal space gives the rank measure. Ordinal performance space is thus generic with respect to performance measures, in that neither the nature nor the number of performance or conduct dimensions is specified by the parameters of the space. The nature of the performance dimensions is not specified by the space because all performance is measured in terms of rank. Nor are the number of dimensions specified by the space, because any number of dimensions can be plotted on the same y-axis—the rank axis.

Strategic position is the position specified for a firm by longitudinal ordinal performance data on the key strategic dimensions with respect to a reference group that generates this space. The environment for evaluating position can be variable within a hierarchy, such as that in Table 10.1. This implies that strategic position is a group-relative as well as a longitudinal and multidimensional concept.

With respect to the dimensionality of strategic position, clearly not all of the possible dimensions of performance for a firm are of equal importance in determining the strategic position of a firm. In the airline industry example in chapters 3 and 4, market share was identified as a key strategic dimension that was being stabilized at the expense of the stability of several other key performance measures. There is not space here to go into methods or procedures for identifying key strategic dimensions, but all have the same underlying motivation, and that is to reduce the complexity of the problem facing a researcher or manager by reducing the number of dimensions that must be considered. In a recent paper, Kuhn (1987) provides a systems-theoretic context for such a process. As Kuhn points out, the strategic positioning process for a firm is both dynamic and relative; it is a homeostatic process that, from the perspective of an observer, takes place in a system composed of the firm, the competition, and the environment of the firm.

The concept of strategic position implies that it is a firm's position relative to a selected reference group or set of reference groups that is of prime importance in determining strategic performance. Strategy should be aimed at improving the position of the firm in the strategic space. Positional emphasis would, for example, avoid the pain of attempting to improve on historical performance in times when absolute increases are nearly impossible. The emphasis would be on improving position vis a vis competition; this might mean moderating a decline in absolute performance to yield an improvement in ordinal position. Emphasis on affecting strategic position would force the consideration of the possible actions and reactions of other firms in the reference group and their effects on the resulting position of the firm.

Conclusion

This book has introduced the concept and presented the basic methodology of longitudinal analysis based on ordinal data. While several articles have appeared in the academic and management literature, this book represents the most complete introduction, development, and sets of applications that is available for ordinal time series analysis. Management researchers in general, and those interested in corporate strategy and policy in particular, have traditionally eschewed the use of ordinal data in their analyses. A reliance on cardinal data alone has resulted in a dearth of longitudinal analyses—at a time when it has become widely recognized that longitudinal analyses are necessary to further our understanding of strategy and policy. Cardinal data have not been generally available in the quantity, and especially in the quality, required for traditional time series analyses. Nor is the situation likely to improve with the retrenchment of government and its withdrawal from the collection and dissemination of time series data regarding the private sector. The replacement of the government in data collection and dissemination operations by private firms that must directly cover the costs of their operations has meant that data quality and quantity have improved in some cases, but that the cost of such data is often prohibitive.

Even if the required cardinal data were available in the quantity and quality desired, the necessity of employing sophisticated mathematical techniques to remove noise and spurious trends from the data, and the depth of understanding required to make the necessary parametric assumptions and interpret their consequences, has placed conventional longitudinal analysis based on cardinal data out of the reach of many managers, analysts, and academic researchers. What has been lacking is a statistical methodology that could be employed with readily available (and not necessarily high quality) data, that did not require unreasonable assumptions to guarantee its results, that did not require arcane mathematics, and that offered a natural interpretation in the context of strategy and policy.

The importance of ordinal time series analysis is that it allows a corporate strategist a relatively simple way to analyze and present longitudinal data on multiple firms, measured along multiple performance dimensions, without making restrictive assumptions about underlying relationships among the observations, and without engaging in a multitude of computations. Further, as was mentioned earlier, the underlying cardinal data can even be somewhat imprecise, yet the ranking approach can still yield some useful results where cardinal analysis might be nearly impossible.

The relation of ordinal to cardinal analysis is not an either/or choice. Cardinal analysis and ordinal analysis can provide complementary information that gives an analyst better strategic information than could be obtained from either methodology alone. Differing methodologies can show different facets of a problem; together they can yield still another facet that can more clearly explain the common ground or identify the assumptions producing different results.

The developments of ordinal analysis and the comparisons of ordinal and cardinal analysis presented in this book have shown that while ordinal data may be less precise than cardinal data in absolute terms, ordinal analysis can yield interpretations of firm behavior that are more precise in a strategic sense. This aspect alone should recommend ordinal methods as strong candidates for use in firm and industry analyses, especially in situations where good data are scarce and where more traditional methodologies may yield misleading interpretations.

NOTE: A computer program is available for IBM personal computers or clones that will compute the rank and information statistics presented in this book. The output from this program is in the form of an ASCII file that can be called into a spreadsheet or graph program to produce output of the type shown in this book. The program runs under PC-DOS or MS-DOS and requires 640K random access memory. A copy of this program and documentation may be obtained by sending $75.00 (U.S. dollars) to ORDSTAT Program, IC^2 Institute, 2815 San Gabriel, Austin, TX 78705. Please specify 3 1/2" or 5 1/4" floppy disks.

Bibliography

"Chip Consortium: Before Congress Antes Up." *Wall Street Journal,* November 17, 1987.

"Chip Wars, Currency Wars." *Washington Post National Weekly Edition,* April 13, 1987, p. 16.

"Fallout from the Trade War in Chips." *Science,* 230 (November 22, 1985): 917-919.

"How Chipmakers Can Survive." *Fortune.* (April 1987): 89.

"Japan is in the Chips—and in Hot Water Here." *Washington Post National Weekly Edition,* April 13, 1987, p. 10.

"The Race that Launched a Thousand Chips." *Washington Post National Weekly Edition,* October 12, 1987, p. 22.

"Semiconductor Industry Survey: Part 1." *Japan Economic Journal* (August 1986).

"Tokyo Reacts Cautiously; Some Firms are Defensive." *Wall Street Journal,* March 30, 1987, p. 10.

"U.S., Japan Begin New Chip Talks, But Tariffs Still Set." *Wall Street Journal,* April 6, 1987, p. 25.

Abell, D. F. and J. S. Hammond. *Strategic Market Planning: Problems and Analytic Approaches.* Englewood Cliffs: Prentice-Hall, 1979.

Adams, F. G., H. Eguchi, and F. Meyer-zu-Schlochtern. *An Econometric Analysis of International Trade.* Paris: Organization for Economic Cooperation and Development, 1969.

Altshuler, A. *Current Issues in Transportation Policy.* Lexington: D. C. Heath, 1979.

Ames, B. C. "Corporate Strategies for a Shrinking Market." *Wall Street Journal,* January 13, 1986, p. 24.

Ansoff, I. *Corporate Strategy.* New York: McGraw-Hill, 1965.

Argresti, A. *Analysis of Ordinal Categorical Data.* New York: John Wiley & Sons, 1984.

Armour, H. O. and D. J. Teece. "Organization Structure and Economic Performance: A Test of the Multidivisional Hypothesis." *Bell Journal of Economics* (Spring 1978): 106-122.

Ashby, W. R. *An Introduction to Cybernetics.* New York: Wiley & Sons, 1956.

Auerbach, S. "Getting Competitive." *Washington Post National Weekly Edition*, December 1986, p. 22.

Bailey, E. E., D. R. Graham, and D. P. Kaplan. *Deregulating the Airlines.* Cambridge: MIT Press, 1985.

Bain, J. S. *Industrial Organization.* 2nd edition, New York: John Wiley & Sons, 1968.

Balakrishnan, S. and B. Wernerfelt. "Technical Change, Competition and Vertical Integration." *Strategic Management Journal* (1986): 347-359.

Bass, F. M. "Profit and the A/S Ratio." *Journal of Advertising Research* 14 (1974): 9-19.

Bass, F. M., P. Cattin, and P. Wittink. "Firm Effects and Industry Effects in the Analysis of Market Structure and Profitability." *Journal of Marketing Research* 15 (1978): 3-10.

Beard, D.W. and G. G. Dess. "Corporate-level Strategy, Business-level Strategy, and Firm Performance." *Academy of Management Journal* 24 (1981): 663-688.

Beaver, W., P. Ketter, and M. Scholes. "The Association Between Market Determined and Accounting Determined Risk Measures." *Accounting Review* (October 1970): 654-682.

Bettis, R. A. "Performance Differences in Related and Unrelated Diversified Firms." *Strategic Management Journal* 2 (October-December 1981): 379-393.

Bettis, R. A. "Modern Financial Theory, Corporate Strategy and Public Policy: Three Conundrums." *Academy of Management Review* 8, 3 (1983): 406-415.

Bettis, R. A. and W. K. Hall. "Diversification Strategy, Accounting Determined Risk and Accounting Determined Return." *Academy of Management Journal* 25, 2 (1982): 254-264.

Bettis, R. A. and V. Mahajan. "Risk/Return Performance of Diversified Firms." *Management Science* 31, 7 (July 1985): 785-799.

Biggadike, R. "The Risky Business of Diversification." *Harvard Business Review* 57, 3 (1988): 103-111.

Boisjoly, R. P. and T. M. Corsi. "The Aftermath of the Motor Carrier Act of 1980: Entry, Exit, and Merger," 258-264. *Proceedings of the 23rd Annual Meeting of the Transportation Research Forum.*

Boston Consulting Group. "Perspectives on Experience." Boston, Mass., 1972.

Bowman, E. H. "A Risk/Return Paradox for Strategic Management." *Sloan Management Review* (Spring 1980): 17-31.

Briskin, L. "The Difference Between Productivity and Competitiveness." *Industrial Management* 29 (May-June 1987): 9-13.

Brockett, P. L. and J. H. B. Kemperman. "Statistical Recognition of Trends in Health Monitoring Systems." *Methods of Information in Medicine* 19 (April 1980): 106-112.

Brozen, Y. "Concentration and Structural and Market Disequilibria." *Antitrust Bulletin* 16 (Summer 1971): 241-248.

Business Week. "Who's Excellent Now?" (Nov. 5, 1984): 87-94.

Buzzell, R. D., B. T. Gale, and R. M. Sultan. "Market Share—A Key to Profitability." *Harvard Business Review* 53, no. 1 (1975): 97-106.

Byrnes, J. L. S. *Diversification Strategies for Regulated and Deregulated Industries: Lessons from the Airlines.* Lexington: D. C. Heath, 1985.

Calantone, R. and R. G. Cooper. "New Product Scenarios: Prospects for Success." *Journal of Marketing* 45 (Spring 1981): 48-80.

Carroll, D. T. "A Disappointing Search for Excellence." *Harvard Business Review* 6 (November-December 1983): 78-88.

Carter, J. C. "An Entropic-Based Partitioning Approach to the Analysis of Competition." Ph. D. diss., Columbia University, 1979.

Caves, D. W., L. R. Christiansen, and M. W. Trethway. "U. S. Trunk Air Carriers, 1972-1977: A Multilateral Comparison of Total Factor Productivity." In *Productivity Measurement in Regulated Industries* edited by T. G. Cowing, and R. E. Stevenson. Academic Press, 1981.

Caves, R. E. and B. S. Yamey. "Risk and Corporate Rates of Return: Comment." *Quarterly Journal of Economics* 85 (August 1971): 513-517.

Caves, R. "Uncertainty, Market Structure and Performance: Galbraith as Conventional Wisdom." In *Industrial Organization and Economic Development,* edited by J. W. Markham and G. F. Papanek, 283-302. Boston: Houghton-Mifflin, 1970.

Caves, R. E. *American Industry: Structure, Conduct, Performance,* 4th edition. Engelwood Cliffs: Prentice-Hall, 1977.

Chandler, A., Jr. *Strategy and Structure: Chapters in the History of the American Industrial Enterprise.* Cambridge: MIT Press, 1962.

Chandrasekaran, G. *Strategy, Structure, Market Concentration and Organization Performance.* Ph. D. diss., State University of New York at Buffalo, 1982.

Chang, Y. and H. Thomas. "The Impact of Diversification Strategy on Risk-Return Performance." *Academy of Management Proceedings* (1987): 2-6.

Charnes, A., W. W. Cooper, D. B. Learner, and F. Y. Phillips. "An MDI Model and an Algorithm for Composite Hypothesis Testing and Estimation in Marketing." *Marketing Science* 3 (Winter 1983): 55-72.

Charnes, A., W. W. Cooper, T. W. Ruefli, D. Devine and D. Thomas. "Comparisons of DEA and Existing Ratio and Regression Systems for Effecting Efficiency Evaluations of Regulated Electric Cooperatives in Texas." In *Research in Governmental and Nonprofit Accounting,*

187-210, edited by J. L. Chan and J. M. Patton, Vol 5, Greenwich: JAI Press, 1989.

Child, A. "Organization Structure, Environment, and Performance: The Role of the Strategic Choice." *Sociology* 6 (1972).

Christensen, C. R., K. R. Andrew, and J. L. Bower. *Business Policy: Text and Cases,* 4th ed., Homewood: R. D. Irwin, 1978.

Christiansen, H. K. and C. A. Montgomery. "Corporate Economic Performance: Diversification Strategy versus Market Structure." *Strategic Management Journal* 2 (1981): 327-343.

Christopher, R. C. "Don't Blame the Japanese." *New York Times Magazine* (October 19, 1986).

Clutterback, D. "The Dangers of Too Much Excellence." In *Strategic Direction,* edited by D. Clutterback, 15, 1986.

Cohen, S. S. and J. Zysman. "Manufacturing Innovation and American Industrial Competitiveness." *Science,* 239 (March 1988): 1110-1115.

Collins, N. R. and L. E. Preston. "Price—Cost Margins and Industry Structure." *Review of Economics and Statistics* 51 (August 1969): 271-286.

Conrad, G. R. and I. H. Plotkin. "Risk/Return: U.S. Industry Pattern." *Harvard Business Review* (March-April 1968): 90-99.

Cooper, R.G. "The Dimensions of Industrial New Product Success and Failure." *Journal of Marketing* 43 (July 1979): 93-103.

Cowing, T. G. and R. E. Stevenson. "Diversification in Major U.S. Airlines." *Transportation Journal* 20, 3 (Spring 1981).

Crock, S. and P. Dwyer. "Looser Antitrust Laws Won't Trim America's Trade Gap." *Business Week* (February 1986).

Cunningham, L. F. and W. R. Wood. "Airline Diversification." *Transportation Journal* (Spring 1983).

Daniel, W. W. *Applied Nonparametric Statistics.* Boston: Houghton Mifflin, 1978.

Day, D. L., W. S. Desarbo, and T. A. Oliva. "Strategy Maps: A Spatial Representation of Intra-Industry Competitive Strategy." *Management Science* 33, 12 (December 1987): 1534-1551.

Day, G. S. "The Product Life Cycle: Analysis and Applications Issues." *Journal of Marketing* (Fall 1981): 60-67.

Demsetz, H. "Industry Structure, Market Rivalry and Public Policy." *Journal of Law and Economics* 16 (April 1973): 1-10.

Diewert, W. E. "The Theory of Total Factor Productivity Measurement in Regulated Industries." In *Productivity Measurement in Regulated Industries,* edited by Thomas G. Cowing and Rodney E. Stevenson. Academic Press, 1981.

Dinneto, D. M., R. McDaniel, Jr., T. W. Ruefli, and J. B. Thomas. "The Use of Ordinal Time Series Analysis in Assessing Policy Inputs and Impacts." *Applied Behavioral Science* 22, 1 (January-February 1986).

Dundas, K. N. M. and P. R. Richardson. "Implementing the Unrelated Product Strategy." *Strategic Management Journal* 3 (1982): 287-301.

Eastham, T. R. "Japan Lobby Hires Best U.S. Advisers." *Japan Times,* January 21, 1986.

Engwall, L. *Models of Industrial Structure.* Lexington: D.C. Heath, 1973.

Finan, W. F. and A. M. LaMond. "Sustaining U.S. Competitiveness in Microelectronics: The Challenge to U.S. Policy." *U. S. Competitiveness in the World Economy,* edited by B. R. Scott and G. C. Lodge, chapter 3. Boston: Harvard Business School Press, 1985.

Fischer, S., M. Parkin, and J. A. Frenkel. "The Economy of Israel." *Carnegie-Rochester Conference Series on Public Policy* 20 (Spring 1984): 7-67.

Fishburn, P. C. *Interval Orders and Interval Graphs: A Study of Partially Ordered Sets.* New York: Wiley-Interscience, 1985.

Fisher, N. and G. R. Hall. "Risk and Corporate Rates of Return." *Quarterly Journal of Economics* 83 (February 1969): 79-92.

Forrester, J. W. "Understanding Social and Economic Change in the United States." In *The Next 25 Years: Crisis and Opportunity,* edited by A. A. Spekke. Washington, D. C.: World Future Society, 1975.

Freund, J. E. and F. J. Williams. *Business Statistics: The Modern Approach.* Englewood Cliffs: Prentice-Hall, 1964.

Friedlaender, A. F. and R. H. Spady. *Freight Transport Regulation.* Cambridge: MIT Press, 1981.

Fruhan, W. *The Fight for Competitive Advantage: A Study of the United States Domestic Trunk Air Carriers.* Boston: Harvard University, Division of Research, 1972.

Galbraith, C. and D. Schendel. "An Empirical Analysis of Strategy Types." *Strategic Management Journal* 4 (1983): 153-173.

Gale, B.T. "Market Share and Rate of Return." *Review of Economics and Statistics* 54 (1972): 412-423.

Gokhale, D. V. and S. Kullback. *The Information in Contingency Tables.* New York: Marcel Dekker, 1978.

Gorman, D. "Recent Economic Performance and Prospects in COMECON." *Barclays Review.* 55, 3 (August 1980): 61-65.

Granger, C. W. J. and M. Hatanaka. *Spectral Analysis of Economic Time Series.* Princeton: Princeton University Press, 1964.

Guenther, G. L. "Performance and International Competitiveness of the U. S. Semiconductor Industry, 1975-88." Congressional Research Service, No. 85-1064E. Washington, D. C.: Library of Congress, 1985.

Hadley, G. *Elementary Statistics.* San Francisco: Holden-Day, 1969.

Hajek, J. and Z. Sidak. *Theory of Rank Tests.* New York: Academic Press, 1967.

Hall, F. L. "World Trade Outlook." *Business America* (July 27, 1981): 1; (February 20, 1984): 2; (August 20, 1984): 2.

Hall, M. and L. Weiss. "Firm Size and Profitability." *Review of Economics and Statistics* 49 (August 1967): 319-331.

Harrigan, K. R. "An Application of Clustering for Strategic Group Analysis." *Strategic Management Journal* 6 (1985): 55-73.

Harris, R. G. and L. A. Sullivan. "Horizontal Merger Policy: Promoting Competition and American Competitiveness." *Antitrust Bulletin* 31, 4 (Winter 1986): 871-933.

Hart, P. E. "Entropy and Other Measures of Concentration." *Journal of the Royal Statistical Society* 134 (1971): 73-85.

Hatten, K. J. "Quantitative Research Methods in Strategic Management" In *Strategic Management*, edited by D. Schendel and C. Hofer. Boston: Little-Brown, 1979.

Hatten, K. J. and D. E. Schendel. "Heterogeneity within an Industry: The Case of the U.S. Brewing Industry, 1952-1971." *Journal of Industrial Economics* 26, 2 (1977): 97-113.

Hatten, K. J., D. E. Schendel, and A. C. Cooper. "A Strategic Model of the U.S. Brewing Industry: 1952 - 1971." *Academy of Management Journal* 21, 4 (1978): 592-610.

Hax, A. C. and N. S. Majluf. *Strategic Management: An Integrative Perspective*. Englewood Cliffs: Prentice-Hall, 1984.

Hayes, R. H. and S. C. Wheelwright. *Restoring Our Competitive Edge— Competing Through Manufacturing*. New York: John Wiley & Sons, 1984.

Hayes, R. H. and S.C. Wheelwright. "Link Manufacturing Process and Product Life-Cycle." *Harvard Business Review* 57, 1 (January-February 1979): 133-140.

Hayes, R. H. and S. G. Wheelwright "The Dynamics of Process-Product Life Cycles." *Harvard Business Review* (March-April 1979): 127-136.

Heggestad, A. A. and S. A. Rhoades. "Concentration and Firm Stability in Commercial Banking." *The Review of Economics and Statistics* 58 (November 1976): 443-452.

Henderson, B. D. *Henderson on Corporate Strategy*. Cambridge: Abt Books, 1979.

Hollander, M. and D. A. Wolfe. *Nonparametrical Statistical Methods*. New York: Wiley, 1973.

Horowitz, A. and I. Horowitz "Entropy, Markov Processes and Competition in the Brewing Industry." *Journal of Industrial Economics* 16 (July 1968): 196-211.

Hunsaker, J. K. "The Changing Shape of America's Airline Industry: An Analysis of the Deregulation Strategies of Five Airlines." *Proceedings of the 22nd Annual Meeting of the Transportation Research Forum*, 1981, pp. 449-456.

Hurdle, G. J. "Leverage, Risk, Market Structure and Profitability." *Review of Economics and Statistics* 56 (November 1974): 478-489.

International Trade Administration. "A Competitive Assessment of the U. S. Semiconductor Manufacturing Equipment Industry." Washington, D. C.: U. S. Department of Commerce, 1985.

International Trade Administration. "An Assessment of U. S. Competitiveness in High Technology Industries." Washington D. C.: U. S. Department of Commerce, 1983.

Jackson, B. B. and B. P. Shapiro. "New Ways to Make Product Line Decisions." *Harvard Business Review* (May-June 1979): 140.

Jacquemin, A. P. and C. H. Berry. "Entropy Measure of Diversification and Corporate Growth." *The Journal of Industrial Economics* 24, 4 (June 1979): 359-369.

Japan Economic Journal. "Semiconductor Industry Survey: Part 1." (August 2, 1986).

Kanter, R. M. "Increasing Competitiveness Without Restructuring." *Management Review* 76 (June 1987): 21ff.

Kendall, M.G. *Rank Correlation Methods* . 4th edition, London: Griffen, 1970.

Kern, K. R. editor. *Corporate Diagrams and Administrative Personnel of the Chemical Industry.* Princeton: Chemical Economic Services, 1964.

Kimberley, J. R. "Data Aggregation in Organizational Research: The Temporal Dimension." *Organizational Studies* 1 (1980): 367-377.

Kimberley, J. R. "Issues in the Design of Longitudinal Organizational Research." *Sociological Methods and Research* 4 (1976): 321-347.

Knight, F. H. *Risk, Uncertainty and Profitability.* New York: Harper Torch Books, 1965.

Kondratieff, N. D. "Die Langen Wellen der Knojunktur." *Archiv fur Socialwissenschaft.* December 1926; translated into English in abridged form by W. Stopler as "The Long Wave of Economic Life." *Review of Economics and Statistics* (Nov. 1935).

Kotler, P. "Competitive Strategies for New Product Marketing Over the Life Cycle." *Management Science* 12 (December 1965): 104-119.

Kotler, P. *Marketing Management: Analysis, Planning and Control,* 4th edition, Englewood Cliffs: Prentice-Hall, 1980.

Kozmetsky, G. "Commercializing Technology: The New Management Challenge." IC^2 Institute, The University of Texas at Austin, 1986.

Kuczmarski, T. D. and S. Silver. "Strategy: The Key to Successful New Product Development." *Management Review* (July 1982): 2640.

Kuhn, A. "System Design for Performance Control and Deregulation: Steersmanship in the New Environment." Berkeley: University of California, Office of Institutional Research, 1987.

Lachica, E. "Task Force Urges Pentagon Subsidies for Chip Makers." *Wall Street Journal*, February 13, 1987), p. 9.

Lachica, E. "U.S. Semiconductor Firms are Knocking Only Small Chips off the Japanese Block." *Wall Street Journal*, June 2, 1987, p. 6.

Lawrence, R. Z. "Can America Compete?" Washington, D. C.: Brookings Institution, 1984.

Lehmann, E. L. *Nonparametrics: Statistical Methods Based on Ranks.* San Francisco: Holden-Day, 1975.

Leibowitz, M. R. "Chip Takeover Targets." *High Technology Business.* September 1987.

Levitt, T. "Exploit the Product Life Cycle." *Harvard Business Review* (November-December 1965): 81-94.

Lieb, R. C. *Transportation: The Domestic System.* Second edition, Reston: Publishing, 1981.

Lindenberg, E. B. and S. A. Ross. "Tobin's q Ratio and Industrial Organization." *Journal of Business* 54, 1 (1981): 1-32.

Luce, R. D. and L. Narens. "Measurement Scales on the Continuum." *Science* 236, 19 (June 1987): 1527-1532.

MacDonald, J. M. "Diversification, Market Growth, and Concentration in U.S. Manufacturing." *Southern Economic Journal* 50, 4 (April 1984): 1098-1111.

Mahajan, V., Y. Wind, and J. Bradford. "Stochastic Dominance Rules for Product Portfolio Analysis." In *TIMS Studies on Marketing Planning,* edited by A. Zoltners. Providence: Institute for Management Sciences, 1981.

Mandell, R. W. *Financing Capital Requirements of the U.S.Airline Industry in the 1980s.* Lexington: D. C. Heath, 1979.

Mansfield, E. "Price Indexes for R and D Inputs, 1969-1983." *Management Science* 33, 1 (January 1987): 124-129.

Markham, J. W. *Conglomerate Enterprise and Corporate Performance* Cambridge: Harvard University Press, 1973.

Marlow, M. L., J. P. Link, and R. P. Trost. "Market Structure and Rivalry: New Evidence with a Non-Linear Model." *The Review of Economics and Statistics* (1985): 678-682.

McClellan, S. T. *The Coming Computer Industry Shakeout: Winners, Losers & Survivors.* New York: John Wiley & Sons, 1984.

McEnally, R. W. "Competition and Dispersion in Rate of Return: A Note." *Journal of Industrial Economics* 25 (September 1976): 69-75.

Melicher, R. W., D. F. Rush, and D. F. Winn. "Degree of Industry Concentration and Market Risk-Return Performance." *Journal of Financial and Quantitative Analysis* (November 1876): 627-635.

Meyer, J. R. and C. V. Oster, editors. *Airline Deregulation: The Early Experience.* Boston: Auburn House, 1981.

Meyer, M. H. and E. B. Roberts. "New Products in Small Technology-Based Firms: A Pilot Study." *Management Science* 32, 7 (July 1986): 806-821.

Miller, D. and P. Friesen. "The Longitudinal Analysis of Organizations." *Management Science* 28, 9 (September 1982): 1013-1034.

Ministry of International Trade and Industry. *White Paper on International Trade* 1955-84. Tokyo, 1985.

Montgomery, C. A. Diversification, Market Structure, and Firm Performance: An Extension of Rumelt's Model. Ph. D. diss., Purdue University, 1979.

Montgomery, C. A. The Measurement of Firm Diversification: Some New Empirical Evidence. *Academy of Management Journal* 25 (1982): 299-307.

Morash, E. A. and C. Enis. "The Effects of Motor Carrier Deregulation: A Stock Market Perspective." *Proceedings of the 23rd Annual Meeting of the Transportation Research Forum* (1982): 256-271.

More, R. "Why Industrial Product Strategic Planning Fails." *Business Quarterly* (Spring 1982): 54-60.

Moyers, R. C. and R. Chatfield. "Market Power and Systematic Risk." *Journal of Economics and Business* 35 (1983): 123-130.

Nathanson, D. A. and J. Cassano. "Organizational Diversity and Performance." *The Wharton Magazine* (Summer 1982): 18-26.

Noyce, R. N. and A. W. Wolff. "High-Tech Trade in the 1980s: The International Challenge and the U.S. Response." *Issues in Science and Technology* (Spring 1986): 61-71.

Palepu, K. "Diversification Strategy, Profit Performance and the Entropy Measure." *Strategic Management Journal* 6 (1985): 239-255.

Peters, T. J. and R. H. Waterman, Jr. *In Search of Excellence: Lessons from America's Best Run Companies.* New York: Harper and Row, 1982.

Phillips, A. "Structure, Conduct and Performance—and Performance, Conduct and Structure?" In *Industrial Organization and Economic Development*, edited by Jesse W. Markham and Gustav F. Papanek, 283-302. Boston: Houghton-Mifflin, 1970.

Phillips, F. Y. "Some Information Theoretic Methods for Management Analysis in Marketing and Resources." Ph.D. diss. The University of Texas at Austin, 1978.

Pitts, R. A. "Strategies and Structures for Diversification." *Academy of Management Journal* 20, 2 (1977): 197-208.

Pitts, R. A. "Diversification Strategies and Policies of Large Diversified Firms." *Journal of Economics and Business* 28, 2 (1976): 181-188.

Poli, R. and V. Cook. "Validity of the Product Life Cycle." *Journal of Business* 42, 4 (1969): 385-400.

Porter, M. E. *Competition in Global Industries.* Boston: Harvard Business School Press, 1986.

Porter, M. E. *Competitive Strategy: Techniques for Analyzing Industries and Competitors.* New York: The Free Press, 1980.

Prescott, J. E., A. K. Kohli, and N. Ventraman "The Market Share—Profitability Relationship: An Empirical Assessment of Major Assertions and Contradictions." *Strategic Management Journal* 7 (1986): 377-394.

Quastler, H. "A Primer on Information Theory" In *Symposium on Information Theory in Biology*, edited by H. P. Yockey, 3-49. New York: Pergammon Press, 1957.

Rabino, S. and A. Wright. "Financial Evaluation of the Product Line." *Journal of Product Innovation Management* 2 (1985): 56-65.

Rabino, S. and H. R. Moskowitz. "Optimizing the Product Development Process: Strategical Implications for New Entrants." *Sloan Management Review* (Spring 1980): 45-51.

Reich, R. B. and E. D. Mankin. "Joint Ventures with Japan Give Away Our Future." *Harvard Business Review* 2 (March-April 1986): 78-86.

Rhoades, S. A. "Entry and Competition in Banking." *Journal of Banking and Finance* 4 (1980): 143-150.

Rhoades, S. A. and R. D. Rutz. "A Reexamination and Extension of the Relationship between Concentration and Firm Rank Stability." *The Review of Economics and Statistics* 63 (August 1981): 446-451.

Rock, M. L. "Taking Issue With 'Excellence.'" *Directors & Boards* 8, 1 (Fall 1983): 5.

Ross, I. M. "The Global Contest in Industrial Competition Has Just Begun." *Research Management* 28, 3 (May-June 1985): 10ff.

Rostow, W. W. "The Developing World in the Fifth Kondratieff Upswing." *Annals of the American Academy of Political and Social Science* 420 (July 1975): 111.

Ruefli, T. W. "Impacts of Deregulation on Performance and Management of the Largest American Transportation Companies." *Technovation,* 5, 35-60. Amsterdam: Elsevier Science Publishers, 1986. Also in *Innovation and Entrepreneurship in Organizations: Strategies for Competitiveness, Deregulation and Privatization,* edited by R. Burton and B. Obel, Amsterdam: Elsevier Science Publishers, 1988.

Ruefli, T. W. "Creative and Innovative Management: A Manifesto for Academia." In *Frontiers in Creative and Innovative Management,* edited by R. L. Kuhn, 277-293. Cambridge: Ballinger, 1985.

Ruefli, T. W. "Ordinal Measures for Strategy and Management Control: Application to the U.S. Airline Industry." *Technovation* 8, 1-3 (1989): 43-70. Also in *Organizational Responses to the New Business Conditions: An Empirical Perspective,* edited by R. Burton, J. D. Forsyth, and B. Obel. Amsterdam: Elsevier, 1989.

Ruefli, T. W. "Mean Variance Approaches to Risk-Return Relationships in Strategy: Paradox Lost." *Management Science* (March 1990): 368-380.

Ruefli, T. W. and C. L. Wilson. "Ordinal Time Series Methodology for Industry and Competitive Analysis." *Management Science* 33 5 (May 1987): 640-661.

Ruefli, T. W., R. Salazar, and C. Wilson. "Relative Rank Analysis: Theory and Application." Working Paper, Austin: IC^2 Institute, The University of Texas at Austin, 1984.

Ruefli, T. W. and C. L. Wilson. "Comparative Relative Rank Analysis for Industry and Competitive Analysis." Working Paper, Austin: IC^2 Institute, The University of Texas at Austin, 1984.

Rumelt, R. P. and R. Wensley. "In Search of Market Share Effect." *Proceedings of the Academy of Management,* 2-6, 1981.

Rumelt, R. P. "Diversification Strategy and Profitability." *Strategic Management Journal* 3 (1982): 359-369.

Rumelt, R. P. *Strategy, Structure and Economic Performance.* Boston: Harvard University, Graduate School of Business Administration, 1974.

Saba, S. "The U.S. and Japanese Electronics Industries: Competition and Cooperation." *Issues in Science and Technology* (Spring 1986): 53-60.

Salazar, R. and T. W. Ruefli. "Concordance Measures for Industry Analysis." Working Paper, Austin: IC^2 Institute, The University of Texas at Austin, 1985.

Salter, M. S. and W. A. Weinhold. *Diversification through Acquisitions: Strategies for Creating Economic Value.* New York: The Free Press, 1979.

Sampson, A. *Empire of the Sky : The Politics, Contents and Cartels of the World Airlines.* New York: Random House, 1984.

Samuelson, L. *A. New Model of World Trade.* Paris: Organization for Economic Coperation and Development, 1973.

Samuelson, R.J. "Chip Industry Joins the Unwise Drift to Managed Trade." *Los Angeles Times*, August 13, 1986, p. 5.

Sanger, D. E. "Pushing America Out of Chips." *New York Times* , June 16, 1985, p. 1F+.

Scherer, F. M. *Industrial Market Structure and Economic Performance.* Chicago: Rand-McNally, 1980.

Schlender, B. R. "Semiconductor Accord with Japan Fails to Aid U.S. Firms, as Intended." *Wall Street Journal* 79,30, February 1987, pp. 1,8.

Schoeffler, S., R. D. Buzzell, and D. F. Heany. "Impact of Strategic Planning on Profit Performance." *Harvard Business Review* 52 (1974): 137-145.

Schramm, R. and R. Sherman. "Profit, Risk Management and 'The Theory of the Firm.'" *Southern Economic Journal* 40 (January 1974): 353-363.

Schumpeter, J.A. *Business Cycles.* New York: McGraw-Hill, 1939.

Scott, B. R. "U.S. Competitiveness: Concepts, Performance, and Implications." In *U.S. Competitiveness in the World Economy,* edited by B. R. Scott and G. C. Lodge. Boston: Harvard Business School Press, 1985.

Scott, B. R. and G. C. Lodge. *U.S. Competitiveness in the World Economy.* Boston: Harvard Business School Press, 1985.

Scott, B. R. and G. C. Lodge. "Introduction" In *U.S. Competitiveness in the World Economy*, edited by B. R. Scott and G. C. Lodge. Boston: Harvard Business School Press, 1985.

Secretariat of the Contracting Parties to the General Agreement on Tariffs and Trade. *International Trade.* Geneva, Switzerland, 1950-1986.

Seventy-fourth American Assembly. "Running Out of Time: Reversing America's Declining Competitiveness." New York: Harriman, November 1987.

Shannon, C. E. and W. Weaver. *The Mathematical Theory of Communication.* Urbana: University of Illinois Press, 1949.

Shepherd, W. G. "The Elements of Market Structure." *Review of Economics and Statistics* 54 (1972): 25-37.

Shuman, J. B. and D. Rosenqu. *The Kondratieff Wave.* New York: World Publishing, 1972.

Smithsonian Institution. "Critical Choices: Fighting Back or Joining Up."
    Washington, D. C.: Executive Working Session on U.S. Electronics
    Industry Competitiveness, June 1986.
Solomon, E. and J. J. Pringle. *An Introduction To Financial Management.*
    Santa Monica: Goodyear Publishing, 1977.
Spady, R. H. *Econometric Estimation of Cost Functions for the Regulated
    Transportation Industries.* New York: Garland Publishing, 1979.
Starr, M. K. *Global Competitiveness.* New York: W. W. Norton, 1988.
Stastistical Yearbook. New York: United Nations, 1953-1981.
Steele, L. W. and B. Hammay. *The Competitive Status of U.S. Industry.*
    Washington, D. C.: National Academy Press, 1985.
Steiner, G. *Strategic Planning.* New York: Free Press, 1979.
Steiner, P. O. *Mergers: Motives, Effects, Policies.* Ann Arbor: University
    of Michigan Press, 1977.
Stevens, S. S. "On the Theory of Scales of Measurement." *Science* 103
    (1946): 677-680.
Stiglitz, H. and C. D. Wilkerson. *Corporate Organization Structure.*
    Studies in Personnel Policy No. 210, New York: National Industrial
    Conference Board, 1968.
Stobaugh, R. and P. Telesio. "Match Manufacturing Policies and Product
    Strategy." *Harvard Business Review* (March-April 1983): 113-120.
Sullivan, T. G. "The Cost of Capital and Market Power of Firms." *Review
    of Economics and Statistics* (May 1978): 209-217.
Sumney, L. W. and R. M. Berger. "Revitalizing the U.S. Semiconductor
    Industry." *Issues in Science and Technology* (Summer 1987): 32-41.
Taneja, N. K. *U. S. International Aviation Policy.* Lexington: D. C. Heath,
    1980.
Teece, D. J. *The Competitive Challenge.* Cambridge: Ballinger, 1987.
Tellis, G. J. and C. M. Crawford. "An Evolutionary Approach to Product
    Growth Theory." *Journal of Marketing* 45 (Fall 1981): 125-132.
Temple, Barker, and Sloane, Inc. *Transportation Strategies for the Eighties.*
    Oak Brook: National Council of Physical Distribution Management,
    1982.
Theil, H. and D. G. Fiebig. *Exploiting Continuity: Maximum Entropy
    Estimation of Continuous Distributions.* Cambridge: Ballinger, 1984.
Thorelli, H. B. and S. C. Burnett. "The Nature of Product Life Cycles for
    Industrial Goods Businesses." *Journal of Marketing 45* (Fall 1981):
    97-108.
Thorelli, H. B. *Strategy + Structure = Performance.* Bloomington: Indiana
    University Press, 1978.
U. S. Department of Transportation Planning. *National Transportation
    Trends and Choices (to the Year 2000).* Washington, D. C., 1978.
United Nations. *Handbook of International Trade and Development
    Statistics.* New York: United Nations, 1983.
"United Nations Conference on Trade and Development." *Review of
    International Trade and Development.* New York: United Nations,
    1969, 1975, and 1977.

United States International Trade Commission. "64K Dynamic Random Access Memory Components from Japan." Washington, D. C., Publication #1735, August 1985.

United States International Trade Commission. "Dynamic Random Access Memory Semiconductors of 256 Kilobits and Above from Japan." Washington, D. C., Publication #1803, January 1986.

United States International Trade Commission. "Erasable Programmable Read Only Memories form Japan." Washington, D. C.: United States Publication #1778, November 1985.

Waldman, P. and B. R. Schlender. "Is a Big Federal Role the Way to Revitalize Semiconductor Firms?" *Wall Street Journal,* 79, 32, February 17, 1987, pp. 1 and 22.

Waldman, P. and E. Lachica. "Chip Producers Press U.S. to Help Form Consortium to Meet Japan's Competition." *Wall Street Journal* 79, 43, March 4, 1987, p. 6.

Weidenbaum, M. L. "Japan Bashing and Foreign Trade." *Society* (May/June 1986): 42+.

Weiner, N. *Cybernetics.* New York: John Wiley & Sons, 1948.

Weiss, L. W. "The Concentration-Profits Relationship and Anti-Trust." In *Industrial Concentration: The New Learning*, edited by H. Goldschmidt, M. Mann and J. Fred. Boston: Little, Brown and Co, 1974.

Wheelwright, S.C. "Restoring the Competitive Edge in U.S. Manufacturing." *California Management Review* 27, 3 (Spring 1985): 26ff.

White, K.K. *Understanding the Company Organization Chart.* Research Study No. 56. New York: American Management Association, 1963.

White Paper on International Trade 1955-1984. Tokyo: Ministry of International Trade and Industry, 1985.

White, R. M. "The Challenge to U. S. Competitiveness." *Science*, 236, 4805 (May 29, 1987): 1041ff.

Williamson, O. E. *Markets and Hierarchies.* New York: The Free Press, 1975.

Wilson, J. W. "Is It Too Late to Save the U. S. Semiconductor Industry?" *Business Week* (August 18, 1986): 62ff.

Wind, Yoram. "A New Procedure for Concept Evaluation." *Journal of Marketing* 37 (October 1973): 2-11.

Wind, Y. "Product Portfolio: A New Approach to the Product Mix Decision." In *Proceedings of the August 1974 American Marketing Association Conference*, edited by Ronald C. Curhan, 460. Chicago: American Marketing Association, 1974.

Wind, Y. "Product-Marketing Planning Models: Concepts, Techniques and Needed Development." In *Analytic Approaches to Product and Marketing Planning,* edited by A. D. Shocker, 41-43. Boston: Boston Marketing Science Institute, April 1979.

Wind, Y. "The Perception of a Firm's Competitive Position" In *Behavioral Models of Market Analysis: Foundations of Marketing Action*, edited by Francisco M. Nicoosia and Yoram Wind, 55-66. Dryden Press, 1980.

Wind, Y. and H. J. Claycamp. "Planning Product Line Strategy: A Matrix Approach." *Journal of Marketing* 40 (January 1976): 2-9.

Wind, Y. and V. Mahajan. "Designing Product and Business Portfolios." *Harvard Business Review* (January-February 1981): 155-165.

Wind, Y. and P. J. Robinson. "Product Positioning: An Application of Multidimensional Scaling" In *Attitude Research in Transition*, edited by R. I. Haley, 155-175. Chicago: American Marketing Association, 1972.

Wind, Y. and T. Saaty. "Marketing Applications of the Analytic Hierarchy Process." *Management Science* 26, 7 (July 1980): 641-658.

Wind, Y. *Product Policy: Concepts, Methods, and Strategy*. Reading: Addison-Wesley, 1981.

Winn, D. N. "On the Relations between Rates of Return, Risk and Market Structure." *Quarterly Journal of Economics* 91 (1977): 153-163.

Woo, C. Y. "Path Analysis of the Relationship Between Market Share, Business-level Conduct and Risk." *Strategic Management Journal* 8 (1987): 149-168.

World Almanac and Book of Facts. New York: Doubleday and Company, 1953-1983.

Wright, R. V. L. "A System for Managing Diversity" In *Marketing in Management and Administrative Action*, edited by S. H. Britt and H. W. Boyd, Jr., New York: McGraw-Hill, 1978.

Wrigley, L. "Divisional Autonomy and Diversification." D.B.A. diss., Harvard University, 1970.

Wycoff, D. D. and D. H. Maister. *The Domestic Airline Industry*. Lexington: D.C. Heath, 1977.

Yearbook of International Trade and Statistics . New York: United Nations, 1981.

Yockey, H. P. *Symposium on Information Theory in Biology*. New York: Pergammon Press, 1957.

Yoon, E., and G. L. Lillien. "New Industrial Product Performance: The Effects of Market Characteristics and Strategy." *Journal of Product Innovation Management* 3 (1985): 134-144.

Young, J. F. *Information Theory*. New York: Wiley Interscience, 1971.

Zufryden, F. S. "A Cojoint Measurement-Based Approach for Optimal New Product Design and Market Segmentation." In *Analytic Approaches to Product and Marketing Planning*, edited by A. D. Shocker, 101. Boston: Boston Marketing Science Institute, April 1979.

Index

About the Editor and Contributors

DONDE ASHMOS received her Ph.D. in Strategic Management from The University of Texas at Austin in 1988. She is currently an Assistant Professor of Management at The University of Texas at San Antonio. She has published articles in the *Academy of Management Review, Journal of Applied Behavioral Science, Interfaces, Human Resource Management, Health Progress,* and *Journal of the National Medical Association.*

MICHELLE BINZEL has a B.A. from Macalester College and received her Ph.D. in Management from The University of Texas at Austin in 1990. She worked as an analyst with Sheshunoff and Co. of Austin, Texas, and is an Associate of the IC^2 Institute. She is currently doing research on the global environment for management strategy.

CAROL CLETTENBERG received her MBA from The University of Texas in 1985. Her work experience includes eight years with Texas Instruments and two and one-half years with Booze, Allen and Hamilton as a Consultant. She currently works for Apple Computers and is Product Manager for Apple A/UX.

ROB L. JONES received his B.A. and MBA from The University of Texas at Austin. He is an Investment Banker with The First Boston Corporation, specializing in public and corporate finance for natural resource companies. He was formerly a Financial Analyst with Sun Company.

GEORGE KOZMETSKY is Director of the IC^2 Institute, Professor of Management and Computer Science, J. Marion West Chair Professor, and former Dean of the College of Business Administration and Graduate School of Business at The University of Texas at Austin. He is also Professor in the Department of Medicine at The University of Texas Health Science Center at San Antonio, and is Executive Associate for Economic Affairs for The University of Texas System. He is the co-founder, a Director, and former Executive Vice President of Teledyne, Inc. Dr. Kozmetsky received a B.A. from the University of Washington and an MBA and D.S.C. from Harvard University.

TIMOTHY W. RUEFLI is Herbert D. Kelleher/M Corp Regents Professor and Chairperson of the Management Department at The University of Texas at Austin, and Frank C. Erwin Jr. Centennial Research Fellow at the IC^2 Institute.

CHESTER L. WILSON has a B.A. in Economics from The University of Texas at Austin. He was a Research Associate at both the Center for Cybernetic Studies and the IC^2 Institute at the University of Texas at Austin.

PIYU YUE received a M.S. degree from Beijing University in 1965, and now is a Ph.D. candidate in Economics at The University of Texas at Austin. She is an Associate of the IC^2 Institute and is currently a Visiting Economist at the Federal Reserve Bank in St. Louis, Missouri.